Moving Meals and

Culinary cultures, diasporic dishes and familial foodways

**Edited by
Tanya M. Cassidy
and Abdullahi Osman El-Tom**

DEMETER

Moving Meals and Migrating Mothers

Culinary cultures, diasporic dishes and familial foodways

Edited by Tanya M. Cassidy and Abdullahi Osman El-Tom

Copyright © 2021 Demeter Press

Demeter Press
2546 10th Line
Bradford, Ontario
Canada, L3Z 3L3
Tel: 289-383-0134
Email: info@demeterpress.org
Website: www.demeterpress.org

Demeter Press logo based on the sculpture "Demeter" by Maria-Luise Bodirsky www.keramik-atelier.bodirsky.de

Printed and Bound in Canada

Front cover artwork: *Teacups,* by Mindy Stricke. From the 2010 series *You Are Not Where You Were*, a *Greetings From Motherland* project.
Typesetting: Michelle Pirovich

Library and Archives Canada Cataloguing in Publication
Title: Moving meals and migrating mothers : culinary cultures, diasporic dishes and familial foodways / edited by Tanya M. Cassidy and Abdullahi Osman El-Tom.
Names: Cassidy, Tanya, editor. | Tom, Abdullahi Osman El- editor.
Description: Includes bibliographical references.
Identifiers: Canadiana 20200375946 | ISBN 9781772583311 (softcover)
Subjects: LCSH: Food, Social aspects. | LCSH: Food habits, Social aspects. | LCSH: Food habits. | LCSH: Women immigrants, Social life and customs. | LCSH: Immigrants, Social life and customs.
Classification: LCC GT2855 .M68 2021 | DDC 394.1/2086912,dc23

Acknowledgments

First, we wish to thank all of the contributors to *Moving Meals and Migrating Mothers: Culinary cultures, diasporic dishes and familial foodways*, whose hard work and perseverance were key to this project coming to fruition. Additionally, we wish to acknowledge Florence Pasche Guignard who also made editorial contributions early in this project, and who was also co-editor with Tanya of these sister volumes *Mothers and Food: Negotiating Foodways from Maternal Perspectives* (Demeter 2016) and *What's Cooking Mom?: Narratives about Food and Family* (Demeter 2015). We also wish to thank the Loewen family for their generous contribution which helped to see this project move forward. We also wish to thank Professor Andrea O'Reilly and the entire team at Demeter Press. This project also received a donation from the *Polish National Agency for Academic Exchange* (NAWA) connected with a project Tanya is working on with Dr Aleksandra Wesolowska. Also, Tanya wishes to thank the School of Nursing, Psychotherapy and Community Health (SNPCH) Research Committee who awarded her funds to support this project. Finally, we would like to acknowledge our families who have supported us over the years in our professional journeys and whose care and support are the true reason we do the work we do.

Contents

Introduction

Tanya M. Cassidy and Abdullahi Osman El-Tom

*M*oving Meals and Migrating Mothers: Culinary cultures, diasporic dishes, and familiar foodways *is about food as a powerful site for the reproduction, reinvention, and sustainment of culture during times of mobility and in the context of intense, often numerous, external forces, including pressures to adapt to the new host culture, increased exposure to biomedical discourse, global capitalism, and globalization more generally. Although the topic of food and migration is a reoccurring theme, particularly in anthropology (Terragni and Roos), few discussions are linked to women, who are often the primary cooks across the globe, north and south, or recognize the intertwined nature of food and mothering (Cassidy; Pasche Guignard). Mothers continue to be the prime carers at home and to shoulder the strenuous duty of feeding their families; in doing so, they retain the power of food as a major pathway for negotiating membership to kin groups, communities, and nations. Such a role becomes more complex during times of tran-sition, mobility, and migration. This is the predicament of many whose voices are included in this volume as well as with both of us who have approached the subject of migration and food from an anthropological theme for many years but who are both migrants (although from different parts of the world) to a country, Ireland, with a turbulent history related to food and famine. We have often worked together to think about how intergenerational food exchanges can be compared cross culturally and over time (Cassidy and El-Tom). Almost every article in this volume combines exegeses of at least two cultures: an original culture left behind and host culture needing to be learned and adapted to.

We have organized this volume around three interrelated themes. We begin by thinking about the food itself, as a cultural object, and how it transfers across borders. Our second theme concentrates on the mothers themselves, thinking about links to maternal identity issues related to making meals. And our third theme is related to inter-generational issues, particularly in relation to infant feeding and broadly related meanings and experiences of feeding children. The contributors, like the topic itself, come from diverse but related disciplines, and their studies deal with different groups, spanning every continent on earth. Their articles cover themes ranging from nutrition, religion, survival, resistance, autonomy, patriarchy, to biomedical hegemony. For this introduction, we intend to confine our comments to the most important theoretical and methodological issues raised in addition to some pressing conclusions made by the contributors.

The first part of this volume concentrates on the meals themselves and begins with a contribution from Florence Pasche Guignard, who was involved as editor originally in this project and coedited the two other companion volumes published with Demeter Press (Cassidy; Pasche Guignard). In her contribution to this volume titled "You Have to Taste Everything! Mothers, Migrations, and French Food Rules," she elevates the role of food itself, comparing French and Canadian food in schools, and highlights the power of food in the formation of ethnic and immigrant identity culture. Using the concept of "culinary citizen-ship," she shows how food transcends the formation of narrow ethnic community membership and is adapted by mothers and institutions to transmit broader national identities. In France, mothers cede their power to schools for feeding their children. They abhor lunch boxes and expect their children to eat in school canteens. Sharing food at the canteen represents identification with the republic evident in commu-nal consumption of food, in opposition to eating separately. The end result produces citizens who are united by food taste and the sharing of food, defying the spirit of individualism imparted by resorting to home-prepared lunch boxes. At the same time, Pasche Guignard argues that culinary citizenship is also instituted in feeding children at home in France. Sharing food at home is stressed; children eat their meals at the table together with their family members. The principle is further enforced by the French gastronomic rule that "kids eat what adults eat."

According to Pasche Guignard's study, North America (by which she means primarily the United States [US] and Canada) demonstrates a different model of gastronomy at home and school. In sharp contrast to the French ethos of sharing, eating, and living together, the North

American way deviates towards a neoliberal ethos that privatizes problems and solutions and at the same time stresses the ideal of consumer choice. US and Canadian schools forgo canteens and demand children be fed via home-prepared lunch boxes. Wealthier mothers, who may lack time to prepare lunch boxes themselves, outsource feeding of their children to private food providers. Feeding American children at home is also structured to augment the US neoliberal tenets. In American homes, children are allowed to eat separately on a couch or anywhere in the house. Cars are supplied with cup holders to enable children to partake in the American habit of eating on the run. Gastronomy serves as a site to reproduce the national ethos desired by the two cultures.

The migration of cooking from the kitchen into the public sphere in recent decades has come with gendered gains and losses. In her contribution entitled "From Happy Meals to Celebrity Chefs: Shifting Attitudes towards Mothers and Traditional Food in Puerto Rico," Maria Elena Rodriguez examines some of the themes related to this phenomenon. The rise of celebrity chefs, mostly male, and the sharp rise in eating outside the home have great implication for gendered gastropolitics. In some ways, the process has led to the increasing popularity of male celebrity chefs coupled with a rapid devaluing of home cooking, once the prime domain of women.

Rodriguez also tells us about her intention to ground her methodology in feminist principles and produce scholarship that positions women's voices in the centre of her study. Moreover, she equally wants to make her study relevant to women's lives and to challenge the erasure of experiences of women of colour. In order to advance the accessibility and reach of her work, she turns to hooks' discussion of theory of liberatory practice. hooks castigates tendencies in feminist theory to indulge in esoteric and convoluted analysis that is inaccessible to the public, including members of the studied groups. We hasten to agree with hooks, noting that this unfortunate choice is rampant in academia at large and not necessarily confined to feminist scholars. Furthermore, hooks also advises feminist scholars on women to connect their theories with the practice of the real lives of women, both inside and outside academia. Rodriguez can indeed take pride in sticking to her promise of creating accessible work, grounded in the lived experience of the women she has studied.

Although the issue of accessibility is easy to take on board, the recommended focus on lived experience has often been promoted for different reasons. Using her own material, Rodriguez gives us some hint regarding the demotion of lived experience. Although the women involved in her study were keen to discuss their lived experience, she was told by one California man that such interviews would be a waste of time. Valuing the lived experiences of women is key to feminist research. Rodriguez further argues that many scholars do not perceive everyday experience of Puerto Rican women as worthy of being studied. Such lived experience belongs to women's work, a domain that has been consistently devalued and treated as unproductive work. She adds that devaluing work traditionally performed by women silences women and mothers and perpetuates the unfair portrait of their roles as unsophisticated, unnecessary, and unimportant. The editors of this volume agree with Rodriguez and present this book as clear evidence of a departure from such views.

Methodological conformists may experience some unease regarding Rodriguez's breach of research codes in her work—that is, her choice of retaining the real names of her informants in her chapter. As researchers know, most research boards and college research ethic committees insist on disguising the informants' identity via the use of aliases and other symbols. Needless to say, this code is used for good reasons—to protect informants from any adverse result of the work. However, this rule comes with its drawbacks. It robs the informants of agency that accrues from participating in the research project. Rodriguez boldly ignores this research code and legitimizes her reason for doing so. Her research participants themselves insisted that their real names appear in the study, as they wanted the readers to share their stories, hear their voices, and recognize their agency in the work. We hope other researchers also realize that their rigid adherence to research rules can undermine the agency of participants, especially when they cannot use their real names.

In modern life, heavily moulded by globalization and corporate-driven food culture, women are increasingly losing their ability to home cook their meals, which threatens their cultural food traditions. Their children are also influenced by modern foodways, and the result is a new dependence on frozen food, takeaway meals, and eating out. This is an unequal contest, which home-cooking women cannot seemingly win. It is also mothers who shoulder the blame for not devoting enough time to home cooking, devaluing food cooked in the home, and the increase of feeding children fast food. The women studied by Rodriguez are also concerned about something else. As they rightly express, food is culture, and culture is an identity. With the loss of their culinary culture, the very identity of that individual is lost.

Managing mealtime for mothers on either side of the borderlands of Mexico and the US is key to Ramona Lee Pérez's article titled "From Flavours of Domesticity to the Taste of Consumption: Routine, Resistance, and Desire in Borderlands Home Cooking." For Pérez, our very tastes are mediated and manipulated by deeply held cultural beliefs and traditions, recalling the French theoretical contributions of Bourdieu. Women have been historically tasked with cooking and feeding at home. However, and unlike celebrity chefs, their role goes unpaid, as they are expected to perform such work out of love, motherly duty, and tradition.

Our second theme concentrates on the producers themselves, specifically the migrating mothers. The Loewen contribution, "Food without Borders: Adaptive Expressions of Mothering," is from a group of family members who remind us that individual identity is anchored in group membership and that food is central to both forming and communicating this identity (Fischler; Howard). Food maintains its importance as a major signifier of identity long after other signifiers are lost, and its associated community is subjected to severe tests in its postmigration existence. It is difficult to retain language postimmigration, let alone subject it to daily use with children who might not have even seen the original homeland of their parents. Food is unique, as it can be frequently made at home and be leveraged for potentially rescuing some basic tenets of the original culture.

The Loewen contribution reflects on the Mennonites of North America, who employ food in a similar and yet different way. By their very nature as an ethnic group engaged in preaching, the Mennonites travel all over the world to spread their message, a message sweetened by the delivery through the Mennonite Central Committee (MCC) Canada of mundane NGO services such as health, water, and education. As they show, food functions as a social glue that transcends borders and keeps the Mennonite members attached to their culture. However, the pressure of the host culture forces these Mennonite mothers to improvise and adapt—a process that places them at the margin of their international Mennonite communities and catapults them into the nebulous position that straddles the divide between the host culture and the original culture back home. Among immigrants, old and new, the longing for home produces a nostalgic memory that can be assuaged by what Hadas Ore calls "nostalgic food" in her contribution titled "Traversing the Mythology of the Female Home Cook: Jewish-Israeli Mothers 'Cooking' Homes in New Zealand." Israeli immigrant women in New Zealand often resort to cooking meals from their homeland to recreate a feeling of being at home. To boost the power of their nostalgic food, these women add depth to the reproduction of their culture via skipping generations, which takes place through retrieval of the authentic and old recipes of their grandmothers instead of simply cooking what their mothers had taught them.

Both the Jewish-Israelis discussed in the contribution by Ore and the Mennonites reported by the Loewens make a strong connection between food pathways and religion. However, such a connection goes much deeper when it comes to the Nepalese Hindu immigrants in US, as explored in Dorothy Abram's contribution titled "Symbol and Sel-Roti: The Taste of Return in Women's Nepali-Bhutanese-Hindu Refugee Identity and Ritual Performance." Mary Douglas popularized the view of food consumption as a ritual—a situation in which handling food becomes rigidly structured and resistant to idiosyncrasy and individual improvisation. Abram discusses how among her participants, food is integrated into religion, thus making it intrinsically ritualistic. She focuses on sel-roti, a type of bread made of rice flour. In its cooking, the batter is poured in a circle with overlapping ends into hot mustard oil.

This is an important part of making the bread, which leads Abram to call sel-roti "the taste of return." Just as circles always return to the beginning, Sel-roti guarantees the return of a loved one or anything desired: a child going to school, an emigrant going away, a prisoner surviving in hostile land, or a family member recovering health following sickness. Sel-roti is accompanied by a major ritual prayer that recurs every year. The ritual connects the devout worshipper with the Goddess and hence attracts spiritual blessing while achieving certain ends, such as the safe return of loved ones as well as the restoration of tranquillity and wealth to family and community.

Abram describes how some scholars see the arduous task of Swasthani rituals, coupled by the fact that women often work in hot kitchens to make sel-roti, as yet another example of women's sub-jugation in an oppressive patriarchal system. Having acknowledged this perspective, however, Abram invites us to think differently. Involvement in sel-roti and its associated rituals is in essence empowering for women, as it allows them to monopolize an important position within the society. These women act as a bridge connecting the living and the dead, the mundane with the divine, and operate as interlocutors with the Goddess to secure the safety of their children, the welfare of their absent relatives, and the fortunes of their families and communities. It is difficult to argue against the power and high status that come with such a role in any given society. In areas where the avenues towards women's self-actualization are somewhat strained, it is difficult to argue against these women's significant role in sel-roti rituals.

The third section of this volume concentrates on the consumers, most often meaning children, and starts by exploring different experiences with feeding infants. In their contribution about Asian mothers in Vancouver, titled "Intersections of Discursive, Social, and Material Contexts of Good Mothering: Asian Immigrant Mothers' Experiences with Infant Feeding and Nutrition in Metro Vancouver," Gwen Chapman and Sandiza Habib alert us to the problem associated with the interplay between biomedical discourse and minority cultures in feeding babies. Focusing on the social and moral regulations of mothers, Chapman and Habib describe infant feeding as a process using Foucault's concept of "governmentality." The concept refers to how individuals volunteer to govern themselves through self-regulation as well as to biopower, which operates through social control over the bodies. Biopower functions through three elements: truth discourses about human life produced and legitimated by modern science and its associated experts; intervention strategies used by relevant bodies, such as hospitals, to enforce required actions and technologies of the self; and individuals governing and reproducing themselves as pliant ethical subject (Foucault; Rabinow and Rose). The fear of panopticism, a situation of sustained surveillance over people, ensures that subjects discipline their bodies and actions through their self-regulation to conform to the diktats of the legitimate wisdom of biomedical expertise. Biomedical discourse legitimates authoritative scientific truth while dismissing discourses belonging to ethnic and minority groups as irrational, primitive, and indicative of immorality, ignorance, and lack of discipline.

In addition, Chapman and Habib direct our attention to an important foundational ideal that underpins the barrage of care and health advice given to mothers in maternity hospitals. Healthcare serves neoliberal ideologies of "self-responsibilization" for raising future workers. Mothers are encouraged to become ideal immigrants and invest in the health of their children, thus meeting the neoliberal ideal of "citizen self-sufficiency" (McLaren and Dyck). Chapman and Habib further argue that the hegemonic discourse and medical advice offered at hospitals never come as a surprise for these immigrant women in Vancouver. Due to globalization and the spread of modern medicine, they are already familiar with these doctrines and had learned a lot of them before they came to Vancouver. This finding challenges the long-held assumption that the West is the locus of modern scientific knowledge, whereas the East serves as the domain for traditional cultural knowledge.

Ruth De Souza's contribution, titled "Going Without: Migrant Mothers, Food, and the Postnatal Ward," deals with similar issues involving medicalization and globalization in her examination of the admission of immigrant mothers into postnatal hospitals in New Zealand. Ethnic food sharing in postnatal hospitals is also demonized for another reason. Such food is blamed for introducing undesirable, unfamiliar, risky, or dangerous smells into the wards. As De Souza writes, maternity hospitals are not as odourless as implied; more often than not, these places are often overwhelmed by the smell of detergent and other medical elements. However, the postnatal practice shows how smell itself becomes politicized and accorded power in the division of the world into "us" and "them," the national and the alien, the insider and outsider. De Souza concludes that the politics of smell in these hospitals "highlights the limitations of sharable ethnicity and palatable multiculturalism."

Nutritional reductionism is the hallmark of hospital feeding philosophy, and this view cannot prevail without the delegitimation of ethnic food. Mothers at postnatal hospitals are thus prevented from sharing food brought in by relatives. In their chapter, "Infant-Feeding Practices among Chinese Mothers in Ireland," Qianling Zhou and Chen Haoyue, discuss how this has particular cultural implications among Chinese immigrant mothers to Ireland in relation to breast-feeding, which is exacerbated by Ireland largely being a bottle-feeding culture. This rule deprives mothers from using their food as vehicle for love, generosity, and belonging, all of which are linked by some mothers to their feeding at the breast. Indeed, those women are encouraged to subsist on tasteless hospital food, as in the official discourse, eating for pleasure is pathologized, and taste is sacrificed in favour of an authorized version of nutrition.

No discussion of home cooking is complete without examining it as a metonym for what Helen Vallianatos in her chapter titled "Migration, Mothers, Meals: Immigrant Mothers' Experiences and Perspectives on Feeding Children" calls "gendered household gastropolitics." In recent years, it has become common to describe the kitchen as one of the last battlegrounds for gender equality. The jury is still out as to how far women have progressed in this respect. Winning the battle is not yet on the cards, although some see little gain in turning the kitchen into a gender battleground in the first place.

Several contributions to this volume show that home cooking remains a woman's work in postimmigration life. We hasten to add that this gendered division of labour is not confined to Non-Western countries. In France, supposedly a bastion of women's liberation, women spend an average of sixty-six minutes per day cooking, whereas men only spend twenty-four (Champagne et al.). The situation in the United Kingdom (UK) is not so different either, as women are seven times more likely to have cooked the last meal and are ten times more likely to have baked the last cake. This unequal kitchen workload seems to prevail even when women are working outside their home, and in some cases, when they are the main breadwinners in the household. The women studied by Vallianatos complain that they end up doing a "double shift"—working outside the home and inside it as well. To add insult to injury, the reluctance of men to venture into the kitchen is not accompanied by a willingness to cede the power that goes with cooking. Men seem to dictate what is being cooked from the comfort of their television armchairs, and they equally retain a strong influence on the food shopping done by their wives. Furthermore, men seem to take advan-tage of the maternal sacrificial instinct many mothers possess. Women are only too willing to extend feeding care that they offer to their children to their husbands as well. As Vallianatos spells out, women eat less and last at home compared to their menfolk. In the UK, men consume twice the calories, more than twice the protein, and three times the fat compared to their female counterparts. Could men's greed be a factor contributing to their rushing to an early grave?

For some feminists, the spectacle of women shouldering the cooking and serving food can be viewed as a mark of female subordination and an outright sign of oppression. It is tempting to say this gender im-balance can be rectified by cajoling men to take an equal share in home cooking. However, Pasche Guignard directs our attention to a different angle of the debate. In France, many women belittle their husband's contribution in the kitchen, saying that the father is only there to help. They do not insist on challenging the dominant responsibility of mothers to feed their children. The women studied by Vallianatos are much harsher, as they actively resist their husband's encroachment into the kitchen. They think they are better off if their men do not cook anything at all, for they just make more mess and cause them more work.

Vallianatos reminds us that women's dominance in the kitchen is a source of power and not necessarily a form of imprisonment. Ethno-graphic studies done in India attest to the many situations in which the mother-in-law commands a high status and controls resources includ-ing money, food, and labour and power over men in the household, including her son. Drawing on Saba Mahmoud's work, Vallianatos criticizes how Western feminists conceptualize agency due to its narrow focus on challenging patriarchy. She proposes a model of engagement with traditional patriarchy with a strategy that may retain the same patriarchal forms while subtly shifting some of its elements in women's favour. In this model, empowerment does not come from capacity to challenge traditional gastronomical hierarchies but from celebrating women's proficiencies in the kitchen (Mahmoud). There is a consensus that control over home cooking comes with power. However, when women relinquish this power by abandoning home cooking, there is no guarantee that their loss is compensated for in the public sphere. Carole Counihan's study in South Italy precisely demonstrates that. In the past, women controlled a third of the household budget that was allocated to food. Through cooking, women asserted themselves as good mothers but also as carers for the elderly and poor, who depend on them. Women also met periodically to make pasta, and these meetings allowed them to devise strategies to negotiate with their husbands and influence the whole community. All that was lost when food became market oriented; women ceased to be housewives, and cooking moved into the public sector. Gradually, men began to dominate food enterprises in the guise of restaurants, bakeries, and pasta factories, and women ended up at the lower level of food making, working as waitresses, cashiers, and secretaries. This change has led Counihan to conclude that changes to foodways amounts to nothing but false liberation for women.

Moving Meals and Migrating Mothers: Culinary cultures, diasporic dishes, and familial foodways offers the reader a global journey exploring the complex relations underlying the exchange of food within families. The book explores complex culinary cultural changes, and how these relate to gendered dynamics as well as to familial and personal autonomy and agency. Thinking about migration, which inherently involves movement, coupled with maternal ties, this book presents a variety of interpretations regarding how food can be both a bridge to memories as well as a barrier to being and becoming. We hope you, the reader, enjoys dining with us. You are always welcome to return for seconds.

Works Cited

Bourdieu, Pierre. *Outline of a Theory of Practice.* Cambridge University Press, 1977.

Cassidy, Tanya, and Abdullahi El-Tom, editors. *Ethnographies of Breastfeeding: Cultural contexts and confrontations.* Bloomsbury Press, 2015.

Cassidy, Tanya, and Abdullahi El-Tom. "Comparing Sharing and

Banking Milk: Issues of Gift Exchange and Community in the Sudan and Ireland." *Giving Breast Milk: Body Ethics and Contemporary Breastfeeding Practice*, edited by Alison Bartlett and Rhonda Shaw. Demeter Press, 2010, pp. 110-21.

Cassidy, Tanya M., and Florence Pasche Guignard, editors. *What's Cooking, Mom? Narratives about Food and Family.* Demeter Press, 2015.

Champagne, Clara Ariane Pailhé, and Anne Solaz. "Le temps domestique et parental des hommes et des femmes: quells facteurs d'évolutions en 25 ans?" *Economie et Statistique*, vol. 480, 2015, pp. 209-42.

Counihan, Carole. "Bread as World: Food Habits and Social Relations in Modernizing Sardinia." *Anthropology Quarterly*, vol. 57, no. 2, 1984, pp. 47-59.

Counihan, Carole. "Female Identity, Food and Power in Contemporary Florence." *Anthropology Quarterly*, vol. 61, no. 2, 1988, pp. 51-62.

Counihan, Carole. *A Tortilla Is Like Life: Food Culture in the San Luis Valley of Colorado.* University of Texas Press, 2009.

Douglas, Mary. "Deciphering a Meal." *Food and Culture: A Reader*, edited by Carole Counihan and Penny van Esterik. Routledge, 1997, pp. 36-54.

Fischler, Claude. "Food, Self and Identity." *Social Science Information*, vol. 27, no. 2, 1988, pp. 267-92.

Foucault, Michel. *Power/Knowledge: Selected Interviews and Other Writings, 1972–1977.* Pantheon, 1980.

Foucault, Michel. "Governmentality." *The Foucault Effect: Studies in Governmentality*, edited by Graham Burchell et al. University of Chicago Press, 1991, pp.87-104.

hooks, bell. *Teaching to Transgress: Education as the Practice of Freedom.* Routledge, 1994.

Howard, J. "Social Psychology of Identities." *Annual Review of Sociology*, vol. 26, 2000, pp. 267-393.

Mahmoud, Saba. *The Islamic Revival and the Feminist Subject.* Princeton University Press, 2005.

McLaren, Arlene, and Isabel Dyck. "Mothering, Human Capital and the Ideal Immigrant." *Women's Studies International Forum*, vol. 27, 2004, pp. 41-53.

Pasche Guignard, Florence, and Tanya Cassidy. *Mothers and Food: Negotiating Foodways from Maternal Perspectives.* Demeter Press, 2016.

Rabinow, Paul, and Nikolas Rose. "Biopower Today." *BioSocieties*, vol. 1, 2006, pp. 195-217.

Terragni, Laura, and Gun Roos. "People Moving with Food from and to Northern Europe: Food, Migration and Multiculturalism." *Anthropology of Food*, 2018, journals.openedition.org/aof/9123. Accessed 1 June 2021.

Wilk, Richard. *Home Cooking in the Global Village: Caribbean Food from Buccaneers to Ecotourists.* Berg Publishers, 2006.

PART I
Moving Meals, Markets, and Mothers

Chapter 1

You Have to Taste Everything! Mothers, Migrations, and French Food Rules

Florence Pasche Guignard

This chapter explores perspectives on food by expatriate mothers, whose accounts are different from those of asylum seekers, refugees, and economic migrants, which are considered by other contributions to this volume. It focuses on cases where mothers emphasize a cultural intentionality in changing countries with a desire to transmit knowledge gained from their host culture, turning their authentic maternal experience into expertise. This chapter concentrates on the motherhood memoirs and parenting advice books by two North American mothers who reflexively relate their temporary experience of feeding their children (and themselves) while living in France. My sources also include school lunch menus (known as plans alimentaires) from France and Canada. Finally, I draw from my own experience of parenting as a newcomer in an urban and multicultural North American context.[1] In order to reflect on the role of mothers and institutions in transmitting national, cultural, and religious identities through food, I use critical discourse analysis grounded in maternal theory. I contrast the perspectives of two North American authors who published motherhood memoirs with those of some mothers in France. In a context of vehement debates on secularism in France, some mothers whose children eat lunch at daycares or at public schools question, for religious or ethical reasons, what visiting North American mothers identified and praised as an essential "French food rule"—that is, "You have to taste everything!" Not an always enforced rule, this motto is rather a guiding principle in imparting taste literacy to children, along with other values regarding food and national identity.

Borrowing these categories from Nicole Constable's work on migrant workers in Hong Kong, I situate the expatriate North American mothers in this chapter at the privileged (and usually financially well-off) end of the economic spectrum, ranging "from privileged to precarious" (92), of people who engage, willingly or under constraint, in temporary or long-term expatriation. International marriage constitutes one of the many reasons for migration; it is also a site where cultural difference around foodways can become a source of mutual enrichment or of tension, both at home and in society. Accompanying a spouse in relocation for an immediate career advancement or seeking better employment for themselves is a frequent reason for the expatriation of wives and mothers. Another rarely acknowledged motive is the desire to experience the potential pedagogic benefits of living abroad (see, for instance, Stephens) in a mode different than touristic. Missionaries (see Loewen's chapter in this volume) frequently count among their motivations a desire to bring others what they consider as a better religion and other improvements, such as better nutrition, health habits, and foodways. Such motivations are often driven by, or are indirectly serving, colonial imperatives.

The narratives and parenting advice books considered in this chapter explore a question that can be read as a reversal of the assumptions of missionary work: What happens when some of the cultural habits—including food habits—of one's host culture start making more sense than those of one's culture of origin? How can one positively learn from the culture into which one has moved? When expatriate mothers eventually move back home, must they bring back with them the meals, food habits, recipes, and, more generally, the lessons they learned abroad? What is culturally distinctive about the ways parents feed and bring up children born in this globalized world of the early twenty-first century? Such questions will be central in this chapter, which examines how North American mothers in different positions apprehend French parenting and French food rules, both at home and at school.

North American Mothers Discover the Secret Wisdom of French Parenting

In *Bringing Up Bébé,* by Pamela Druckerman (2012), and *French Kids Eat Everything,* by Karen Le Billon (2012), two North American mothers turn their individual encounter with French parenting into a narrative and into an explicit set of rules and advice. Both authors also subsequently published a parenting advice book. While these best-sellers tend to idealize French children, families, mothers, and the institutions they interact with, they also ignore or silence the challenges posed to some mothers in France by the state-mandated school lunch programs known as "la cantine scolaire." In the following, I situate these maternal narratives and advice books in a context where gastronomy and its enforcement, both at home and at school, shape a distinctive normative cultural identity. Some aspects of this French ideal of national culinary diversity also happen to erase the cultural and religious diversity of the very children who are being fed in the absence of their mothers.

Pamela Druckerman

Pamela Druckerman is an American journalist who had three children while living in Paris with her British spouse. The United Kingdom (UK) edition of her memoir was initially titled *French Children Don't Throw Food. Parenting Secrets from Paris.* It was retitled *Bringing Up Bébé* for the US and Canadian markets, with the subtitle *One American Mother Discovers the Wisdom of French Parenting.* This successful book was translated into several languages. In 2014, it was published as *Bébé made in France. Quels sont les secrets de notre éducation?*[2] addressing French and wider francophone readerships.

Druckerman explores many aspects of childrearing in France. Significantly, she starts her book with a description of her strategy when eating out with her husband and their first child, then eighteen months old, which consists of finishing their meals as quickly as possible. This contrasts with the common behaviour of French families in the restaurants they visit:

> After a few more restaurant meals, I notice that the French families all around us don't look like they're in hell. Weirdly, they look like they're on vacation. French children the same age

as Bean are sitting contentedly in their high chairs, waiting for their food, or eating fish and even vegetables. There's no shrieking or whining. Everyone is having one course at a time. And there's no debris around their tables. (Druckerman 2)

Her observations are a starting point for her enquiry into how the French parents in her rather privileged Paris neighbourhood educate their children. She attempts to identify which "invisible, civilizing force at their tables" (3) seems to be absent from hers, which leads her to realize that "it's not just mealtime that's different" (14). She goes on: "I hadn't thought I was supposed to admire French parenting. It isn't a thing, like French fashion or French cheese. No one visits Paris to soak up the local views on parental authority and guilt management" (3).

The 2014 paperback edition of *Bringing Up Bébé* is combined with Druckerman's second book, published in 2013 and entitled *Bébé Day by Day: 100 Keys to French Parenting*, where she offers a condensed version of her advice and tips. The title of the fourth chapter of *Bébé Day by Day* is "Bébé Gourmet," and the appendix includes "Favorite Recipes from the Parisian Crèche" as well as a sample of weekly lunch menus at the daycare. It is significant that *Bringing Up Bébé* opens with the scene at the restaurant and that the first chapter focuses on food and feeding. These topics are again dealt with in the twelfth chapter, "You Just Have to Taste It." This title reflects an imperative central to a predominant understanding of feeding children in France, both at home and at school: The idea is to encourage children to taste everything (without necessarily finishing up their plates).

Karen Le Billon

Karen Le Billon, an academic researcher from Vancouver, offers another narrative in the motherhood memoir genre (though with much more focus on her two daughters and her French husband rather than just on herself). Whereas Druckerman shares her experience of trying a French approach to food, sleep arrangements and patterns, play, politeness, and other issues, Le Billon's central focus in *French Kids Eat Everything* concerns food and mealtimes—within the family, at school, at restaurants, and as guests. The book is structured around experiences that translate into narratives. The author then formulates these ten French food rules summed up on the cover.

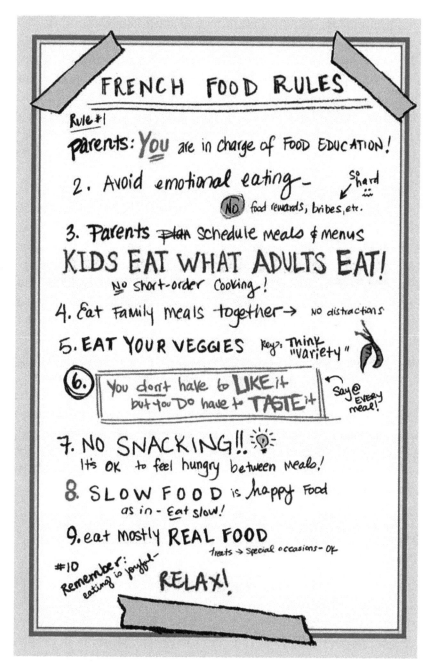

Figure 1. Back Cover of *French Kids Eat Everything*

The complete—and programmatic—subtitle of Le Billon's first Canadian edition of the book reads as follows: {AND YOURS CAN TOO} *How Our Family Moved to France, Cured Picky Eating, Banned Snacking, and Discovered 10 Simple Rules for Raising Happy, Healthy Eaters.* The phrasing "and yours can too," which was deleted from subsequent editions, goes beyond the simple statement and may sound like a reproach to some readers: And yours *should* too but do not because of your inappropriate approach. It might also be a promise: And yours *will* too, if you follow the ten simple rules outlined in this book.

Like Druckerman, Le Billon went on to publish a second book, turning her ten food rules into a practical parenting manual focused on food and mealtime, grounded in a "playful parenting" approach. In *Getting to YUM, The 7 Secrets of Raising Eager Eaters* (2014), Le Billon carefully and consistently addresses "parents" rather than "mothers." However, feminine figures—assumed to be mothers—illustrate the book cover and the pages of *French Kids Eat Everything* and of *Getting to YUM.* Druckerman's books are also illustrated prominently with mothers rather than parents with visibly diverse gender identities other than feminine. In examining the intersection of feeding and parenting, Le Billon's usage of "parents" may sound more inclusive and generic, but it may obscure the reality that mothers, most of whom identify as cisgender women, still do most of the domestic carework, childcare work, and food preparation (Champagne et al.). However, in line with a more general trend, I will use "parenting" rather than "mothering" to refer to "maternal practices" that constitute "maternal work" (as defined by Ruddick 17).

Moving North American Mothers and French Parenting

Druckerman's and Le Billon's books, as well as their mediations (websites, blogs, reviews, media interviews with the authors, etc.) have recently called attention to what North American media have dubbed "French parenting." This expression refers to a cluster of principles more common in the education of children in France than in North America. However, not all French parents engage in this style of education, and many parents who are not French also follow some of these principles. French parenting is an object of study from the perspectives of psychology and sociology, including through cross-cultural comparison (for instance by Suizzo), but without much emphasis on food and feeding. French parenting expands well beyond the national borders of France to other francophone and even broader European contexts where the ideology of intensive mothering (Hays)[3] and theories of attachment parenting have a less powerful hold on mothers than they have in the United States (US), Canada, and other anglophone countries presently (Ennis).

Although the parenting secrets featured in Druckerman's book could have also probably come from other places, they come from Paris, the capital of France, a country that retains a strong association with the prestige of gastronomy and the promise of good taste. However, Druckerman makes it clear that these parenting secrets could also be retrieved from the past. On Druckerman's website page promoting *Bébé Day by Day*, we read: "This little book of lessons will help American parents reclaim a common-sense era of family life that is still the norm in France. Its timeless advice, written in pithy, practical prose, will be appreciated by parents and grandparents alike."[4] The book positions certain practices as those of a past common-sense era, which American parents can no longer access. Through accounting for her own exploration of similar and still alive practices in France, Druckerman claims to provide "a hundred keys" to reopen the door to such wisdom and, perhaps, what some regard as traditional family structures and values. Both Druckerman and Le Billon are in stable heterosexual partnerships and do not intend to explore what different situations (for instance, two women in a same-sex parental couple) may involve in terms of parenting, feeding children, and gender roles.

Other authors have used their own experience of moving abroad, and the shock of return, to question common practices of North American parenting. Judith Warner, who is also a journalist, has written about the contrast of her experience of motherhood in France and in the suburbs of Washington DC in her book *Perfect Madness, Motherhood in an Age of Anxiety*. The *Battle Hymn of the Tiger Mother*, by Amy Chua, is another example, as the author positions Chinese mothering as a challenge to North American parenting, though without an international move of her own family. Such books do not focus only on which aspects of another type of parenting, sometimes presented as "foreign," are considered as more effective. Rather, these essays and narratives point out what might not work optimally in the prevailing current modes of parenting in contemporary middle-class North America in general (Druckerman 4) and, specifically, in the domains of food and feeding children, which is also marked by high standards of intensive mothering.

Druckerman and Le Billon position American parents (read: mothers) as in need of help. Their own status as authoritative experts does not derive from any title or diploma. Rather, they are experts because of their authentic maternal experience. Furthermore, they are able to express themselves through a narrative and to quote relevant studies in the fields of medicine, health, nutrition, and education to back up their personal claims. The mother as author becomes a mediator between two parenting and food cultures, having experienced the best of French parenting and known the worst of American parenting. The expert "international mother" is aware of the pressures put on mothers in both contexts as well as of the supports available to them—or lacking—on both sides of the Atlantic.

Mothers Moving Back

The Worst of Both Worlds?

Le Billon recounts the reverse cultural shock she experiences upon moving back to Vancouver.[5] She explains how she tries to maintain her family's new eating habits and recounts her unsuccessful attempts to set up a hot lunch program at her daughter's daycare in Canada. Despite the parents' interest in Le Billon's project, the daycare did not really support her idea. She suspects that the parents she surveyed were "as picky as their children" (196-97), or, maybe, they were just concerned by reports about experiences of other school lunch programs that failed to meet requirements in terms of quality/cost ratio, health, and safety. Some children benefit from eating at the cantine, where they will access food that is more nutritious, balanced, and healthier than what they would eat at home, but it is also true that some children will have better meals at home. In France, the cantine is "part of the means to decrease social disparities" (Bouzar 78). From a purely nutritional point of view, school lunches are, on average, good enough,[6] although they may not be as perfect as Le Billon and Druckerman describe them. In France, some groups voice their dissatisfaction not about the quality of the food but about cultural issues (see below).

The resistance Le Billon meets (196) from other parents in Vancouver can be summed up as a series of concerns over cultural and religious dietary restrictions, food allergies, picky eating, fear of institutional food (as opposed to the preferred and healthier family food), a general need to be in control of one's child's diet, and a strong emphasis on preserving individual choice. Some of the reasons for this resistance are precisely what the French approach relegates to the background. The common good, which consists in imparting taste literacy and healthy nutrition, trumps individual concerns. In terms of public health, this certainly yields results, although the lower obesity rates in France (compared to North America) cannot be attributed exclusively to the existence of subsidized hot school lunch programs.

Translating the "French food rules" into North American cultural expectations will not work easily, in part because of the predominance of an individualistic approach to solving problems regarding food and health concerns. It is difficult to move such food rules into a context influenced by a neoliberal ethos that privatizes both problems and solutions and that places so much insistence on the idea of consumer choice. In France, parents' committees likely would exercise pressure at the local level in order to make the school lunch better, if needed (for instance, by having more locally sourced produce or organic food on the menu). A North American solution to the same issue would most probably be individualistic, and mothers would be in charge of implementing it. The mother would remove the child from the lunch program and put together a packed lunch for them instead, or in wealthier communities, the school would outsource a good quality lunch to an external and more expensive caterer (thus potentially excluding from the program families who cannot afford it).

Structural Differences: What Is So Different about Parenting and Food?

The French food rules identified by Druckerman and clearly delineated by Le Billon cannot simply move as such to a North American context, without even mentioning that these rules do not work for all mothers and children in France itself. Picky eating also exists, but it is dealt with differently because of the structural differences in how meals and feeding times are organized and because of different approaches in parenting. Mentioning all divergences in the food and parenting cultures is beyond the scope of this chapter. I also leave aside considerations about how socioeconomic criteria and social capital determine to a great extent access to healthy diets through the purchase of a variety of high-quality foods and their preparation with sufficient time and skills. Instead, I focus on particular points that make a difference to mothers who feed their children or let their children be fed by others.

Cooking a fresh and healthy family dinner from scratch has become a notorious performance of good motherhood and thus a maternal achievement in the North American context. There, the family dinner is branded as a "principal and indispensable component of optimally functioning families" (Kinser and Denker 12; see also Kinser). Getting one's children to eat—and even more so to appreciate—what is served to them is a maternal performance. In France, in contrast, a mother who prepares family dinners on a daily basis does not seem to be rewarded with particular merit or appreciation. Her (unpaid) work, as a woman and as a mother, is taken for granted. For a father, though, this work might be recognized as helping out or as doing more than the average French husband does.[7] The participation of fathers in the preparation, serving, supervision, and cleaning up of meals is not extensively questioned. Fathers are there to help, which is better than nothing, but the idea that the responsibility of feeding at home is principally or even exclusively that of mothers remains largely unchallenged. Discussing the issue of gender equality in her chapter titled "I adore this baguette," Druckerman concludes that "If you drop the forlorn hope of fifty-fifty equality, it becomes easier to enjoy the fact that some urban French husbands do quite a lot of childcare, cooking, and dishwashing" (193) after remarking that "None of this follows the American feminist script" (192). Complaining about their partners not participating as much as they should in either household management tasks or in childrearing does not change the effective distribution of labour. Thus, all strategies to limit the amount of housework are worth consideration, and not systematically engaging in short-order cooking is one of them. French mothers emphasize cooking for the family rather than for the children. Desires and taste preferences of children, though acknowledged, are not central to the preparation of the home-cooked meal. Sitting at the table[8] together with one's children and eating with them (rather than monitoring their meal or serving them constantly) does not per se constitute an instance of intensive mothering (as defined in Hays; see note 3). Responding to Amber Kinser's critique of the family meal as an expression of intensive mothering, I argue that what brings in the intensity is not sitting at the table but rather attending to the (older) child's needs throughout the meal while disregarding one's own.

Another structural difference in children's feeding that has a direct impact on mothers is precisely the existence of an affordable (for most) cantine scolaire. School is one site where French mothers pass on to others the power to feed their children while, nevertheless, still being responsible for their general outcomes in terms of health and social acceptability. Paid employment is the norm for a majority of mothers in France, and thus most children eat at the cantine. Mothers generally do not have to cook or pack a lunch.[9] As described by Le Billon, parents check the school lunch menu, which is posted at the school's gate or online (35-36). Mothers adapt their home dinner plans so that the child does not eat the same type of dish twice in the same day or in the same week (e.g., pasta for lunch and lasagna for dinner). Unless they join the school's parents committee, mothers have no direct power to decide what the school will serve their children. Inversely, the public school lunch menu has an influence over the family dinner, at home, in the private sphere. Mothers adapt to the school's decisions and not the opposite. The case of nut-free zones or entirely nut-free schools in North America constitutes a contrastive example: The entire school, as well as all other parents who prepare their kid's school lunches in their own kitchens, adapt to the dietary requirements of one or several children to limit the risk of possibly life-threatening allergic reactions.

These structural differences make it difficult to apply the French food rules consistently in a North American context. Not only do Druckerman and Le Billon write about their own experience, but they also try to pass on some tips in parenting. In part because of such structural differences, and because of the general lack of interest or support from communities, they resort to and advise a more individual strategy: Both Druckerman and Le Billon go on to publish, after their memoir, a parenting advice book offering concrete solutions to implement in one's own home. Another reason, though, may prevent the implementation of the French food rules: the politics of religious accommodation that is much more developed in North America than in France. In contrast, the notion that the public school—and to some extent its users—ought to be secular, or laïc, prevails in France, in a context of increasing tensions around such issues. The next section of this chapter turns to this point.

Tasty Nationalism: Banning Ketchup and Giving No Other Option

Water is available without restriction. Salt and dressing (mayonnaise, vinaigrette, ketchup) are not freely available and are served according to dishes. Bread must be freely available.
—Article 2 of a 2011 decree on the nutritional quality of meals served at school (Arrêté)

Together at the Table of the (Maternal) Republic

In 2011, an official decree[10] banned ketchup from being freely available to children in the cantines of primary schools in France. Not only nutrition but also culture was invoked for this restriction. In an interview with the *Daily Mail*, Christophe Hébert, chairman of the National Association of Directors of Collective Restaurants, declared that "We have to ensure children become familiar with French recipes so that they can hand them down to the next generation and that they need to know that in France food means conviviality, sharing and having a good time at the table."[11] How occasional consumption of reasonably sized portions of ketchup threatens conviviality is not obvious, but it is clear that, from this perspective, ketchup stands for an unwanted "Americanization" (Fantasia 204) and "McDonaldization" (Légasse qtd. in Chérel) of food in a country where fast food and junk food remain the exception not the rule. In the 1990s, McDonalds was indeed marketed to French customers as a family restaurant and as a typical example of American cuisine (Fantasia). This is still the case now. McDonalds and other fast food chains established in this market are also considered family restaurants because they serve familiar food—a food whose taste is consistent, with soft textures (that need not be chewed) and no bitterness. Such food is not considered kids' food but as childish and not appropriate for the everyday diet of both adults and children. However, French parents do not feel guilty about occasionally taking their children to McDonalds; the Happy Meal is a special treat, not an everyday fare. Definitions of "kids' food" diverge from those in a North American context (a *National Post* article on the topic by food journalist Adam McDowell is aptly titled "Death to the Chicken Finger"). In *Bringing Up Bébé,* Druckerman observes: "Why is it that so many of the American kids I meet are on mono-diets of pasta or white rice, or eat only a narrow menu of 'kids' foods, whereas my daughter's French friends eat fish, vegetables, and practically everything else? And how is it that, except for a specific time in the afternoon, French kids don't snack?" (Druckerman 3). This viewpoint sharply contrasts with the "kids eat what adults eat," which is Le Billon's third French food rule (see Figure 1). The cultural implication and hidden fear of ketchup, and all that it stands for, is that children who consume it on a regular basis will never develop a culturally adequate taste for stronger tastes, such as blue cheese or oysters. In addition, fast food chains do not serve wine (or any alcohol)—the grown-up beverage par excellence in a country known for its wine.

Because it implies a potential or actual loss of culinary diversity and traditions (Légasse qtd. by Chérel; Fantasia), the standardization of food is regarded as a threat. In other contexts, imported foodstuff or foodways threaten the authority of mothers regarding food and feeding (see Rodriguez in this volume). In France, banning ketchup is a way to curb this threat in the public sphere of the school.

This ban was accompanied with a renewed emphasis not just on food literacy but on taste literacy and conviviality. In most French cantines, just like at home, children use regular, reusable plates and cutlery and not compartmented food trays, in which the food is dumped directly, or disposable plastic or paper plates. Corroborating the importance of eating together, Stéphane Papi notes that "In France, gastronomy constitutes a strong cultural element, and commensality is considered as an important moment of encounter and exchanges, as much in the family as in the social sphere" (1). Sharing a meal is seen as a foundation to the vivre ensemble (living together), which also takes place in the schools of the French Republic under the form of manger ensemble (eating together).

Another reaction consists not in excluding certain foodstuff, like ketchup, but students with dietary restrictions for their inability to participate in an ideal French culinary citizenship, as defined by the imperative of tasting everything. Determining the extent to which some particular exclusions (of certified halal food or of students who demand to consume it) serve an Islamophobic agenda under the cover of secularism deserves another, more detailed discussion, which is beyond the scope of this chapter.[12] In the following, I focus again on how maternal roles connect, for better or for worse, to contested notions of "culinary citizenship" (Mannur), "culinary nationalism," (Parkhurst Ferguson), or even what I call "tasty nationalism." I also point out that expatriate moving mothers, such as Druckerman and Le Billon, writing on feeding French children, do not engage with such notions.

In her study of the foodways of South Asian communities in the diaspora, food studies scholar Anita Mannur defines a type of food-based citizenship as "that which grants subjects the ability to claim and inhabit certain identitarian positions via their relationship to food" (29). Here, the concept of "culinary citizenship" is advanced to explain how people understand their relationship to their country through food and eating. Focusing on France and discussing cookbooks and recipes as "primary indicators of identity" (102), Priscilla Parkhurst Ferguson discusses another relevant notion, that of "culinary nationalism." She uses France as the most "striking example of a 'culinary country,' one where cuisine and nation are seen to coincide" (Parkhurst Ferguson 102). Building on these two notions—that of culinary citizenship and that of culinary nationalism—I argue that a form of tasty nationalism is subtly at work in the cantine scolaire.

The public school lunch is not only a meal shared with peers but also an event that builds up what the secular French state defines as appropriate citizenship. During lunch, children sit together as subsidized guests at the table of the Republic and are indirectly fed by the state. Mothers are absent from schools, where the act of feeding children nevertheless retains its association with the feminine; unsurprisingly, most cantine workers are women and the nation itself is thought of as feminine.[13] As many have stressed in recent debates about accommodations for religious dietary restrictions, participation in the school lunch program is not mandatory. However, it is, for many, not an optional state-funded convenience; for many mothers this program allows them to participate full-time in the workforce.

As Adam McDowell aptly remarks "typical French cantine ... stick [sic] mostly to French dishes." The recipes collected by Le Billon, the sample menus in Druckerman's book, and the dozens of menus from French cantines that I have collected[14] indeed consist mostly in traditional French cuisine. Although gustatory curiosity in children is highly valued, the range of dishes generally remains within the very rich culinary repertoire of French cuisine, for which during the twentieth century, "the local [became] the national" (Parkhust Ferguson 104). Does the internal diversity of French cuisine mean there is no need to add more international dishes, with only a few exceptions, to the school menu? Are logistics a real constraint? Or is there an implicit agenda of cultural formatting, of a culturally normative taste lagging behind the apparent diversity and balance of the menus of the French cantine scolaire? In comparison, more international dishes are on the menus that I collected from Canadian caterers delivering meals to school-aged children in Toronto and Vancouver. For instance, Foodie Kids Inc., a catering company based in Vancouver, serves school lunches that include such dishes as tofu teriyaki rolls, orange ginger chicken, and samosa. Of course, these are not meant to reflect an authentic (a contested term) cuisine of these specific countries, but it does give children a chance to be exposed to a variety of tastes or, at least, to become aware that people, elsewhere or right next door, eat different foods. On a previous, 2015 version of their website, Foodie Kids Inc. stated that they strived "to introduce Vancouver children to the multicultural cuisine they'll encounter in the real world.[15]Another company, Real Food for Real Kids, based in Toronto, has a substantial statement of values on their website: "North American food culture has seen a steady decline in recent generations, characterized by a dangerous slide away from nutritious and locally-grown whole foods, and toward cheap, highly processed 'convenience foods.'"[16] This company also features a diverse repertoire and, in addition, always offers a choice between a vegetarian and an omnivore subscription for school lunches. Both Canadian caterers give a choice to children: Two menus are available, one which offers a healthy and balanced version of a well-known dish, and another option.[17]

Motherland and Food

The French cantine's menus that I analyzed often placed some emphasis on the recipes made with local products or rooted in a regional cuisine repertoire (see Figure 2).

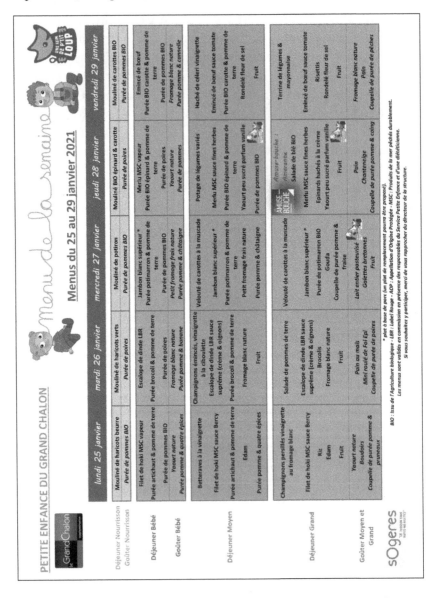

Figure 2. Public School Lunch Menus from Châlon-sur-Saône, France, in January 2021; the logo with a cow and a calf indicates that the dairy products come from local farms

Can such marking be read as a sign of anchoring the cantine's cuisine in the terroir—that is, tying food to place and, in the same move, rooting children in a specific territory to the motherland? At school, not only a culinary heritage but also the values of the Republic are imparted to children through the sense of taste. Children are being modelled into (future) good citizens who will fully participate in society. Participation in the school meal means tasting everything (goûter de tout) as well as disregarding one's own aversions or preferences, including the religious or ethical imperatives that the family or community might also transmit to the child, or enforce.

Even in the most recent debates, few commentators suggested that the state should stop offering a school lunch or that French parents who do not wish their child to eat the food served at the cantine, for whichever reason, should adopt the North American approach, consisting of bringing packed homemade lunches to school. The cantine scolaire as a state-sponsored institution is rarely questioned. The contents of the menus, however, are under increased scrutiny. Arguing that "the vegetarian meal [is] the most secular of all"[18] (Bélier), some have suggested that removing meat altogether was a practical and secular solution to enable children to eat together, at the table of the Republic. Even without discussing contentious political issues around communitarianism and secularism,[19] would it be easy to implement a vegetarian option while maintaining a focus on transmitting a French culinary heritage? In France, vegetarianism remains as an alternative, marginal, and contested choice (Larue). Even if it comprises vegetarian dishes (quiche, green lentils de Puy and other beans, and many sorts of cheese-based dishes), French cuisine is not typically a vegetarian-based cuisine. Vegetarian meals could be a solution only if they include sources of protein that are not traditional French food, such as tofu or tempeh. Could local production of, for instance, tofu even meet the demand if all school restaurants in France were to switch to completely vegetarian menus overnight? In the menus that I collected and in those featured in Druckerman and Le Billon's books, the central course of the meal is meat, while vegetarian options are rare. Recipes with meat, poultry, fish, seafood, and other edible animal flesh[20] constitute the main sections of most generalist French cookbooks, with few exceptions.

An implicit partnership between mothers and schools takes place around the school lunch: Mothers are expected to raise their babies and introduce them to a variety of food so that they do not become picky eaters by the time they start the école maternelle at the age of between two and a half and three. Children must be fit to be cared for by caregivers other than their parents and trained to obey instructions. Ideally, a child should also be débrouillard—a term that can be translated as prepared to be independent and resourceful. They must be used to tasting new foods, even if they are not required, in principle, to finish all the items on their plate. In parallel, the school will also enforce what is regarded as proper etiquette. Disruptive behaviours, such as playing with or throwing food, are not tolerated, both at school and at home. *French Kids Don't Throw Food*, the title of the UK edition of Druckerman's first book, reflects this rule for table manners. The same basic principles are widely shared within French society and are enforced at school and in most homes. In this sense, the school reinforces the education to taste as well as the table manners that parents—in fact mostly mothers—impart to their children. Mothers who do not agree with some of these principles, such as this imperative to taste a little bit of everything on the plate when this goes against their religious or ethical values, face what Sara Ruddick identifies as the tension between two of the fundamental actions of maternal thinking: the first is preservative love, and the other is training for social acceptability (65-81 and 103-123). What the mother regards as right and desires to transmit to her child may not correspond to what the state outlines as social acceptability. The mother is facing two equally demanding imperatives—that of the state which schools (future) citizens through their stomachs and that of enforcing dietary restrictions imposed by specific religious or philosophical traditions.

Mothers who openly question the quality or the content of the meals may appear not only as excessively anxious mothers but also as suspicious, disruptive citizens. For some of them, letting the school feed their child is a compromise and a risk, a competition in the formation of a distinct cultural identity through specific foodways. Although they have little agency, mothers nevertheless are held accountable. They delegate the control of what is on the menu to the school, but they remain responsible for what their children effectively eat or fail to eat. Whether they are citizens or residents in France, many (though not all) who identify as Muslims observe dietary restrictions to different extents. Some may avoid pork or refuse to eat any type of meat unless it is certified halal. What makes the position of Muslim mothers different from that of other mothers who question the menu, for instance vegetarian mothers, is that they are held accountable for their children's diets by their relatives and their community if there is a strong emphasis placed on consuming only halal products.

Echoing Mannur's statement that "food often serves to mark defining moments in marking ethnicity for communities that live through and against the vagaries of diasporized realities, marred by racism and xenophobia" (7-8), as is the case in other countries, food is often used in France as a marker of identity and of national cohesion[21] or of resistance to it. As intense debates between religious and secularist[22] traditions exist in France, some interpret the refusal to eat certain foods or to eat at certain moments (e.g., day fasting during Ramadan) as a refusal to assimilate or even as resistance to adopting and conforming to a uniform national identity.

The school lunch becomes another occasion to publicly express religious belonging.[23] Whereas it was previously sufficient for a majority of Muslims in France to just avoid pork, the current trend is to avoid meats lacking halal certification and to control the lists of all ingredients in order to make sure that no illicit ones (e.g., non-halal gelatine) are hidden. The shift from halal meat to halal food (Bergeaud-Blackler) or even halal lifestyles (including specific halal sports facilities, banking institutions, etc.) is documented in France (Bergeaud-Blackler; Bouzar) and is still a topic of debate that this chapter cannot fully engage with.

Once in her entire book, Le Billon very briefly acknowledges the problem in a parenthesis: "The French approach levels the playing field (although the exclusion of Muslim children due to the lack of halal foods is a longstanding issue)" (47).[24] This levelling of the playing field—that is, this uniformizing aspect of French culture that imparts values through food has its drawbacks—as no reasonable accommodation can be considered on the ground of religious or, even less so, cultural difference. Except for medically documented cases of allergies, no accommodation will be permitted: All children eat the same food, at the same time, in the same manner and this reinforces an esprit de corps. The commensality boosts the sense of belonging (sentiment d'appartenance) or, in the opposite, of exclusion. Whereas in North

America, the issues revolving around feeding children at home and at school raise mainly public health concern (access to nutritious food, prevention of disease, etc.), in France, such issues are also cultural. The children of expatriate North American mothers may not encounter any other issue than their initial reluctance to taste everything, which the French food rules will eventually overcome. However, mothers who deal with religious or ethical imperatives and choose to observe dietary restrictions (and wish to pass them onto their children) face other issues in using state-sponsored public facilities, such as the cantine scolaire. Which is more important to whom? Is it the respect of religious or ethical imperative or the participation in society as culinary citizens? Will state-sponsored structures find ways to continue inviting all children as subsidized guests at the table of the Republic, or will mothers have to find privatized solutions? Debates on such matters are recurring and intensifying. Solutions are implemented on a local basis, where some cities accept the "secular vegetarian" meal not as a nutritional or tasty ideal but as a "compromise" (Bouzar 83). Those who engage in these debates (such as parents, politicians, religious authorities, or anthropologists, to name only a few) rarely mention as a solution the lunchbox brought from home (and likely prepared by mothers rather than by someone else).

Concluding Remarks

The accounts examined in this chapter, written by two North American mothers temporarily taking residence in France, are undoubtedly authentic. As intended in a motherhood memoir genre, they also are personal and, thus, selective. They tend to construct an idealized image of French mothers, children, families, and the institutions with which they interact, in particular public schools and their cantines. They overlook several issues at the intersection of parenting, food, identity, and belonging, in particular the downsides of an approach to feeding children that leaves little room to personal preference, ethical or religious imperatives, and intercultural sensibility. By pointing out what works best in France, these authors highlight, by contrast, what is not producing desirable results in North America. They offer to remedy the culturally sustained phenomenon of picky eating through applying a set of rules. The problem is that one cannot simply transpose to North America the good tips and French food rules given by Le Billon and Druckerman; some of these rules will not work because they depend on support systems and social structures that are available to mothers in France but not in North America. These rules also work because of a broad cultural consensus in France regarding food and feeding children: Mothers, other caregivers (including grandparents), the cantine's staff, and teachers generally agree on the same principles. Marginalization, not accommodation, most likely awaits those who disagree with the content of the school's plates and with the "you have to taste everything" rule. French culinary national(ist) identity itself contrasts with both Americanized foodways, perceived as dangerous and undesirable, and with specific dietary restrictions. Those motivated by religious imperatives, in particular those of observant Muslims, may render difficult participation in commensality in public settings such as the cantines scolaires. Mothers of these children are the ones likely to have to carry further their demands for accommodations.

Because individual attempts at reforming the school's food system at a local level are unsuccessful, the two North American authors find another way to share their solution to what they clearly identify as a problem: They write parenting advice books. The advice and rules given in the parenting advice books *Bébé Day by Day* (Druckerman) and *Getting to YUM* (Le Billon) offer practical solutions to implement in one's own home. They might work for the middle-class primary readership addressed by Druckerman and Le Billon in a precise domain: Practices that depend only or foremost on mothers and that concern food practices in the home and in the family can be implemented. Those that involve collective structures and social interactions might prove more difficult to bring about. The required changes concern not just the food but the parenting approach in general. They might come at odds with some tenets of typical modes of childrearing in contemporary North America that place children and their preferences—not just their needs—at the centre of family life, as in the pervasive ideology of intensive mothering.

In their position as visiting foreigners, Le Billon and Druckerman do not engage with the issue of a French tasty nationalism deployed to serve the ideological purpose of vivre ensemble (living together). For children attending the public school lunch program, this goal translates into a manger ensemble that their mothers should prepare them for:

They eat the same dish and sit as equals at the table of the Republic. In the absence of their mothers, they become rooted in the terroir and the territory of the motherland through traditional recipes and locally sourced food, served by the generous and maternal hand of the state.

Endnotes

1. I have previously written about such an experience from a partially autoethnographic perspective in motherhood studies (Pasche Guignard and Guignard).

2. The Anglicism is in the original French title, which can be translated as *Made in France Baby. What Are The Secrets of Our Child-Rearing?*.

3. Sharon Hays defines intensive mothering as "a gendered model that advises mothers to expend a tremendous amount of time, energy, and money in raising their children" (x).

4. pameladruckerman.com/bebe-day-by-day/. Accessed 16 Apr. 2021.

5. She does so in the penultimate chapter ("The Best of Both Worlds," 177-202).

6. To my knowledge, there are no initiatives as famous and mediated as those of celebrity chef Jamie Oliver in the US and the UK (for instance, the documentary series *Jamie's School Dinners*) to improve the quality of the meals served at la cantine in France. Although there certainly is room for improvement in some school restaurants, issues are not resolved through privatized or dramatically mediatized initiatives.

7. The repartition of housework in France is clearly gendered. In 2010, women spent on average sixty-six minutes per day cooking, and men only twenty-four (Champagne).

8. A typical meal in France is eaten at the table, not on a couch or anywhere else in the house. A comparative "spatial analysis of feeding children" (Johnson) also yields interesting contrasts. The internal structure of houses, kitchens, and dining rooms determines feeding arrangements to some extent. Feeding North American children is often done "on the run" (Johnson 83): There are cup holders in car seats and on strollers (both for the adult and for the child), a vast choice in snack packs, boxes, sippy cups, individual portions, etc. All these allow for feeding children in contexts other than domestic.

9. Exceptions will be allowed in the case of medically documented severe allergies. A supervised lunch program where each child brings their own packed lunch is not the norm. Either students eat at the cantine, or they go back home for lunch.

10. The original decree "Arrêté du 30 septembre 2011 relatif à la qualité nutritionnelle des repas servis dans le cadre de la restauration scolaire" in French reads: "L'eau est à disposition sans restriction. Le sel et les sauces (mayonnaise, vinaigrette, ketchup) ne sont pas en libre accès et sont servis en fonction des plats. Le pain doit être disponible en libre accès" (Arrêté du 30 septembre 2011).

11. http://www.dailymail.co.uk/news/article-2045733/French-ration-tomato-sauce-school-canteens-limits-baguettes.html#ixzz3U BraUZ5X.

12. In some instances, under the cover of laïcité, some cities where an alternative to pork had always been available previously, sometimes for over thirty years, no longer offer this option. The Observatoire de la laïcité (observatory on secularism) reminded in a press release (communiqué de presse à propos de la restauration scolaire) that laïcité could not be used as a reason for not proposing an alternative menu for the school lunch program. It remains perfectly legal, however, to serve only one menu, which may contain pork, but laïcité could not be used as a justification for this.

13. The notion of motherland translates as la mère patrie. Another example is the figure of Marianne, a personification of France, that appears in many governmental logos, in official documents, and in postal stamps.

14. My original research collected samples of menus in 2015 and 2016 that were available online. More recent menus tend to follow the same patterns.

15. www.foodiekidsinc.com/delicious-meals/. Accessed 30 Mar. 2015.

16. www.rfrk.com/about-rfrk/#values. Accessed 16 Apr. 2021.

17. Ethnic foods are considered as more adventurous and thus positioned as alternatives to a norm, which raises another series of questions about privilege and who decides what constitutes a norm.

18. Also see Papi; Bélier et al.

19. Dounia Bouzar engages in such discussion on the basis of a case

study in Lyon, where a vegetarian option was systematically available. The vegetarian meals, however, were not conceived as strictly vegetarian since fish was served.

20. Snails and eels are not frequently consumed, and I could not find any school lunch menu featuring them.

21. Examples featured in (mostly regional) French media include the apéros saucisson-pinard. These began in 2010 to protest against the use of public streets adjacent to mosques for the Friday prayer. Such events are still held occasionally. These apéros consist in sharing food, namely pork dry sausages (saucisson) and wine (pinard, a slang word for wine).

22. I distinguish between "secular" and "secularist" in order to mark the French propensity to impose a certain comprehension of secularism, la laïcité. Other forms of secularism tolerate to a greater extent than French legislation the expression of belonging to specific religious communities or traditions through the display of religious symbols in the public sphere, including in schools (at least for students, if not also for teachers). French laïcité is now transformed into laïcisme, a form of radicalized secularism (Fernando).

23. Disruptions of a supposedly religiously neutral space during the public school lunchtime are not, however, exclusive to France. North American examples of behaviours or practices that are singled out as religiously disruptive rarely pertain to the contents of the school cafeteria's lunch, since the option of bringing a packed lunch is given. Rather, they involve gestures or vocal expressions of faith, such as saying grace or praying to bless the food or give thanks before eating.

24. Other communities, which could rely on more resources, have solved the issue by creating their own private, religious schools. There are, for instance, Jewish schools, where Jewish dietary laws are observed in the school. The lunch served to children is kosher.

Works Cited

"Arrêté du 30 septembre 2011 relatif à la qualité nutritionnelle des repas servis dans le cadre de la restauration scolaire." *Journal officiel de la République française*, vol. 229, 2 Oct. 2011, www.legifrance.gouv.fr/jorf/id/JORFTEXT000024614763. Accessed 8 June 2021.

Bélier, Sandrine et al. "Le repas végétarien, le plus laïc de tous." *Le Monde*, 23 Mar. 2015, www.lemonde.fr/idees/article/2015/03/26/ le-repas-vegetarien-le-plus-laique-de-tous_4602163_3232.html# 24TbKMqrFKVJZqpG.99. Accessed 2 Jun 2021.

Bergeaud-Blackler, Florence. "De la viande halal à l'halal food: comment le halal s'est développé en France." *Revue européenne des migrations internationales*, vol. 21, no. 3, 2005, pp. 125-47.

Bergeaud-Blackler, Florence. "L'école au défi de l'espace alimentaire halal " *Histoire, monde et cultures religieuses*, vol. 4, no. 32, 2014, pp. 103-18.

Bouzar, Dounia. "Des cimetières et des cantines à Lyon. Une gestion laïque de la diversité par l'élargissement de la norme générale." *Quand le religieux fait conflit: Désaccords, négociations ou arrangements*, edited by Anne-Sophie Lamine, Presses Universitaires de Rennes, 2014, pp. 77-94.

Champagne, Clara, Ariane Pailhé, and Anne Solaz. "Le temps domestique et parental des hommes et des femmes: quels facteurs d'évolutions en 25 ans?" *Economie et statistique* 478-479-480, 2015, pp. 209-42.

Chérel, Guillaume. "Périco Légasse: "La macdonaldisation est un impérialisme économico-culturel." *L'Humanité*. 8 Jan. 2013, www. humanite.fr/societe/perico-legasse-la-macdonaldisation-est-un-imperial-512316. Accessed 2 June 2021.

Chua, Amy. *Battle Hymn of the Tiger Mother*. Penguin Books, 2011.

Constable, Nicole. *Born out of Place: Migrant Mothers and the Politics of International Labor*. University of California Press, 2014.

Daily Mail. "France to Ration Tomato Ketchup in School Canteens to Keep Its Kids French." *The Daily Mail*, 6 Oct. 2011. www.dailymail.co.uk/ news/article-2045733/French-ration-tomato-sauce-school-canteens-limits-baguettes.html#ixzz3UBraUZ5X. Accessed 2 June 2021.

Druckerman, Pamela. *Bringing Up Bébé. One American Mother Discovers the Wisdom of French Parenting*. The Penguin Press, 2012.

Druckerman, Pamela. *Bébé Made in France. Quels sont les secrets de notre éducation?* Flammarion, 2013.

Druckerman, Pamela. *French Children Don't Throw Food*. Black Swan, 2013.

Druckerman, Pamela. *Bébé Day by Day. 100 Keys to French Parenting.* The Penguin Press, 2013.

Ennis, Linda, editor. *Intensive Mothering: The Cultural Contradictions of Motherhood.* Demeter Press, 2014.

Fantasia, Rick. "Fast Food in France." *Theory and Society,* vol. 24, no. 2, 1995, pp. 201-43.

Fernando, Mayanthi L. *The Republic Unsettled: Muslim French and the Contradictions of Secularism.* Duke University Press, 2014.

Foodies Inc. "Delicious Meals." *Foodie Kids,* foodiekidsinc.com/delicious-meals/. Accessed 30 Mar. 2015.

Hays, Sharon. *The Cultural Contradictions of Motherhood.* Yale University Press, 1996.

Johnson, Jennifer. "Mothering and Food Work in the Nuclear Family Home: A Spatial Analysis of Feeding Children." *Mothers and Food. Negotiating Foodways from Maternal Perspectives,* edited by Florence Pasche Guignard and Tanya M. Cassidy, Demeter Press, 2016, pp. 275-87.

Kinser, Amber. "At the Core of the Work/Life Balance Myth: Motherhood and Family Dinners." *What Do Mothers Need? Motherhood Activists and Scholars Speak Out on Maternal Empowerment for the 21st Century,* edited by Andrea O'Reilly, Demeter Press, 2012, pp. 316-30.

Kinser, Amber E. and Denker, Katherine E. "Feeding without Apology: Maternal Navigations of Distal Discourses in Family Meal Labor." *Mothers and Food. Negotiating Foodways from Maternal Perspectives,* edited by Florence Pasche Guignard and Tanya M. Cassidy, Demeter Press, 2016, pp. 11-27.

Larue, Renan. *Le végétarisme et ses ennemis: vingt-cinq siècles de débats.* Presses universitaires de France, 2015.

Le Billon, Karen. *French Kids Eat Everything {And Yours Can Too}: How Our Family Moved to France, Cured Picky Eating, Banned Snacking, and Discovered 10 Simple Rules for Raising Happy, Healthy Eaters.* Harper Collins, 2012.

Le Billon, Karen. *Getting to YUM. The 7 Secrets of Raising Eager Eaters.* HarperCollins, 2014.

Mannur, Anita. *Culinary Fictions: Food in South Asian Diasporic Culture.* Temple University Press, 2010.

McDowell, Adam. "Death to the Chicken Finger. How We Created an Entire Generation of Unsophisticated, Picky Eaters—And Why We Must Stop the Tasteless Cycle." *National Post*, 11 Feb. 2015, news.nationalpost.com/the-kids-menu/. Accessed 2 June 2021.

Observatoire de la laïcité. "Communiqué de presse à propos de la restauration scolaire." *Gouvernement de France*, 17 mars 2015, www.gouvernement.fr/sites/default/files/contenu/piece-jointe/2015/03/communique_odl_restauration_scolaire_17_03_2015.pdf. Accessed 2 June 2021.

Papi, Stéphane. "Islam, laïcité et commensalité dans les cantines scolaires publiques. Ou comment continuer à manger ensemble 'à la table de la République.'" *Hommes et migrations. Revue française de référence sur les dynamiques migratoires*, vol. 1296, 2012, pp. 126-35.

Parkhurst Ferguson, Priscilla. *Word of Mouth: What We Talk About When We Talk About Food.* University of California Press, 2014.

Pasche Guignard, Florence, and Thomas Guignard. "Scary Candy, Goldfish Crackers, and Kale Chips. Feeding and Parenting our New Canadian Daughter in Toronto." *What's Cooking, Mom? Narratives about Food and Family* edited by Tanya M. Cassidy and Florence Pasche Guignard, Demeter Press, 2015, pp. 138-48.

Real Food for Real Kids. "About Real Food for Real Kids." *RFRK*, www.rfrk.com/about-rfrk/#values. Accessed 16 Apr. 2021.

Ruddick, Sara. *Maternal Thinking. Towards a Politics of Peace.* Ballantine Books, 1989.

Stephens, Meredith. "The Rebellious Bento Box: Slapdash Western Mothering in Perfectionist Japan." *What's Cooking, Mom? Narratives about Food and Family*, edited by Florence Pasche Guignard and Tanya Cassidy, Demeter Press, 2015, pp. 160-70.

Suizzo, Marie-Anne. "French Parents' Cultural Models and Child-rearing Beliefs." *International Journal of Behavioral Development*, vol. 26, no. 4, 2002, pp. 297-307

Suizzo, Marie-Anne. "French and American Mothers' Childrearing Beliefs: Stimulating, Responding, and Long-Term Goals." *Journal of Cross-Cultural Psychology* 35, 2004, pp. 606-26.

Warner, Judith. *Perfect Madness: Motherhood in the Age of Anxiety.* Penguin, 2006.

Chapter 2

From Happy Meals to Celebrity Chefs: Shifting Attitudes towards Mothers and Traditional Food in Puerto Rico

Maria Elena Rodriguez

Para mí, la comida—más que simplemente ingerir alimento—es un canal de comunicación. Y de mantener la familia unida, o de reunir amistades y personas que hace tiempo no se ven. Para mí, yo creo que la comida es bien importante. Bien importante.

For me, food—more than simply ingesting nourishment—is a channel of communication. And to maintain the family together, or to reunite with friends or people that you haven't seen in a long time. For me, I believe that food is very important. Very important.

—Gloria
Fajardo, Puerto Rico
August 2012

I n the island of Puerto Rico, rich and varied historical influences have produced a complex food culture that is constantly being reshaped by numerous global and political forces. The contemporary Puerto Rican food system offers a unique opportunity to explore how societal notions surrounding gender and food are simultaneously constructed and disrupted. In this chapter, I examine how Puerto Rican women negotiate mothering, cultural identity, and foodways within an increasingly globalized and Americanized food system. This discussion centres around two main themes. First, that women's food work in the home has been steadily devalued in recent years, whereas the male celebrity chef persona has grown in popularity. And second, that women are often blamed for a loss of culinary culture in the home by depending too heavily on fast foods because of their busy lives. I situate this discussion within the broader context of colonialism and the historically ambiguous political relationship between the United States (US) and Puerto Rico. By drawing connections between the experiences of Puerto Rican women in the home and the larger island context, I hope to further a discourse on the unique gendered dynamics of the Puerto Rican food system, grounded in local women's experiences.

Research Design and Methodology

This work is derived from semistructured interviews I conducted during the summer of 2012 with twenty women in and around Fajardo, Puerto Rico. Fajardo is a medium-sized Puerto Rican city with a large working-class population, located on the eastern coast of the island. Historically, the economy of Fajardo has been driven by agriculture, fishing, and small-scale manufacturing, although it has shifted in recent years to include more tourism. Fajardo has also been the site of an increasing influx of American-owned grocery stores and fast-food chains, including the opening of the island's very first Walmart in 1992. These recent changes have drastically altered the landscape and consumption patterns of local residents.

I centred this inquiry on women in Puerto Rico because I believe they play a crucial and complex role in the transfer of cultural knowledge and values within Puerto Rican society, as also described by Loewen, Loewen, and Loewen Shepherd in this volume. In approaching this work, I drew heavily from Meredith Abarca's *charlas culinarias*, Carole Counihan's food-centred life histories, and the traditions of oral history and *testimonios* (Abarca; Acevedo; Counihan). These methods allowed me to formulate a critical feminist research framework that aims to centre historically marginalized people and experiences. Using food as a starting point, I sought to weave together individual voices into a collective narrative. I also drew from my lived experience as a working-class, Queer woman of colour, who was raised in the US by a Puerto Rican mother and white father. My transnational identity and mixed heritage formed my own backdrop to this research and my interpretation of it.

In conducting this research, I have sought to ground my methodology in feminist principles in order to produce scholarship that centres women's voices, is relevant to women's lives, and challenges the erasure of experiences of women of colour. In my efforts to increase the accessibility and reach of my work, I drew upon bell hooks' discussion of theory as a liberatory practice. hooks rejects the notion that theoretical work, and specifically feminist theory, should be written in a way that furthers the disconnect between lived realities and academic scholarship. Instead, she proposes that theory can be expressed as a "lived experience of critical thinking, of reflection and analysis" and subsequently draws the connection between theory and practice in the real lives of women both inside and outside of academia (hooks).

Although many women's voices contributed to my overall understanding of these topics, in this chapter, I focus on the perspectives of three particular interview participants. In preparation for the interviews conducted in 2012, I established informed oral consent and provided each participant with the choice to use their own name or to use a pseudonym. Out of the twenty women who participated in an interview, not one person asked for confidentiality at that time. Interestingly, a number of interview participants felt strongly that they did want their names to be connected with the study, expressing excitement at being recognized for contributing to university research. In 2021, I was able to re-establish consent with two of the three interviewees featured here; therefore, the names and identifying features of those two interviewees are real. The participants are as follows:

- Anna Gonzalez: a Puerto Rican woman raised in New York City, who later moved to Luquillo, a town close to Fajardo. At the time of our interview, she was in her mid-sixties.
- Zuleyka Ponce: a Puerto Rican woman originally from Fajardo. At the time of our interview, she was in her mid-twenties and working in the accounting field.
- Gloria (pseudonym): a Puerto Rican woman born and raised in Vieques. At the time of our interview, she was in her mid-thirties and working at a marina in Fajardo.

Historical and Political Background

The cultural roots of people who call Puerto Rico home are the product of a merging of many different peoples, most predominantly Indigenous Taíno, enslaved Africans, and Spanish colonists. These three groups converged over five hundred years ago when Spanish colonizers arrived at the island they named Puerto Rico and embarked on a mission to subjugate Indigenous people and their resources. As a result of the Spanish-Cuban-American War, the US gained control over Puerto Rico in 1898 and has retained ownership of the island ever since (Whalen and Vazquez-Hernandez). Developing as a nation consistently under some form of colonial control has had numerous far-reaching implications for the political views and ways of life for contemporary Puerto Rican people.

Puerto Ricans both living in the US and on the island were granted US citizenship in 1917 through the Jones-Shafroth Act. Even though the political status of the island remained largely unchanged, this shift in citizenship of island nationals marked the end of any meaningful Puerto Rican citizenship in a legal sense. Puerto Rico was defined as an unincorporated territory and would remain so for the next thirty years (Whalen and Vazquez-Hernandez). In 1952, Puerto Rico was subsequently established as an *Estado Libre Asociado,* or commonwealth, of the US. This political designation allowed the US to determine which aspects of governance would be legislated federally and which aspects would be self-governed on the island. Moving forwards, the US federal government retained control in Puerto Rico over the military, citizenship, immigration, currency, foreign affairs, trade, transportation, communication, and the judicial system (Duany; Whalen and Vazquez-Hernandez). Puerto Ricans maintained their US citizenship, although to this day they cannot vote for president of the US and also lack voting representation in Congress. These circumstances have led to a somewhat disjointed sense of nationalism and citizenship for many Puerto Ricans.

Since acquiring Puerto Rico from the Spanish in 1898, the US has employed numerous strategies in an attempt to Americanize the island and its people. In early Americanization programs, English was temporarily declared as the official language, particularly in the school system (Acosta-Belen et al.). Food assistance and distribution programs targeted the poor populations of Puerto Rico's rural countryside and growing cities. These programs distributed processed American food staples, such as canned vegetables, white bread, evaporated milk, cheddar cheese, crackers, and peanut butter. In the school system, breakfast and lunch programs were institutionalized with the goal of teaching poor Puerto Ricans "proper nutrition," which was based primarily on 1950s American dietary trends (Santiago). Many of these programs were successful in combatting malnutrition and reducing child mortality; however, they almost always ignored cultural food practices (Gonzalez). Although many of these historical tactics have either ended or become more subtle in nature, they have left an indelible mark on Puerto Rican lives and culinary culture.

Within the context of an increasingly ambiguous political situation and the impact of Americanization practices, Puerto Ricans navigate the food system in a multitude of ways. These narratives are tightly bound to the island's history, the legacy of colonialism, and the various policies put in place by US governance. The intersection of gender, culture, and foodways offers an opportunity to consider how Americanization has produced an air of devaluation—with specific reference to traditional Puerto Rican cuisine as well as the women who have historically prepared it.

Shifting Attitudes on the Value of Women's Work

Early on in my research, I was met with strong resistance from those who did not acknowledge the inherent value in studying women's experiences with food. One Puerto Rican man living in California went so far as to urge me to only interview Puerto Rico's renowned male chefs and forget about wasting my time "interviewing housewives." The fact that lived experiences of everyday Puerto Rican women are often not considered noteworthy enough for research, points toward a key issue—what has been traditionally considered "women's work" in the household has been steadily devalued by society as unproductive and uncultured work. De-valuing work traditionally performed by women and dismissing the value of women's food-centred experiences both serve to perpetuate the silencing of women's and mother's voices as unsophisticated, unnecessary, and unimportant.

A complementary issue is the worth placed on professional cooking, a field in Puerto Rico that is heavily dominated by men. Interview participant Gloria described this situation in detail:

> Como del trabajo, era bien raro ver un hombre cocinar. Era bien raro. En la casa de mis papás, los hombres pensaban: "Yo proveo el dinero, usted vaya al supermercado y usted prepara la comida." ... Sin embargo, desde los tiempos de los abuelos ... en el área de la cocina, en las áreas fueras como los restaurantes y demás, los que han predominado en la cocina siempre han sido los hombres más que mujeres. No sé a qué se debe ese fenómeno, pero casi siempre todas las personas que trabajan como profesional en la cocina y en confección de alimentos son los hombres. Las mujeres - vas a ver una que otra chef, pero no el volumen de hombres. Así que, se contradicen de que las mujeres son para la cocina porque son mayormente en la casa, pero en el ámbito profesional son los hombres los que están en la calle confeccionando alimentos.

Within the scope of work [in the home], it was very rare to see a man cooking. It was very rare. In my parents' house, the men said: "I supply the money; you go to the supermarket and prepare the food." ... Nevertheless, since my grandparents' time ... in the arena of the kitchen, like in restaurants, the ones who have predominated in the kitchen were always the men more than women. I don't know what to attribute this phenomenon to, but almost always the people who work as a professional in the kitchen and in the preparing of food are men. The women—you will see a chef here and there but not at the frequency of men. So, it's a contradiction that women are meant to be in the kitchen because yes, they are mostly in the home, but in the professional sphere, it is men who are out there preparing food.

I saw this firsthand as I attended a *feria gastronómica* (gastronomic fair) during my time in Puerto Rico. This fair featured renowned chefs and restaurant owners from the western region of Puerto Rico, and most were men. Even the postcard I received advertising the event reflected this; the card showed pictures of twelve featured chefs, eleven of whom were men. At the fair, I visited many of the booths and collected flyers advertising restaurants and culinary schools. Of the culinary school flyers I collected, all of the images depicting students were of men; the images were accompanied by text urging the reader to "earn a certificate in culinary arts" or exclaiming "You *too* can be a professional!"

This imagery, and the underrepresentation of women at the fair, both serve to further this conceptualization of successful chefs as predominantly male and those cooking in the home as predominantly female. The celebration of men as professional chefs and the devaluation of culinary work in the home offers men more social power and privilege than is afforded to women. Since women are not generally compensated for work performed in the home, men obtaining prestige as professional or celebrity chefs reflects the economic inequities faced by women in the food system. Men receive fame and a paycheck from their food work, whereas women are expected to cook for their families out of love, motherly duty, and tradition.

In one interview I conducted with two successful female restaurant owners and chefs, they alluded to their success in the restaurant business as being related to them not having children. As a lesbian couple, the fact that they did not have a "traditional" family makeup with children to care for allowed them to become more successful as culinary professionals. This situation reinforces the idea that women, who often are expected to be the main caretakers of children and the family, are not afforded the same opportunities as men in the culinary field because of these very roles they are expected to fulfill.

Mothers and Fast Food in Puerto Rico

A related shift in the eating practices of Puerto Ricans over the last fifty years has seen fewer meals being eaten in the home and more use of outside sources of food. The consumption of fast-food has skyrocketed, as parents have sought more convenient and affordable options for feeding their families. More parents—particularly mothers—have transitioned out of home-based domestic or agricultural work as a necessity for survival in today's economy. Additionally, more parents now take advantage of daycare and school-feeding programs to supplement their children's nutrition, both of which can provide huge benefits to resource-limited families. However, these changes have also resulted in new attitudes towards the role mothers play in the care and feeding of their children, including a discourse that is often rooted in blame.

In considering the expansion of fast-food in Puerto Rico, it is necessary to examine the assumptions that are made about the local culture in relation to fast-food. A 2005 *Caribbean Business* article on the fast-food industry in Puerto Rico states that with "sales reaching over $1 billion, the island's fast-food industry is satisfying the local market's changing lifestyles." This same article also offers a gendered explanation for why fast-food establishments have been so successful in the island. Quoting a representative of McDonald's, the article states: "The family structure is different from what it used to be 30 years ago. Mom has become the gatekeeper of the family, and there is less time to eat at home every single day" (Rosa).

Interview participant Anna Gonzalez discussed the impact of fast-food on the food choices of Puerto Rican youth as well as the pace of life in relation to fast-food:

Es que la juventud, tú le presentas un plato de arroz y habichuelas y mejor dice, "No, yo quiero nuggets." Y ahí es que están los problemas. Que la influencia es negativa por ese sentido, que los niños se acostumbran a comer mucha comida de fast food, si tú los acostumbras. Y como a veces es más fácil, y el estilo de vida te obliga a ir a un fast food, y comprarle por la ventanilla y sigues caminando y sigues haciendo lo que estás haciendo y sigues trabajando ... Pero eso es lo negativo, que les influye. La influencia es en que se acostumbran muy ligero y entonces no les gusta la comida que uno tiene en casa.

It's just that the youth, you give them a plate of rice and beans and they say "No, I want nuggets." And there's where the problems are. The influence is negative in this sense, children get accustomed to eating a lot of fast-food, if you accustom them to that. And how many times your lifestyle obligates you to eat fast-food and buy it from the drive-through window and continue on and continue what you are doing and continue working.... This is the negative ... that they are very easily accustomed and then they don't like the food that they have at home.

Anna describes a situation in which the negative influence of fast-food in Puerto Rico would cause children to reject their own cultural foods in favor of "nuggets" or other fast-food items. She says that this stems from parents causing their children to become overly accustomed to eating fast-food, to the point where they prefer it over what they would be eating at home. Anna also comments on how she feels the very lifestyle that many Puerto Ricans lead obligates them to feed their families from the drive-through window. Because of lack of time and the need to move on to other things or to continue working, parents are restricted to the easier and quicker option. This has serious repercussions, she argues, in the ways that children become accustomed to eating fast-food and the loss of a desire to eat more culturally significant foods.

Many other women I interviewed made similar comments regarding the fast-paced lifestyles people lead, the decrease in time available for cooking or sharing meals with family at home, and the impacts this has had on their diet. Gloria related the pace of life in Puerto Rico to the relationship between the island and the US:

Los restaurantes de comida rápida así, a mí nos han impactado tanto. Aparte del stress de vida y lo rápido, lo ligero que vivo. Y todo es en cualquier esquina, vas para el trabajo y desayunas, pareces del trabajo, almuerzas en el carro. Y sigues haciendo más cosas y más cosas y mientras más saturada se ve la gente, más obligada se ve en comer afuera, porque no hay tiempo para cocinar. No hay tiempo, imagínate, no hay tiempo para cocinar. No hay tiempo para sembrar.... Estamos viviendo al estilo americano aquí. No somos estado pero nos comportamos como tal en muchos aspectos. Nos gustan las cosas fáciles y rápidas.

Fast-food restaurants, in my opinion, have impacted us a lot. Apart from the stress of life and the fast pace, the quickness that I live. And all of this is on any street corner; you go to work and have breakfast, come out from work, and have lunch in your car. And you continue doing more things and more things, and meanwhile you see people more swamped, more obligated to eat outside, because there is no time to cook. There is no time, believe me, there is no time to cook. There is no time to grow food....We are living the American lifestyle here. We are not a state, but we act like it in many ways. We like things easy and fast.

Beyond the issue of lack of time, Gloria spoke at length about how American influence, in the form of changes to the food system, has affected Puerto Rican identity and mentality as a nation.

Aquí en Puerto Rico nosotros tenemos mucha influencia, nosotros como pueblo, es bien pobre nuestra propia identidad. Aquí cualquiera viene y planta bandera. Los fast foods especialmente ... ahora tu miras así, está inundado, invadido de los fast foods ... Aquí todo lo que ponen la gente lo apoya y lo aprueba. Siguen creciendo ... y la competencia en el mercado hasta que lo que tenemos hoy en día, que estamos saturados de comida chatarra, prácticamente, porque todo tienen preservativos, y comida que se guarda por tanto tiempo a la hora de la verdad no es nada saludable. Y aquí mayormente la comida que encuentras es de los Estados Unidos. Acá nosotros somos relacionados con los Estados Unidos ... no es estado, pero estamos relacionados. Y allá es donde empiezan a buscar cada cadena a poner su fast food, su línea de restaurantes y entonces se viene la competencia, la competencia de pollo, que si Popeye's, Kentucky, Church's. Y entonces viene el Chili's viene el Longhorn ... Y aquí todo el puertorriqueño lo patrocinan todo, aunque no lo entienda, aunque no lo usen, lo patrocinan.

Here in Puerto Rico, we have a lot of influence, us as a people, our own identity is very weak. Here anyone comes along and plants their flag. Fast foods especially now you look around, we're inundated, invaded with fast food. ... Here, anything that is established, people support it and try it. And [fast food establishments] continue growing ... and the competition in the market expands until what we have today ... that we are saturated with junk food, practically, because everything has preservatives, and food that keeps for a long time truthfully is not healthy. And here for the most part, the food you see is from the United States. Here, we have a relationship with the United States ... we are not a state, but we have a relationship. And that's where they start to establish every fast-food chain, their chain of restaurants and then comes more competition ... whether it's Popeye's, Kentucky, Church's. And then comes Chili's and Longhorn [...] and here Puerto Ricans support everything; even if they don't understand it, even if they don't use it, they support it.

In this quote, Gloria relates the expansion of fast-food chains in Puerto Rico to the political relationship between the island and the US. To her, the two issues are related because the island has this relationship with the US, which makes it much easier for fast-food chains to enter the island and set up their restaurants. Her discussion of Puerto Rican identity in relation to fast food is fascinating because she comments that the Puerto Rican identity is weak, which many have argued is a result of so many years of colonization and economic stagnation. She also discusses how she believes that Puerto Ricans support these new outside chains "even if they don't understand it, even if they don't use it." This is related to other discussions I have had that compared this high level of consumerism on the island to the desire to be seen as a modern people. Some Puerto Ricans have internalized a negative view of themselves as being backward or behind the times, potentially as a result of early Americanization programs or more contemporary US-promoted industrialization and modernization efforts. There may be a connection between these US efforts to modernize the island and its people and the internalization of this identity. A symptom of this internalized identity of needing to become more modern could be the high level of conspicuous consumption and the need to try and support new modern trends and conveniences, such as fast food.

In her ethnographic work with Mexican-American women in Antonito, Colorado, Carole Counihan argues that the industrialization and globalization of the food system has affected not only how people in Antonito eat but "also how their changing foodways reflect a challenge to the survival of their culture and economic autonomy" (Counihan, "A Tortilla"). She discusses how industrialized foods have altered not only the way the foods themselves taste but also the cultural or personal connotations those foods hold for the people consuming them. Counihan's exploration of food and family dynamics in Florence, Italy, also reflects these shifts, as she documented the impacts to Italian food culture through the introduction of fast food coupled with more mothers working outside of the home (Counihan, "Around the Tuscan Table"). This was echoed in my research when women, like Anna, described how changes from eating more traditional diets to consuming more fast food manifested in a loss of local food culture.

We have recently seen an increase in the academic scholarship looking specifically at the relationship between globalization and food cultures, of which the proliferation of fast food restaurants is a part of. Akil Gupta discusses the global movement of cuisines, showing how the global production, distribution, and consumption of food and spices provide a rich case to examine cultural transaction and exchange. By considering globalization from this point of view, Gupta discusses how the "movement of crops, changing culinary practices, and shifting habits of food consumption" have played a critical and undervalued role in shaping local identity and culture. In his examination of globalization and food culture in Belize, Richard Wilk provides an additional viewpoint on the effect of the globalized movement of food and people on cultures. He argues that forces such as globalization, tourism, and global capitalism do not automatically result in a "steamrolling" of culture and identity. Instead, he shows how in Belize, these forces have interacted with local culture and fuelled the emergence of a highly transnational and creolized identity, as evidenced through culinary culture (Wilk). This concept of a creolized and transnational identity is particularly relevant in the case of Puerto Rico, given its political history.

In our interview, Zuleyka Ponce described the connection between food and identity in this way:

La comida, la cultura, eso es lo que identifica a las personas de que país son. Y es como la identidad de uno, si eso se pierde, entonces ya no va a haber puertorriqueños.

Food, culture, this is what identifies people and what country they are from. And it's the identity of someone; if this is lost, then there won't be any Puerto Ricans anymore.

The above excerpt came after I had asked about the increased availability of fast food on the island, and we had talked in depth about its impact. Zuleyka's words are incredibly powerful here, as they link the cultural identity of Puerto Ricans to their traditional foods and argue that if we lose these cultural markers, we lose Puerto Ricans themselves. This assertation becomes even more complex as we consider the role of gender in the ways cultural traditions are expected to be taught and passed down through generations.

While we were discussing why fewer women cook at home nowadays, Zuleyka offered this explanation:

Por el tiempo, ahora la vida está más dura que antes. Para mí, antes las mujeres estaban más en la casa y se dedicaban más a la cocina; pero ahora todos salen a trabajar, mujeres y hombres, y la mujer también llega cansada y no se va a poner a trabajar en la cocina después de estar todo el día trabajando; y también eso hace que compren más comida afuera. Yo lo veo así.

Because of time, life now is more difficult than before. In my opinion, women spent more time in the home, and they dedicated themselves more to cooking; but now everyone goes to work, women and men, and the woman also arrives tired and doesn't set herself to work in the kitchen after spending the whole day working; and this also makes it so that they buy more food outside. This is how I see it.

Zuleyka's argument reinforces notions surrounding the impact that women working outside the home has on family eating patterns. I saw a striking example of this, as one of the women I interviewed for this project fed her young children fast food the night I interviewed her because she did not have time to do the interview as well as cook, help her children complete their homework, and so on. This same woman owned a health food store and spoke passionately about her desire to cook using whole ingredients and to ensure her children were eating healthily. Even this woman, who was so committed to a healthy lifestyle, relied on fast food occasionally when her schedule did not allow for cooking at home. I noted the sense of self-criticism and failure when she spoke about her difficulty in providing her young children with a wholesome diet given the busy life she led as a successful small business owner.

This research indicates that mothers often bear the brunt of blame for providing their families with nutritionally deficient food, regardless of their various family and professional commitments. Women are both the ones expected to provide for the family's nutritional needs and the ones at fault when they no longer have time to prepare wholesome home-cooked meals. Although men excel in the professional culinary world as described earlier in this chapter, they do not have to make the choice between cooking and family because for them it is a profession. Women often carry this burden, even when they have their own professions outside of the home. As they lean more heavily on fast food, frozen foods, or prepared packaged items, mothers are criticized for the loss of culinary culture, whereas successful male chefs are celebrated. This concept is made evident by the strong emphasis placed on the connection between food and cultural identity. In the case of Puerto Rico, colonial history and the impact of the US on the fabric of Puerto Rican lives are both closely intertwined with the island's sense of identity as it relates to culturally significant foods

Some of my own preliminary conclusions can be problematized when considering the complexity of food systems, gender dynamics, and personal autonomy and agency. My argument does not discount the experiences of mothers who may enjoy fast food, who dislike cooking, or who benefit from the savings in time and cost that fast food offers them. I acknowledge the diversity of women's experiences as well as personal interest and rejection of often oppressive gender roles and norms. What is most concerning to me is the creation of a US-focused rhetoric that undermines the value of Puerto Rican food traditions and women's contributions to the food system, however varied they may be. Many women I interviewed spoke strongly about how culinary traditions are often intimately related to a person's cultural or national identity. Some women talked openly about the dominating influence of the US on the island's cultural food heritage. I think this is particularly important when considering younger generations growing up in a time period when US influence on the food system in Puerto Rico is ever-increasing as new American fast-food chains set their sights on the Puerto Rican market.

Specifically regarding the notion of globalization and food systems, my critique of these changes does not necessarily make my stance antiglobalization. What I take issue with is the way that globalization of the food system in Puerto Rico has been spearheaded primarily by corporate interests, with little to no regard for the people of Puerto Rico. This corporate-driven globalization, paired with the ongoing Americanization of Puerto Rican lives, has greatly affected the ability of Puerto Rican people to sustain their cultural food traditions. Although globalized changes to the local food system in Puerto Rico may be inevitable, they also need to allow for the expression of agency and self-determination, particularly when it comes to experiences of women and mothers.

In sum, large-scale shifts within the Puerto Rican food system and economy have created a situation in which connection to traditional food culture is at stake and values surrounding food work are unbalanced. Because women have historically been tasked with the duty of caring for and feeding their families, this shift away from eating meals at home places blame on mothers who feed their children fast food. This dynamic places an even heavier burden of blame upon poor and working-class women as the main consumers of fast food and therefore the ones most to blame for a loss of traditional food culture in the home. This discourse can be problematized when considering the contemporary strains placed on mothers who participate more frequently in economic activities outside the home in order to survive in increasingly difficult financial times. Additionally, as mothers are blamed for changing food values at home, the culinary work they do is simultaneously devalued in comparison to celebrated male chefs. To address these issues, we need a local food system that both supports the preservation of Puerto Rican culinary heritage and values the diverse contributions of Puerto Rican mothers.

Works Cited

Abarca, Meredith E. "Los Chilaquiles de Mi 'amá: The Language of Everyday Cooking." In *Pilaf, Pozole, and Pad Thai: American Women and Ethnic Food*, edited by Sherrie A. Inness, University of Massachusetts Press, 2001, pp. 119-44.

Abarca, Meredith E. *Voices in the Kitchen: Views of Food and the World from Working-Class Mexican and Mexican American Women*. Texas A&M University Press, 2006.

Acevedo, Luz del Alba, editor. *Telling to Live: Latina Feminist Testimonios*. Duke University Press, 2001.

Acosta-Belen, Edna, et al. *"Adios, Borinquen Querida": The Puerto Rican Diaspora, Its History, and Contributions*. Center for Latino, Latin American, and Caribbean Studies, 2000.

Counihan, Carole M. *Around the Tuscan Table: Food, Family, and Gender in Twentieth-Century Florence*. Routledge, 2004.

Counihan, Carole M. *A Tortilla Is Like Life: Food and Culture in the San Luis Valley of Colorado*. University of Texas Press, 2009.

Duany, Jorge. *Puerto Rican Nation on the Move: Identities on the Island and in the United States.* University of North Carolina Press, 2002.

González, Elisa M. "Nurturing the Citizens of the Future: Milk Stations and Child Nutrition in Puerto Rico, 1929–60." *Medical History,* vol. 59, no. 2, 2015, pp. 177-98.

Gupta, Akhil. "A Different History of the Present: The Movement of Crops, Cuisines, and Globalization." *Curried Cultures: Globalization, Food, and South Asia,* edited by Ray Krishnendu and Tulasi Srinivas, University of California Press, 2012, pp. 24-46.

hooks, bell. "Theory as Liberatory Practice." *Teaching to Transgress: Education as the Practice of Freedom.* Routledge, 1994.

Rosa, Taina. "The Fast-Food Industry." *Caribbean Business,* 2005, www.puertorico-herald.org/issues2/2005/vol09n30/CBFastFood.html. Accessed 2 June 2021.

Santiago, Esmeralda. *When I Was Puerto Rican.* Vintage Books, 1993.

Whalen, Carmen Teresa, and Victor Vazquez-Hernandez, editors. *The Puerto Rican Diaspora: Historical Perspectives.* Temple University Press, 2005.

Wilk, Richard. *Home Cooking in the Global Village: Caribbean Food from Buccaneers to Ecotourists.* Berg Publishers, 2006.

Chapter 3

From Flavours of Domesticity to the Taste of Consumption: Routine, Resistance, and Desire in Borderlands Home Cooking

Ramona Lee Pérez

This chapter illuminates disjunctures in the ideology and practice of mothering by exploring the flavours of domesticity in the Mexico-United States (US) borderlands. Applying an oral history approach and lifecycle analysis to women's food narratives, I map the contours of regional home cooking (cocina casera), notions of taste (sabor), the critical persona of housewife (ama de casa), and tensions between cultural persistence and socioeconomic change. Drawing from comparative ethnographic field research on food habits in southern New Mexico and northern Chihuahua, I analyze the memories and culinary routines of two grandmothers living on either side of the border to show how Mexican and Mexican American women manage mealtimes through food routines, improvisational shortcuts, and the cultivation of gastronomic desire. This work contributes to understandings of kinship, mothering, and nurturance, provides historical and political-economic contextualization of changing food habits in the borderlands region, offers ethnographic documentation of household cooking practices, and gives voice to women's experience of their everyday lives.

My argument rests upon interlocking concepts foundational to regional domestic and intellectual life, namely con la cocina se mama and sabor, charla, and "theorizing from the flesh." The folk saying, "con la cocina de mama," loosely translated as "cooking with one's mother," reflects a cultural predilection for maternal nurturance through food. A multivalent term, "cocina" is first a verb denoting cooking as an activity. "Doing gender" (West and Zimmerman) as they are "doing cooking" (Certeau), women perform mothering (Butler) as they execute tasks for food preparation. "Cocina" also demarcates the space of the kitchen, a focal point of household life and the place for making and partaking of family meals (Christie; Marte). As such, the cocina is where people not only congregate to prepare and consume food but also share in one another's company and enact the connective tissue of kinship; they arrive at table to practice their relationships to one another in gender- and generation-differentiated hierarchies. Commensal meals, in contrast, are a time to inculcate group values, establish behavioral norms, share information and beliefs, and ratify the structure of the family (Weismantel). Finally, "cocina" also translates as cuisine, a system of interrelated edibles and their preparation methods, techniques, and modes of serving (Velasquez de Leon). As the codification of taste profiles that imbues foods with historical and cultural significance, cocina is also the systematic training of palates as mothers bring meals to the table.

The related concept of sabor means taste, flavour, or savour and is arguably the dominant cultural aesthetic of Mexican and Mexican American domestic life. Sabor is the epistemological foundation for good mothering.[1] Suggesting a phenomenological (Alcoff; Merleau-Ponty) and embodied perspective (Csordas; Stoller; Weiss), sabor demands reflexive gustation and evokes critical pleasure derived from investing time and focused attention on an edible experience as well as an appreciation for the tactile, olfactory, visual, auditory, and social flavour of cocina. A humanist and liberatory practice of everyday epicureanism, sabor is a structure of feeling precipitated into habitual conduct (Williams), the habitus arising from a sensorially dense social field (Bourdieu), and a critical ethos (Geertz) of borderlands culture. For example, el sabor de casa (taste of home) simultaneously evokes tasty comida casera (home cooking), the gender/kinship role of ama de casa (commonly translated as housewife but literally master of the home), and the realm of domestic life. Con la cocina se mama and sabor—thus intertwine in an embodied ideology of nurturance that mothers navigate through cooking for themselves and others.

The theoretical framework for my work emerged directly from informal fieldwork conversations in which ethnographic interlocutors acted as organic intellectuals (Gramsci) during the reconfiguring of the research agenda (Smith) as they expounded upon critical cultural concepts. To engage women's articulation of their embodied expertise, I developed "kitchen table ethnography" (Pérez), a reflexive research praxis similar to food-based life histories (Counihan) and Meredith Abarca's charlas culinarias (culinary chats) to foster dialogues about food and its role in regional cultural production. This process of making meaning through sharing personal, situated experiences echoes two key characteristics of borderlands feminist scholarship—namely, using testimonio (biographical testimonial literature) and reported conver-sation as forms of data (Abarca; Anzaldúa and Moraga; Behar; Castañeda et al.; Chavez; Cisneros; Rodriguez; Torres) and the concept of intersectional embodiment as lived experience and politically informed epistemological strategy (Anzaldúa; Castillo; Pérez; Sandoval; Trujillo), or "theory in the flesh" (Moraga).[2]

Research setting, Methods, and Sample

Based upon thirteen months of comparative, multisited, and cross-border ethnographic fieldwork on the food habits of Mexican and Mexican American women, this chapter focuses on the experiences of two elderly women, one from either side of the border. To situate the research and explain how their oral histories exemplify national and regional patterns of changing mothering roles, I first establish the ethnographic context, including important historical, economic, and cultural trends. I then summarize the research methodology and study sample. Next, I provide a brief sketch of the two women upon whom this chapter rests and explain how their personal histories exemplify trends apparent among other consultants. Finally, I present the interview data with these key consultants and analyze their stories according to the themes arising from participant observation with the entire research sample group.

The kitchens where I conducted the research are all located in the

Chihuahuan desert, an apparently endless horizon that straddles the Mexico and US border. Covering central and southern New Mexico and the northern half of Chihuahua as well as parts of Texas, Arizona, Coahuila, Durango, Zacatecas, and Nuevo León, it is one of the largest deserts in the Americas. With an average elevation of 4000 feet (420 meters) and over 350 days of sunshine, rainfall is less than 9 inches (22.86 cm) per year while the temperature ranges from 40 degrees Fahrenheit in the winter to the low 100s in the summer. This harsh climate combined with the area's history as a frontier territory under Spanish colonialism frustrated attempts at settlement and economic development; the area has also been the site for a series of important historical events, including the Mexican-American War, a century of skirmishes with the Apaches, and the Mexican Revolution. Later, the land would serve as the grounds for NAFTA[3]-era factories, which boasted unregulated labour and offshoring policies, narcotrafficking, and a continuing series of brutal femicides. All of this contributes to a cultural narrative identifying the region as a *país bárbaro* (savage country) (Jordán).

I conducted fieldwork in July 2000 and from July 2002 to July 2003 in Las Cruces, New Mexico, in the southwestern US and in Casas Grandes/Nuevo Casas Grandes, Chihuahua, in northern Mexico; I travelled biweekly between the two research sites. Twin towns located about 100 miles (160 kilometres) south of the international border and about 200 miles (320 kilometres) each from the state capital and the border city of Cuidad Juarez/El Paso to the north, Casas Grandes was the site of a Columbian trade centre, Paquimé, dating back to 700 BC (1974) prior to the arrival of Spanish colonial expeditions in 1536 (Resendez) and 1565 (Sen Venero). The colonial settlement of Casas Grandes began in 1661 with a mission and then a settler's outpost in 1825; Nuevo Casas Grandes was founded on the opposite side of the river in 1879 as a station for the Río Grande, Sierra Madre, and Pacific railroads (Sen Venero). Casas Grandes now boasts a total population of seventy thousand, and about a third of residents works in manufacturing, whereas the remainder works in agriculture or food processing industries, service trades, or the public sector (INEGI). Las Cruces, founded in 1849 as part of the Treaty of Guadalupe Hidalgo ending the Mexican American War, sits only 50 miles (80 kilometres) from Cuidad Juarez (Mora). Las Cruces has a current population just under one hundred thousand, and the public sector dominates local employment, along with food cultivation and processing as well as a growing service industry (Census). Cotton and alfalfa are grown as export crops on both sides of the border while a range of produce is cultivated for local and national markets.

Fieldwork consisted of extensive participation observation and oral history interviews, which were conducted in both sites. First, I documented the regional food economy through reviewing the census data, mapping and surveying farms, ranches, food processing and shipping companies, grocery stores, farmers' markets, specialty shops, and restaurants, as well as interviewing a range of local political and economic leaders to establish the ethnographic context for the study. I then recruited initial research participants from a variety of settings, such as churches, women's groups, and senior centres, as well as from local research sponsors. More women joined the study via snowball sampling and social network analysis. I conducted semistructured interviews focusing on oral history, social networks, and food habits with thirty-six Mexican origin women, some of whom were biologically or socially related. They lived in Las Cruces, New Mexico, and in Casas Grandes/Nuevos Casas Grandes, Chihuahua.

Respondents ranged from working poor to upper-middle class and from eighteen to eighty years old. They were mostly Catholic and represented a broad spectrum of educational achievement, work history, residential mobility, and use of ethnic labels. Respondents were born and raised in a variety of locales, including rural villages in the border states of New Mexico and Texas or in the border states of Chihuahua and Sonora in Mexico, among camps of migrant agricultural labourers, in a smelter town, and in urban settings throughout the US, Mexico, and Latin America. Age and class rather than nationality shaped educational achievement and labour history. One third hold or are pursuing professional degrees. Approximately one sixth of the total did not complete elementary school. Predominantly Catholic, the sample also includes Pentecostal and Mormon women in Las Cruces and Casas Grandes respectively. All were actively engaged with their religious communities, either through prayer at home, attending regular services, observing the ritual calendar, or volunteering at their local church. Some women cooked meals for parish staff, cooked prepared feasts for church holiday celebrations, and sold food for parish fundraisers. Despite similarities in these basic demographics, the international border delineated significant differences in terms of life experience and attitudes towards food and family.

The twenty Mexican women in the sample demonstrated greater residential stability. The vast majority had lived most of their lives in northern Chihuahua. Fifteen of these women were born either in their current county of residence or in neighbouring counties; three were born in the nearby border city of Cuidad Juarez/El Paso, and the final two in the neighbouring Mexican state of Sonora. Of the sixteen Mexican American women, only four were raised in their current county of residence. Another four hailed from northern New Mexico, four from west Texas, and one from Florida. The final three, one of whom was undocumented and was living in the US without legal residency, had migrated as adults from rural communities in northern Chihuahua. Whatever the history of residential mobility, all participants emphasized their natal states as an important identity label. Casas Grandes residents commonly referred to themselves as Mexicana or Norteña (north Mexican). Mexicana was also popular among first-generation immigrants to the US, whereas the US-born women over fifty typically identified as Hispanic, although a few preferred Mexican. Those born in northern New Mexico commonly used Hispanic or Spanish; US-born women thirty and under favoured Chicana and Latina. Others referred to themselves as Hispanic, Mexican, Chicana, Latina, Mexicana, or Norteña according to context.[4]

In both research sites, kin and social networks extended across multiple geopolitical boundaries. Although most Casa Grandes participants had a high density of immediate kin living within a radius of twenty miles, they also reported extended networks stretching across Chihuahua and northern Mexico and down to Mexico City, with sizeable contingents in ten other Mexican states as well as six US western and southwestern states, plus Hawaii, Canada, and China. Genealogical inquiries illustrated a gradual process of urbanization over the last three generations and also evidenced historical migration trends and the impact of the US program of repatriation efforts during the Great Depression. Las Cruces women also claimed residential proximity and frequent socializing with relatives, but smaller family sizes resulted in simpler kin networks. They reported family in town, throughout the state and in nearby El Paso, across seven different western, southwestern, and Midwestern states, and in Florida. With the exception of three first-generation immigrants, most emphasized kin living in the US, although one third-generation woman also cited relatives across northern Mexico and in Mexico City.

Aside from residential mobility and social networks, the international border also delineates differential integration into the market economy. Eighty per cent of women in the US sample had direct experience with wage labour. Among those over sixty, work outside the home was often restricted to years before marriage or after children started school. The majority of women between eighteen and sixty years of age either studied or worked outside the home. A few women at the edges of the class demographic—working poor and upper middle class—were homemakers and/or generated income from home-based businesses. Among the Mexican sample, most married women over forty-five did not work outside the home, although middle- and upper-middle-class women often operated a family or home-based business. In contrast, over 90 per cent of the twenty-five to forty-five year-old group on both sides of the border work full-time, usually as teachers, nurses, and secretaries. Elderly Mexican women commonly described their occupation as el hogar (the home) even when they operated small businesses out of the home.

Life History Snapshots: Tencha and Pat

Born in 1923, three years after the end of the Mexican Revolution, in the serrano[5] of northwestern Chihuahua, Doña[6] Hortensia "Tencha" Ortega Madrid left school at age twelve to help her mother at home. She married at fifteen and moved to Nuevos Casas Grandes, where she lived in the same house, built by her husband in Colonia Obrera (the worker's neighbourhood), for over four decades. At age eighty, Tencha describes herself as an ama de casa (homemaker), spouse, and head of a prolific dynasty numbering over 150 people who form a web of kinship that covers Chihuahua, encompasses northern Mexico, and traverses the border. After seven decades of reproductive labour—raising six brothers and sisters, twelve children of her own, as well as many of her own fifty-two grandchildren, seventy-two great-grandchildren, and even her four great-great grandchildren—Tencha remained dedicated to her daily routine of cooking for others. Recorded interviews with Tencha are often a jumble of a telephone ringing, roosters crowing, a screen door slamming, utensils clinking, and a cacophony of voices indecipherably intertwined—all evidence of dense social networks and high frequency of interpersonal contact.

Porfiria "Pat" Flores-Lucero was born in 1926 in northern New Mexico. At eighteen, she left home to work in California's WWII-era shipyards. She married at nineteen, moved to Oklahoma, divorced a few months later, worked briefly in Utah, and moved back to New Mexico. Her second marriage, to an Air Force officer, lasted twenty-four years, spanned three military bases in New Mexico and California, and provides the context for most of her memories of cooking for others. After twenty-four years as a wife and mother, Pat divorced and entered her second phase of wage labour, namely twenty-two years at a furniture store in Santa Barbara, California. She retired at sixty-two and moved to live closer to her children, first her youngest son in Phoenix, Arizona, and then her daughter and eldest son in Las Cruces and El Paso, respectively. By age seventy-seven, Pat lived alone in a one-bedroom apartment in a senior housing complex in Las Cruces and volunteered a few hours a week in a local senior services program. In contrast to Tencha, Pat's life history highlights residential mobility, greater integration into the global economy, and smaller kin networks; the arc of her autobiographical narrative deemphasizes biological reproductivity in favour of a personal chronology characterized by independence and consumerism.

As representatives of the grandmother generation, Tencha and Pat both demonstrate deep historical perspective and display the authority of "core" figures in their respective social networks (Alvarez; Lomnitz and Pérez-Lizaur). As border residents, their stories suggest regional patterns in kinship, nurturance, and domestic ideology, and they reveal nationally differentiated trends in women's wage labour and personal mobility. Articulate and engaging interlocutors, their first-person narratives provide intimate perspective on the experience of mothering and the conflict between reproductive and productive labour over the course of seven decades. Framed by issues raised throughout the research sample, these interviews illustrate the scope of sabor, the multiple dimensions of cocina and the evolution of mothering in the borderlands. With the theoretical and ethnographic framework now established, I now proceed to analysis the key themes in narratives of con la cocina se mama—namely, the reliance on routines and shortcuts, gendered food habits, and gastronomic desire.

Routines and Resistance: Food Cycles and Cocina Floja

Borderlands mothers develop a series of routines and shortcuts for managing the daily nutritional needs of an entire household over several decades and life stages. In terms of temporal organization, provisioning and menu planning tend towards repetition of preferred flavours, ingredients, and recipes in a set of household food cycles, which are patterned according to women's marketplace engagement as workers and consumers as well as their personal expertise in and commitment to reproductive labour. Mexican women generally articulate a longer time span than Mexican American women when planning domestic culinary production, preferring a quincena (fifteen days) or even a monthly food cycle rather than a weekly calendar. Whereas Mexican women expressed a general aversion to a weekly food cycle—which was often expressed as a concern that family members would get bored with eating the same food—Mexican American women did not display similar concerns. Key to the success of household meal planning and the continuing cultivation of sabor is the resistance strategy of cocina floja, a subgenre of tricks for domestic food preparation. Roughly translated as "lazy cookery," these shortcuts were referenced by the majority of research consultants.

When on the schedule of preparing family menus when her children were young, Pat remembers consistent daily and weekly menu cycles:

In the morning, I would usually fix them cereal. They didn't care much for eggs, except on Saturday. And pancakes they liked. Then for lunch, I had to put in peanut butter and jelly. That's all they wanted. All the time! Then they'd come home from school and have cookies and milk. Of course in the evening, I had to cook a lot of good food 'cause my ex was a big eater. He never liked dessert, so my kids never grew up with pies and cakes and stuff like that. Just cookies. I'd fix enchiladas and tacos, and you know, and beans. Every Monday, I had to have beans. Frijoles with chile and meat, pork or ground beef, but always with chile and beans, then fried potatoes and either tortillas or sopaipillas. That was every Monday....We just ate tuna fish on Friday.... For

Sunday dinner I would fix chicken or ham ... mostly it was just gringo food you know, vegetables and salads and stuff like that.

Pat's reflection illustrates that the more disposable income available in a given household, whether as a woman's own earned income or the steady salary of her spouse, the more likely she is to integrate a short food cycle with cocina floja strategies, such as large-batch cooking, recycling leftovers, and using packaged foods. Pat baked cookies for afterschool snacks on a weekly basis and turned the Monday pot of stewed pinto beans into refried beans for subsequent meals. Disposable income also increases reliance on shortcuts like packaged foods and American mainstream dishes, even when Mexican cocina casera staples remain central to meal planning routine. The prevalence of boxed cereal, peanut butter and jelly, and canned tuna all highlight the rapid industrialization of the US food supply that took place from the 1920s through the 1950s (Bentley; Levenstein; Shapiro), which drastically changed family consumption habits, particularly children's food preferences. The Mexican-style meat and potatoes dinners that Pat served, alternating with "gringo meals" like roast chicken and salad, contrast sharply with nostalgic reminiscences about her rural childhood in northern New Mexico.

Compared to her own mother's handmade tortillas, green beans straight from the kitchen garden, and milk and meat from a local relative's livestock, Pat's grocery store provisioning system is an exercise in cocina floja, which is idealize historical or rural diets as lacking shortcuts. Pat also discusses her own mother's pan huevona (lazy woman's bread) as well as baking soda biscuits as compared to loaves of home-baked yeast bread; other interviewees also expounded on bistec huevona (lazy woman's steak), sopita floja (lazy women's rice dish), and dozens of other lazy dishes. The generational differences of cocina floja, similar to Mexican versus Mexican American versions, rest in frequency of use, incorporation of industrially produced foods, and especially the attitudes of the speakers when reflecting on cooking shortcuts. Mexican women tend to be self-deprecating when revealing cocina floja strategies versus the privileged attitudes of Mexican American mothers. A subset of Mexican American cookbooks popularized by small publishers, most notably *Mexican Recipe Shortcuts or the Casserolization of the Classics* (Duran), elevate lazy cookery to its own art form. Overall, Pat's evolving food cycle reflects the gradual transition towards industrialized *sabor*, which characterizes the US food supply since the postwar era, American women's entry into the wage labour and consumer marketplace, and an increasing reliance on explicit strategies for cocina floja. While living and working in a WWII-era shipyard in Oakland, California, Pat got a crash course in the consumer habits that later would shape her family's diet: "I remember walking to the shipyard," she recalls "and they had this snack stand on the way and I would stop and buy me something for lunch." Disconnected from home and family and with disposable income at hand, Pat learned to buy her meals, a habit she would later foster in her children:

> We used to go out to a restaurant, or we would go to McDonald's or a drive-in or some, you know, like Sonic [a chain of drive-in fast-food restaurants]. It wasn't a Sonic, but it was something like it. And we used to go to the NCO [Non-Commissioned Officers] Club for breakfast on Sunday morning, and the kids thought they were so grown up because they'd order Shirley Temples, and we used to take them out to eat. Now I stop in at McDonald's, or else my daughter and I go to Herbert's [a local restaurant] or the Spanish Kitchen or there's another one on Solano.... They sell good Mexican food there.

Although Pat was a housewife for a quarter of a century, postwar standards of living meant that she and her family came to expect restaurant meals as part of their weekly meal routine. Eating out functions as the ultimate form of cocina floja in which the entire cooking, serving, and cleaning process is outsourced to a local business. The trend continues with her grandchildren who are already accustomed to restaurant and fast food outings. Family food habits are tied to Pat's attitude towards meal preparation: "Now, I'm not a cook. I don't cook except for when my kids ask me to fix them enchiladas on Saturday. That's when I cook. Other than that, if it doesn't go in the microwave, I don't cook. I've gotten very lazy, and I think I'm entitled to it.... For a long time I cooked, I cleaned, I washed, I ironed. No more." Her reliance on weekly food cycles and cocina floja strategies of packaged foods and eating out contrasts with the experience of women in a historically linked but nationally distinct context on the Mexican side of the border.

Because of a lag in women's entry into the paid workforce when compared to the US, Mexican amas de casa tend towards a more complex temporal and sociospatial organization of food cycles than their Mexican American counterparts. Successful provisioning rests on intricate organizational systems for managing household resources. Tencha consciously synchronizes the household budget with overlapping calendrical, seasonal, and ritual cycles, as well as social capital and obligations, which are all facilitated by her extended personal networks, access to transportation, storage constraints, family gastronomic preferences, and her own culinary skill. Preferring a system of monthly provisioning and *quincena* (a two-week cycle) menus, which are complemented by the regional harvest calendar, Tencha speaks about the financial limitations of her domestic food cycle while insisting on her right to sabor:

Me, I buy groceries each month because we're retired and the day the check arrives; the eighth, the ninth [of the month] is when I go buy. Good! Yes, I continue buying groceries ... but the day I go grocery shopping, I buy enough for the whole month. Sugar, coffee, oil and sausage, cheese, meat. I bring them home, and I put them in the refrigerator. I bring pot roast. I bring chops, cutlets.... I make one thing and then I make another.... And then more napkins, coffee, toilet paper, canned foods, canned tuna, canned milk, corn, green beans. I bring all of this, so I have it here ... salt ... oil... Then in between, in the middle of the month, well, if something runs out, then I buy it. If run out of a meat that I want to eat, then I go for more.

Although Tencha's preference for a monthly provisioning system appears to result from the financial constraints of her fixed, low-income household without access to disposable funds, the longer food cycle is also an artifact of the postwar proliferation of household appliances increasing food storage and cooking capacity[7] combined with seasonal provisioning patterns within the regional farming-ranching economy. Several north Mexican interviewees reminisced about monthly trips from rural homes into town in order to stock up on dry goods, whereas perishable items, such as dairy, meat, and produce, were cultivated by each family. Even though she no longer lives in the rural setting of her youth and tends to purchase meat and dairy from local markets, Tencha retains multiple links to the agricultural provisioning cycle.

> Just now they brought me new beans. Jose [her eldest son] just brought me a round barrel of beans the day before yesterday. Oh! I don't buy beans for the whole year. That one who called just now, he harvests the beans and brings me a sack, and it lasts the whole season. Sometimes he even brings a sack or two of [dried] red chile, and there I have it for the whole season. And a lady I know from Las Cruces brings me sacks of onions. They last me a good season.... I always have beans, and when I don't, well, I buy some. Look right now, I don't have the sack [of beans], but look, there I have my onions.

The pattern of harvesting with the seasons and storing basic foodstuffs throughout the year is fundamental to regional culture. Chihuahuan cuisine is shaped by its rugged mountain and steppe terrain and high altitude desert climate as well as its history as a frontier colony and crucible of the Mexican Revolution in northern Mexico (Frías Neve and Vargas Valdez). Such conditions led to a regional cuisine distinguished by centuries-old food preservation techniques, namely dehydration, canning, and cheese making. These methods impart unique flavours to popular recipes while synchronizing culinary production with local growing seasons and sense of sabor.

Tencha demonstrates her technical skills in lengthy accounts of her canning technique, whereas her time and resource-management abilities, coupled with anticipatory cocina floja, are revealed in the variety and durability of her store.

> Tencha: Now I'm making a little *conserva* [homemade preserves] for myself.... Right now. I'm making some tomato.

> Author: But you have others?

> Tencha: Yes, peach, apple, quince. I have everything.... I was going to open this so you can see here. Open it and see. Open it! I have quince. I have tomato.... I have quince, apple, yes. I have everything.... And there in the cupboard, that one, I have. I have *chile*, tomato, pumpkin, corn, green beans, every variety [of vegetable]. And here it's just fruit of every kind. I have everything, everything harvested here.... I have everything

preserved for the winter.

Canning has a special place in the northern Mexican household food cycle, occurring at the intersection of seasonal harvest calendars, provisioning routines, and domestic strategies of cocina floja. When pressed for a quick recipe (e.g., meat sautéed in a premade tomato-chile sauce), an easy side dish (e.g., preserved cactus paddles and green beans), or when low on fresh produce during the winter months, Tencha is prepared with a pantry full of homemade *conserva*. Aside from traditional methods of food preservation, Tencha also uses modern food preservation techniques to plan for the predictable instances of cocina floja.

> Tencha: Now I'm cooking some [beans], and I'll put them in little bags in the freezer, and when I want to refry beans, I just empty them out. In little bags in the freezer, beans keep very well.
>
> Author: How long do they keep?
>
> Tencha: However long, 'cause they get taken. There are times that Manuela [her neighbour] comes, or my daughters-in-law [and say], "Oh! I didn't put on any beans!" And I tell them, "There are some frozen ones. Take them."

Once foods are preserved, they can be used as instant additions to meal preparation.

Preparing for the eventual necessity of lazy meals is thus part of the household cooking routine and is built into the weekly and annual food cycle.

Searching for Sabor: Cultivating Gastronomic Desire

Given the overarching regional ideology of motherly nurturance and the necessary invention of household strategies, such as food cycles and cocina floja, in order to meet their obligations, how do women exercise a personal sense of taste? Tencha answers as follows:

> What do I like to eat? Well, what should I tell you? I like everything! Like, Ismael says, they want to tell me that I'm very mañosa [crafty]. I don't want to deny myself chile or anything to

eat because if I feel—and then my brother comes over, and he scolds me about why I eat sugar. He scolds me! Would you believe he's one of the youngest? I'm the oldest of the entire family.

In this declaration of epicurean zeal, Tencha is pleased to report her unofficial title of mañosa, a colloquialism describing a person whose delight in food verges on the sybaritic. Embracing the pleasures of eating through a personal gastronomy based on local crops and regional recipes, she deflects accusations of gluttony by dedicating her passion for sabor to the benefit of others, industrious cookery reflecting an unremitting commitment to the cultivation and indulgence of taste. Although nowadays she has lower caloric needs and is subject to dietary guidelines meant to allay encroaching diabetes and heart disease, Tencha still insists on consuming restricted food like sugar and red chile, such is her dedication to the pursuit of flavour. This excerpt from her culinary narrative also illuminates a significant trend in cross-gender relationships: Men, whether her father, brothers, or eldest son, may attempt to contain or control her exuberance, but she retains ownership over her cravings and her cooking. When she confesses to being mañosa, Tencha posits her epicurean self against gender and age discipline and implies that women have more taste than men because they are obligated to communication as an everyday aesthetic. Although gustation is predicated on individual experience, it can only flourish in shared experience. Tasty food thus engenders tasty talk.

Contrasting her gourmandism with the dietary patterns of her husband, a man who, in her opinion, has lost his appetite, Tencha elucidates the intensity of her passion for eating.

Tencha: Don Mariano prefers eating only sweets. Yes, pure sweets. Well, pure sweets [for] breakfast, lunch, and dinner, and for me pure enchiladas. I like them better than tacos.

Author: Why?

Tencha: Well, who knows. "To eat chile," says Ismael. "You'll see how good this little salsa is for eggs. It's not too spicy."

Author: So how often do you have enchiladas?

Tencha: No, I eat them frequently, but no, [I] don't think it's every day. Sometimes I don't make them for an entire week. Yes, I like them a lot. I also like milanesa a lot. Well, I like everything! I like cocido in this season. In the winter, I really like stews and I like pozole. I don't like menudo.... I like tamales a lot too.... My son that was just here, he brings them to me often because he goes to El Trebol bakery and sometimes when he goes the tamales are just arrived, and here he comes with my bag of tamales.

Beginning with quiet criticism of her spouse's inferior sabor and then celebrating how her children share her more refined sense of taste, Tencha proceeds to enumerate her favourite dishes from pan dulce (fresh-baked, sugar-crusted pastries) and milanesa (breaded chicken cutlets) to mole (poultry stewed in spicy chocolate sauce) and tamales (large, stuffed cornmeal dumplings steamed in corn husks). Although in other conversations she outlines a detailed nutritional model in which the elderly should not eat too many meats or spicy foods, Tencha joyously confesses a penchant for enchiladas (fried corn tortillas doused in red chile sauce and layered with grated cheese and chopped onions), milanesa, and especially pozole (pork and hominy stew flavoured with red chile). She also expounds upon seasonal recipes like cocido (meat and vegetable stews kept hot on the stove to ward off the chill of winter in the high desert). Beyond her personal gratification, Tencha's refined sabor is a form of cultural capital good for cultivating social standing and interpersonal relationships. From frozen beans parceled out to wayward daughters-in-law to the tastiest tamales in town delivered by her eldest son, desired foods are plentiful in her kitchen.

In contrast to Tencha's family- and cooking-based model of sabor, Pat's perspective rests upon her identity as a food consumer. She reveals personal taste preferences only in nostalgic reminiscence of childhood eating experiences or in emphatic declarations of gastronomic independence:

[We grew] green peas ... we called them alberjones. I used to go out there [to the garden]. She had to get me out of there 'cause I'd eat a whole bunch and get sick. They were so good, fresh, fresh! And then she'd have a lot of corn. We used to get the husks off and put it on top of the stove and brown it real good and eat it like that.... She [mom] used to make the best calabacitas (squash) with corn.... She'd scrape [the corn] off the cob and fix it with onions and cheese, and oh, it was so good! And her tortillas were out of this world. I was never able to make them like she did.... And capirotada [bread pudding].... She made it so good with the bread and the raisins and pine nuts, which she would hoard so I or my brothers wouldn't get into them and eat them. And then she'd put in cinnamon and make carmelado. She would put sugar on the stove to melt, and it would turn into caramel, and she'd put it in [the bread pudding], and oh, it was so good!

Freshness, particularly straight-from-the-garden produce, is a key feature of sabor. When reminiscing about her mother's garden, Pat exhales deeply and speaks with animation, proclaiming her food preferences as she outlines elements of regional cookery. This quote also reveals the importance of abundance in her childhood culinary cosmology. Easy access to favourite ingredients fosters the repeated gastronomic experience essential for constructing good taste. A whole bunch of homegrown peas, corn, squash, and pine nuts as well as homemade tortillas and holiday dessert all created a surfeit of flavour in dishes, which Pat repeatedly declares as "so good."

After testifying to her continuing nostalgic desire for the comida sabrosa (delicious meals) of her youth—made possible by the embodied expertise of her partially blind mother—Pat's personal relationship with cooking is strangely apathetic: I bought them Home Bakes [frozen dinners] ... but it's kind of a hassle.... I was gonna fix them Saturday but then I got lazy and didn't do it. This is chicken, mashed potatoes, and biscuits. And what I was gonna do, I was gonna put in carrots and peas so we could have the vegetables, too." Pat's diet nowadays contrasts sharply with the homegrown meals of her early childhood, and that difference is reflected in her embodied culinary epistemology. Rather than punctuating her story by gesturing the dimensions of foodstuffs or miming cooking techniques demonstrating embodied cooking knowledge like the elderly Mexican women who participated in this study, Pat simply walks to the freezer, extracts a box and bag, points to illustrated labels, and returns the items to the freezer. From microwaveable dinners to canned fruits, frozen vegetables and plastic wrapped tortillas, packaged food fractures the cook's relationship with food preparation, negating embodied knowledge as it reduces time and effort spent in the kitchen. Frozen dinners, precut produce, and microwave technology can be combined for a complete meal in a few minutes, but the extent of Pat's alienation from cooking surfaces is the ultimate paean to cocina floja, as she admits, "I got lazy and didn't do it." Packaged foods simplify the cooking process, but for Pat, if she has to enter the kitchen, it is not convenient enough.

When asked about her current favourite meals, Pat's response reflects childhood taste socialization, reinforces her antipathy towards domestic labour, and highlights her identity as a food consumer rather than an active proponent of sabor: "[I love] pork chops! And a salad. I love peas with carrots or without, but I love peas. And a salad. Not really a salad but pork chops and mashed potatoes and gravy. That's my favourite food, but I don't make it very often. Yeah, that's my favourite. That and McChicken. I love McChicken and fries and my strawberry milkshake." Another conversation confirmed Pat's attachment to McDonald's: "Every Sunday I have a McChicken and fries. I go from church to the stores. I go to Kmart. I go from there to McDonald's and get me a McChicken and fries. But that's me."

These excerpts reveal several important aspects of Pat's changed palate. First, she chooses as her hallmark dish a stereotypically masculine meal of broiled meat. Initially, she makes a concession to nutrition and the kitchen garden of her youth by adding peas, carrots, and a salad to the menu, but in the end, she retracts the greens entirely and reiterates her preference for pork chops and mashed potatoes. Her selection begs the question why this meal is so tasty to her. Feminist analysis might presume that Pat rejects salad in favour of pork chops in a deliberate reversal of gendered taste ideology. Linda Shapiro documents the historical construction of a feminine penchant for vegetables and a masculine taste for meat. Claiming a meat-and-potatoes meal as her own favourite asserts her right to privileges of masculinity as earned through decades as a divorcee and long-term engagement with the labour market. Pat declared repeatedly in multiple interviews that "I don't need a man," establishing her financial, emotional, and gastronomic independence from patriarchal regulation.

This independence, however, comes at a price. Pat's most frequent meal is an icon of the global consumer economy. When she asserts, "I love McChicken and fries and my strawberry milkshake," she declares allegiance to the branded convenience of the golden arches over the kitchen garden sabor, as maintained by her mother in 1930s northern

New Mexico and Tencha on the opposite side of the border. Pat repeatedly applies the word "me," "my," and "mine" only when discussing McDonald's meals, indicating her important relationship with fast food. Tasty home-cooked meals were from a time when Pat belonged to her mother; the obligation of cooking fulfilled with simplifying routines and cocina floja shortcuts was from when she belonged to her husband and children. Fast food, from coffee and a roll during her factory days to McChicken and strawberry shake after church, is Pat's version of feminist fare. When she visits McDonald's, she feels empowered by the ability to make, and pay for, her own choices. Rather than preparing meals to please others, she buys food for her own gratification. Financial independence allows Pat to disengage from reproductive labour, but it also limits her potential sabor to whatever her money can buy. The pinnacle of commercial capitalism, fast food thus represents both the market ideal of freedom of choice and the decline of embodied production of taste.

Degusto Ergo Sum: I Taste Therefore I Am

Detailing the characteristics of borderlands regional cuisine, this chapter explores how industrialization and women's entrance into the workforce affect the practice of cooking, household diet, and concepts of taste and family relationship. While professing values such as diligence, frugality, generosity, improvisation, and breadth of food knowledge, twenty-first-century borderlands women cheat expectations of self-sacrificing nurturance by modifying domestic cookery through strategies of resistance and personal gratification. Tencha and Pat negotiate key cultural concepts of sabor and con la cocina se mama as they navigate culturally preferred gender roles and capitalist disembodiment with discursive, productive, and consumer strategies. Tencha inscribes motherhood by engaging family, friends, and the convenience of small appliances to support her continued fulfillment of the housewife role, even as she declares gastronomic independence with her strong taste preferences. Pat twice relocated to live closer to her grandchildren and chooses to express nurturance in nondomestic contexts, and when she takes her family out to eat rather than cooking for them at home, she ratifies kin ties while modelling versions of gastronomy and femininity different than those she learned as a child.

In the context of the rugged independence of this frontier region and the rising tide of global consumer capitalism, autonomy is key to a reformulated culinary consciousness that is dedicated to gastronomic emancipation and liberation from culinary drudgery.

This work makes multiple contributions to anthropology, oral history, and the interdisciplinary studies of food and the Mexico-US border. As an overarching theory of taste, the notion of sabor enhances the study of the senses as it can anchor phenomenological research. Kitchen table ethnography models reflexive research methods and collaborative epistemology for scholars interested in oral history and dialogic analysis, whereas highlighting women's narratives of nurturance balances literature on gender oppression. Already rich in work on folklore and popular culture, border studies benefits from ethnographic research on regional food habits and women's domestic routines, and food studies grows from ethnographic and theoretical perspectives of borderlands cultural practice.

Endnotes

1. Abarca's related definition of sazón refers to a cook's embodied capacity to create flavour.
2. See Karen Mary Davalos for an analytical assessment of significant works using testimonio and "theory in the flesh."
3. NAFTA refers to the 1994 North American Free Trade Agreement signed by Canada, Mexico, and the US.
4. Ana Castillo and Patricia Zavella explore the significance of borderland women's ethnic labels.
5. Ana Maria Alonso and Daniel Nugent explain how Chihuahua's serrano, or the desert highlands region, served as frontier realm of colonial settlement caught in a hundred-year battle with local Indigenous populations; it was also the site of conflict during the Mexican-American War, home of Pancho Villa, and location of some of the fiercest battles of the Mexican Revolution. Building on Jordan, Alonso and Nugent argue that this fraught history shaped a cultural character of hardy independence and strict gender roles based upon principles of valour/honour for men and virtue for women.
6. "Doña" is an honorific title for married women meaning "ma'am."

7. For a thorough discussion of the impact of household appliances on *cocina*, see Emma Pérez, chapter 4.

Works Cited

Abarca, Meredith. *Voices in the Kitchen: Views of Food and the World from Working-Class Mexican American Women.* Texas A&M Press, 2006.

Alcoff, Linda Martín. "Merleau-Ponty y la Teoría Feminista sobre la Experiencia." *MORA*, vol. 5, 1999, pp. 122-38.

Alonso, Ana Maria. *Thread of Blood: Colonialism, Revolution, and Gender on Mexico's Northern Frontier.* University of Arizona Press, 1995.

Alvarez, Robert R. *La Familia: Migration and Adaptation in Baja and Alta California, 1800–1975.* University of California Press, 1987.

Anzaldúa, Gloria. *Borderlands/La Frontera: The New Mestiza.* Aunt Lute Books, 2012.

Anzaldúa, Gloria, and Cherrie Moraga. *This Bridge Called My Back: Writings by Radical Women of Color.* Aunt Lute / Kitchen Table Press, 1983.

Behar, Ruth. *Translated Woman: Crossing the Border with Esperanza's Story.* Beacon, 2003.

Bentley, Amy. *Eating for Victory: Food Rationing and Politics of Domesticity.* University of Illinois Press, 1998.

Bourdieu, Pierre. *Outline of a Theory of Practice.* Cambridge University Press, 1977.

Butler, Judith. "Performative Acts and Gender Constitution: An Essay in Phenomenology and Feminist Theory." *Theatre Journal*, vol. 40, no. 4, 1988, pp. 519-31

Castañeda, Antonia, et al., editors. *Gender on the Borderlands: The Frontiers Reader.* University of Nebraska Press, 2007.

Castillo, Ana. *Massacre of the Dreamers: Essays on Xicanisma.* University of New Mexico Press, 2014.

Certeau, Michel de. *The Practice of Everyday Life, Vol. 2: Living and Cooking.* University of Minnesota Press, 1998

Chavez, Denise. *A Taco Testimony: Meditations on Family, Food and Culture.* Rio Nuevo Publishers, 2006.

Christie, Maria Elisa. *Kitchenspace: Women, Fiestas and Everyday Life in Central Mexico.* University of Texas Press, 2008.

Cisneros, Sandra. *A House of My Own: Stories from My Life.* Knopf, 2015.

Counihan, Carole. *Around the Tuscan Table: Food, Family and Gender in Twentieth Century Florence.* Routledge, 2004.

Counihan, Carole. *A Tortillas Is Like Life: Food and Culture in the San Luis Valley of Colorado.* University of Texas Press, 2010.

Csordas, Thomas J. *Embodiment and Experience: The Existential Ground of Culture and the Self.* Cambridge University Press, 1995.

Davalos, Karen Mary. "*Sin Vergüenza*: The New Chicana Cultural Studies." *Feminist Studies*, vol. 34, no. 1-2, 2008, pp. 151-71.

Frías Neve Marcela, and Jesús Vargas Valdez. 1996. *Cocina Regional de Chihuahua.* Cuidad de Chihuahua: Ediciones Nueva Vizcaya.

Gamboa, Maggie. *Recetas del Valle: Recipes from Mexico, Spain and the Desert.* Saint Albert the Great and Newman Center, Del Valle Printing and Graphics, 1988.

Geertz, Clifford. *The Interpretation of Cultures.* Hutchinson, 1973.

Gramsci, Antonio. *Selections from the Prison Notebooks.* International Publishers, 1971.

Jordán, Fernando. *Crónica de un País Bárbardo.* Centro Libraro la Prensa, 1981.

Latina Feminist Group. *Telling to Live: Latina Feminist Testimonios.* Duke University Press, 2001.

Levenstein, Harvey A. *Revolution at the Table: The Transformation of the American Diet.* University of California Press, 2003.

Lomnitz, Larissa A., and Pérez-Lizaur. *A Mexican Elite Family, 1820-1980.* Cambridge University Press, 1988.

Marte, Lidia. "Foodmaps: Tracing Boundaries of Home through Food Relations." *Food and Foodways*, vol. 15, no. 3-4, 2007, pp. 261-89.

Merleau-Ponty, Maurice. *The Phenomenology of Perception.* Routledge, 2002.

Mora, Anthony P. *Border Dilemmas: Racial and National Uncertainties in New Mexico, 1848-1912.* Duke University Press, 2010.

Nugent, Daniel. *Spent Cartridges of Revolution: An Anthropological History of Namiquipa Chihuahua.* University of Chicago Press, 1993.

Pérez, Emma. *The Decolonial Imaginary: Writing Chicanas into History.* Indiana University Press, 1999.

Pérez, Ramona Lee. *Tasting Culture: Food, Family and Flavor in Greater Mexico.* New York University, PhD dissertation.

Pérez, Ramona Lee. "Interviewing Epistemologies: From Life History to Kitchen Table Ethnography." *Research Methods for Anthropological Studies of Food and Nutrition,* edited by J. Brett and J. Chrzan, Berghahn Books., 2017, pp. 47-57.

Rodríguez, Rosana Paula. "El Poder del Testimonio, Experiencias de Mujeres." *Estudos Feministas,* vol. 21, no. 3, 2013, pp. 1149-69.

Sandoval, Chela. *Methodology of the Oppressed.* University of Minnesota, 1994.

Sen Venero, Maria Isabel. *Historia de Chihuahua.* Centro Libraro la Prensa, 1998.

Shapiro, Linda. *Perfection Salad: Women and Cooking at the Turn of the Century.* Farrar, Straus and Giroux, 1986.

Shapiro, Linda. *Something from the Oven: Reinventing Dinner in 1950s America.* Viking, 2004.

Smith, Linda Tuhiwai. *Decolonizing Methodologies: Research and Indigenous Peoples.* Zed Books, 1999.

Stoller, Paul. *Sensuous Scholarship.* University of Pennsylvania Press, 1997.

Torres, Eden. *Chicana without Apology: The New Chicana Cultural Studies.* Routledge, 2004.

Trujillo, Carla. *Living Chicana Theory.* Third Woman Press, 1997.

Velazquez de Leon, Josefina. *Mexican Cook Book Devoted to American Homes: Recipes of Mexican Cookery of Each Region of the Mexican Country, Adopting Its Ingredients, to the Elements That Can Be Substituted in the Northern Part of the United States, Central Republic and South.* Escuela de Cocina Velazquez de Leon, 1961.

Weismantel, Mary. "Making Kin: Kinship Theory and Zumbagua Adoptions." *American Ethnologist,* vol. 22, no. 4, 1995, pp. 685-704.

Weiss, Gail. *Body Images: Embodiment as Intercorporeality.* Routledge, 1999.

West, Candace, and Don H. Zimmerman. "Doing Gender." *Gender and Society,* vol. 1, no. 2, 1987, pp. 125-51.

Williams, Raymond. *Marxism and Literature*. Oxford University Press, 1977.

Zavella, Patricia. "Feminist Insider Dilemmas: Constructing Ethnic Identity with Chicana Informants." *Frontiers,* vol. 13, no. 3, 1993, pp. 53-76.

PART II

Migrating Mothers, Performing Identity through Making Meals

Chapter 4

Food without Borders: Adaptive Expressions of Mothering

William Loewen, Gladys Loewen,
and Sharon Loewen Shepherd

Historically, mothers have held primary responsibility for family culinary traditions—preserving, cooking, and serving food. What a family eats is contextual and is shaped by multiple environmental forces, the family's social identity, and the individual choices made by the parents in general, mothers in particular. Using a social identity lens, this chapter examines themes and changes in mothering and food in one Mennonite family. Anne Loewen, mother of the authors of this chapter, born in Siberia at the time of the Russian Revolution, immigrated to Canada as a child with her parents. Through marriage and subsequent ordination as a missionary she lived in Colombia, Peru, Zambia, Togo, France, United States, and Canada, each posting impacted her food choices and preparation. This chapter examines how Canadian Mennonite culinary traditions shifted by tracking notable changes in Mennonite cookbooks and explores how the traditions of the Loewen family paralleled or deviated from the Mennonite group pattern.

Theoretical Context

George Mead states that one's sense of self "arises in social experience ... and that it is impossible to conceive of self arising outside of social experience" (140). Group membership is a foundation of an individual's identity (Turner 18; Ashforth and Maelm 20; Howard 367), and food is central to both forming and communicating that identity (Fischler 275; Gumerman 109), even after other cultural markers of that identity such as language have disappeared, as Vallianatos observes in this volume. Every person eats, and eating is both a nutritional and symbolic function (Fischler 275).

E. N. Anderson notes that "Food communicates class, ethnic group, lifestyle affiliation, and other social positions" (124). Rice, potatoes, or beans as a main staple is indicative of culture; hamburger versus filet mignon can delineate class. Economics and lifestyle determine how and where we obtain food. What we eat, where we eat, how we eat, and with whom we eat is informative of our social identity in a global world.

Marlene Epp describes the identity of women as being closely linked to food in families ("The Semiotics of Zwieback" 314-315), arguing the kitchen is the only place where women have power in a male-dominated culture (*Mennonite* 246). Women generally control the acquisition and preparation of food for the family, as they are central players in daily food preparation. They also maintain a key role in managing transitions in contextual family changes. A family may move to another country where food staples, produce, and spices are foreign. Even in a familiar setting, events such as war, drought, economic downturns, or national food trends may alter food availability. Women are pivotal in protecting family diet, ensuring familiarity and comfort, while managing food shifts during a time of change.

Food and food preparation are often a key piece of a woman's identity, especially her cultural and social identity, as noted in this volume by De Souza, Ore, and Rodriguez. Food shifts can affect a woman's identity as she contends with changes in food accessibility, food preparation, and the meaning of food in other settings. Ore suggests that mothers use cooking to bring a sense of comfort to the home and to keep memories and traditions alive when negotiating changes in environment and culture. Yet attempting to maintain past food practices may also separate women from others in the new environment. Women who compromise and adapt in new environments often experience internal changes, which can lead towards alienation within their own cultural community (Epp, "Pioneers" 148), giving them a feeling of being an outsider (Schmidt, Zimmerman, and Reschly 3).

In summary, using the social identity lens, a mother constructs her identity through a process of resisting and complying with social and cultural expectations that confront her. Global economics, religion, politics, and culture have a bearing on social expectations and influence the development of a person's identity. A mother's sense of self depends on how she handles the social and cultural expectations of others, her own desires, and the manner in which she balances this interplay.

Historical Context

North American Mennonites generally consist of two groups: Swiss Mennonites from southern Germany, France, and Switzerland who immigrated to North America in the 1700s, and Russian Mennonites from northern Germany and Holland who migrated first to Russia and then between 1880 and 1930 and again after World War Two (WWII) to North America (Epp, *Mennonite* 25-26). The historical and narrative content of this chapter focuses on the Russian Mennonite experience, whereas the cookbook section reflects the global Mennonite community.

The Mennonite tradition was to be in the world but not of the world as followers would live separately in protected, religious communities (Umble 40). In the late 1920s, Canadian Mennonite immigrants founded Yarrow, British Columbia (BC), a farming village reminiscent of their Russian/German heritage, designed to insulate villagers from outside influences (Neufeldt 24). Men and women worked together on small farms raising animals, planting fruit trees, and growing gardens; cooking was viewed as women's work. Women used fruit for platz[1] and perishki[2] and dried fruit for moos[3]; cabbage for cabbage rolls, sauerkraut, and borscht[4]; and cucumbers and dill for pickles. Cow's milk was used for making butter, bread and zwieback,[5] and cottage cheese, which was used to make varenike.[6] These familiar foods formed the bulk of their diet; they were the ethnic markers of their heritage (Epp "The Semiotics of Zwieback" 318; Staebler, 6), occupying an important role in church and community events—such as funerals, picnics, and weddings. It was women's responsibility to preserve fruit, vegetables, and meat for the winter, as Mennonites lived off the land whenever possible. "Mennonite tradition taught them [Mennonite believers] to be thrifty" (Mock 164)—a frugal approach using leftover fruit and vegetables by pickling watermelon rind and making Chow-Chow, a vegetable relish at the end of the garden season. They roasted wheat, grinding it to make a coffee-like drink called prips (Epp, "The Semiotics of Zwieback" 319). During the Mennonite migrations of the 1920s and 1940s out of Russia, Mennonite women baked and packed thousands of roasted zwieback for the journey, as dry-roasted zwieback can last several months without be-coming stale (Epp, "The Semiotics of Zwieback" 327); it served as thrifty migration survival food.

Figure 1. Pan of Fresh Zwieback at Mennonite Church Picnic, Siberia, 2010, Gladys Loewen, Digital Photo.

The Mennonite immigration to Canada and the events of WWII brought changes to their diet, agricultural practices, preservation of food, and employment. Poverty and the Great Depression forced fathers, sons, and daughters to work in the hop fields surrounding Yarrow (Kauffman, "Hop Season" 175), as family members worked to eke out a living. Later, strawberry and raspberry farms flourished in the rich soil of the Fraser Valley (Kauffman, "Our Raspberry World" 165), providing income. Recognizing their acute need, entrepreneurial Mennonites launched a commercial economy with a cannery, general store, butcher shop, gas station, and farm-related services alongside the agrarian economy (Neufeldt et al. 151).

The Mennonite lifestyle promoted quiet, simple values with the church at the heart of community life. Church was held multiple times per week with attendance expected. The church taught that direct communication with God existed through conversion as well as a personal pledge to follow God's will, which, for some, meant a call to mission work (B. Loewen et al. 123; J. Loewen and Prieb 120; Rawlyk 121, 143). In this "lived religion" (Braude 249), faith and fervour went hand-in-hand in answering God's call. The Yarrow Mennonite Brethren (MB) Church had an active Bible school and a Canadian and foreign missions programme, which sent "one foreign missionary for approximately every 120 members" (Penner 61); they were viewed as "apostles of the church sent to the 'heathen.' ... There was no greater calling" (Penner 55). Missionary work was placed on a "pedestal ... representing a higher standard of Christian obedience" (J. Loewen and A. Loewen 429). The missionary call was glorified in the church setting, as spiritual wealth superseded personal wealth, creating a dependence on the largesse of the home church for financial support (J. Loewen and A. Loewen 429).

Missionary work changed the complexion of the Mennonite Church from its origins in sixteenth-century Europe through its expansion through migration to North America. By 1948, Mennonite church membership records showed 262,187 members: 71 per cent North America, 20 per cent from Europe, and 8 per cent from mission work in Indonesia, Brazil, Mexico, and Paraguay (Bender et al.). By 2012, Mennonite membership had swelled to 1,774,720, with a significant change in the location of members: 30 per cent from North America, 3 per cent from Europe, and the remaining 67 per cent from twenty-one African countries, fifteen Asian and Pacific countries, and twenty-two Latin American and Caribbean countries (Bender et al.). Migration and mission efforts produced a globalized Mennonite identity, non-western nation Mennonites now the majority, transitioning from a primarily Caucasian to a multicultural identity.

North American Mennonite Food Changes

The extensive missions outreach resulted in notable shifts pertaining to the Mennonite identity and lifestyle. An early global shift was evidenced in the kitchen, as it shows changes in "food ways ... the site at which the old and new worlds meet" (Epp, "The Semiotics of Zwieback" 315). As women moved about in the larger community of non-Mennonites, they read cookbooks, attended potlucks, and exchanged recipes with friends, neighbours, and work colleagues, which introduced them to previously unknown ingredients. Mennonite women who travelled to foreign countries had direct exposure to new foods and ingredients (Anderson 203). To explore and document these changes in Mennonite cooking, the authors reviewed a variety of Mennonite cookbooks, choosing the cookbooks from the Mennonite Central Committee[7] (MCC) *World Community Cookbook* series as they span all Mennonite factions.

The first in the cookbook series, *More-with-Less*, begins with a premise of worldwide hunger and the need for "Christians [to] respond in a caring-sharing way in a world with limited food resources" (Longacre 9). Doris Janzen Longacre advocates eating simply and healthily, being aware of the Western propensity to overspend money, overeat, and overindulge in protein, sugar, and processed foods. The cookbook promotes frugal, nutritious eating through homemade soups, stews, and casseroles that allowed a portion of meat to serve more people. Women were given traditional Euro-Mennonite fare—such as Swiss Mennonite scrapple[8] shoofly pie[9] as well as Russian Mennonite borscht and varenike—and new ideas to try in the kitchen. This cookbook fit with a largely Euro-Mennonite community, as it mirrored the simple, frugal Mennonite lifestyle (Mock 267-268) and helped to mould "a Mennonite identity based on the principles of discipleship and simple living ... shaping ideology and values" (Epp, *Mennonite* 246).

Extending the Table, the second book, uses "changes and trends in North American eating patterns" (Schalbach 20) as a way to convey a message of global interconnectedness. It offers international recipes containing vignettes about the source of the recipe, allowing the reader to "enter into the lives and situations of these people and to be changed by them" (Schalbach 7). The recipes reflect what "people learned to eat as they lived, worked and grew to know others" (Schalbach 22) in mission placements. Mennonites were zealous in sending missionaries to spread the gospel worldwide (Penner 60) and MCC workers undertook countless international community projects. They brought back a multiplicity of lifestyle and food experiences that inspired *Extending the Table* recipes. The cookbook contains a nutritional guide to sodium, cholesterol, saturated fats, and fiber content; metric conversion; and a glossary of foods new to the Western world—cilantro, bulgur, tempeh, quinoa, and plantain.[10] Proceeds from the cookbooks supported the Mennonite Board of Mission's goal "to foster an awareness about its work overseas" (Mock 268), heralding the global shift in Mennonite identity.

Simply in Season (Lind and Hockman-Wert), the third cookbook, espouses a paradigm shift from eating for convenience to eating fresh, local, and seasonal food for health gains, which helps to support local food producers and sustain the environment. The authors of the cookbook endorse local farmers' markets, seasonal produce stands, and pick-your-own farms to eat what is grown nearby. The benefits include freshness, variety, taste, as well as nutrition for the consumer and economic gain for the local grower. The cookbook also recommends consuming less animal protein and eating organic, vegetarian food to optimize personal and environmental health benefits. It organizes vegetables by season and includes dishes, such as nutty cauliflower skillet, red lentil curry, and black bean–sweet potato burritos, which promote a sustainable, healthy way of life that reduces one's carbon footprint.

Family Narrative

Anne Enns Loewen was born in 1922 on a self-sustaining family farm in Siberia but was largely raised on a small farm in Yarrow, BC, where eking out a living was the norm. The bread-rich diet from their wheat farm in Russia continued in Yarrow, which was the only viable diet during the Great Depression. Women in the family made bread, zwiebach, varenike, perishki, and platz without recipes; young girls learned by osmosis at the feet of older women. Anne, the seventh of nine children, became her mother's housekeeper after sixth grade, as her older sisters left home (A. Loewen, Personal interview; B. Loewen et al. 131). Under her mother's supervision, she would "pick cukes in the afternoon & pickled dills ... make meals, clean house, laundry" (A. Loewen, Journal Book, August 23). She would also preserve fruits and vegetables and make borscht and chicken noodle soup for the family.

In addition to housekeeping, Anne was actively involved in church life, singing in the choir and teaching Sunday School. In the summer, she travelled with church leaders teaching Daily Vacation Bible School for children in nearby communities. Young Anne heard many missionary speakers at the MB Church and read several books about mission work in the Yarrow Bible School, piquing her interest in that calling. Following a meeting at church about missions, she wrote: "I am glad that I have the assurance of being called to work. I am glad I have yielded" (Enns, February 4, 1945).

In 1945, an acquaintance from Yarrow, Jacob A. Loewen, proposed marriage to Anne. His proposal included a commitment to mission work with the MB Mission Board, requiring a college education. Anne accepted Jacob's proposal feeling a calling from God; she was eager to obtain an education. Following ordination as missionaries by the MB Church, they travelled to Tabor College in Kansas to study mission and linguistics in preparation for a mission assignment. Although their college fees were covered by the Mission Board, they struggled to pay living expenses. Each looked for ways to earn money; Jacob preached at local churches for a small stipend, whereas Anne found temporary work as a cook in the dormitory over the Christmas holidays: "I can only praise the Lord again for the wisdom & strength. He gave so liberally for the work in the College kitchen" (Enns, December 22, 1945).

The young couple studied for two years, and in 1947, they received their mission assignment to Colombia, South America. Anne, her husband, and a baby daughter travelled by ship to Colombia and began missionary life on the banks of a river in the Chocó jungle next to a Wounaan native village (B. Loewen et al. 132). Two more daughters were born in the Colombian jungle during their stay. Anne had three roles—missionary, wife, and mother—each with varying levels of importance at different times, although mothering had the highest priority. Food preparation and choices created an instantaneous learning curve, as life in the jungle was unfamiliar to Anne. Staples such as flour, sugar, rice, and canned milk arrived periodically by commercial barges, a seven-hour trip; fresh milk was unavailable.

Figure 2. Rice Barges in the Chocó, Colombia, Circa 1950, Jacob A. Loewen, Slide.

The effort of adapting familiar foods in another culture was educational. Anne tried to bake cakes, cookies and bread using flour, but in the humid jungle heat, flour was constantly wormy; her daughters grew adept at picking out worms from baked goods (M. Epp 114). Anne's husband recounted the situation of two single female missionaries who drank lime juice each morning, as orange juice was unavailable. They wondered why their efforts to establish a church yielded so little gain until their native maid informed them that in local culture, women drank lime juice as a contraceptive; thus the unmarried women's morals seemed suspect (J. Loewen, *The Christian Encounter* 5). Anne's eyes were opened to her own biases (A. Loewen, Journal Book III, March 12) when she used her wedding china for meals with fellow missionaries who came to visit. As natives peered curiously through the screen door during these gatherings, Anne was humbled by the realization that she had given no thought to inviting the Wounaan people, assuming that they preferred eating their own foods using their hands. She changed her thinking and began to include Indigenous members for mealtime invitations served on china. Even so, she taught the use of a spoon for eating, perhaps a combination of hygiene concerns and her own discomfort with Indigenous eating habits.

The type of fresh produce available changed dramatically from Yarrow to Chocó. Anne's children grew up picking tropical fruit—fresh bananas, papayas, guamas,[11] and guavas—from trees. Anne still missed familiar North American fruits, and after receiving a monetary gift from a relative, she purchased imported apples, an uncommon fruit in Colombia. Daughter Gladys remembers receiving four apples, a precious commodity to savour, but she found apples dry and unappealing compared to tropical fruits. Without telling her parents, she sold the apples to older students at her missionary boarding school, buying candy with the gain. The Loewen children adapted to the Colombian treats of sucking on sugarcane sticks to extract the sweet liquid and letting panela[12] cubes melt in their mouth.

During her missionary years, Anne's food borders began to expand and change as she adapted to local ingredients first in the Chocó and later in the city of Cali, Colombia. She began making San Cocho,[13] using yucca in place of potatoes, cooking rice with lentils, and frying sliced platanos like the Wounaan, or peeling and baking them whole in the oven in Cali. Rice became the family staple because of local availability and family preference. Anne learned to shop at local open-air markets, bargaining for and purchasing most of what the family ate. Anne had staff in Colombia to assist with food preparation, cleanup, and child minding to free her for missionary duties, but food remained Anne's domain as she controlled the menu and the kitchen.

After leaving Colombia in 1957, Anne, Jacob and their four children lived in Washington and Kansas where, with familiar food items readily available, she resumed many of the vestiges of her early Mennonite cooking. She once again baked bread, zwieback, perishki and platz, and canned summer fruits and vegetables purchased from local farmers. However, the grocery store began stocking packaged meat, boxed cereals, gelatin, pudding, cake mixes, Wonder Bread, and tin cans of preserved fruits, vegetables, and soups. Now a working mother teaching foreign languages, Anne appreciated the time-saving help of these conveniences, readily incorporating them into her kitchen. Dream Whip—an imitation whipped cream made from processed powder beaten with milk—became a popular dessert topping while peaches in tin cans replaced home-canned peaches. Although Anne's food borders shifted partially to the convenient, as she learned to make one-dish hamburger casseroles, she included foods from Colombia—rice made with onion, lentils with rice, fritos—fried slices of green bananas. Other modified international recipes included curried meatballs with vegetables on rice, and porcupines.[14] The tried and true Mennonite fare was generally relegated to suppers with Mennonite visitors or food packed into the car for family vacations. Anne's children fondly recall picnics with fried chicken, homemade buns, and dill pickles as well as perishki on family trips—remnants of her Mennonite heritage.

In 1965, Anne and her family moved to Lima, Peru, adding another international experience. Processed convenience food was either unavailable or imported and expensive, so Anne returned to cooking from scratch. She baked bread, cookies, and cakes and made mayonnaise, mustard, Thousand Island dressing, tartar sauce, and home-made GrapeNuts cereal. She combined shopping for fresh vegetables and fruit in an open air market, bargaining with vendors in Spanish with the convenience of purchasing staples at a fixed-price in a supermarket or neighbourhood bodega.[15] Anne tried adapting her husband's favourite date bars by using tamarind fruit, thinking their colour and consistency would substitute well. The result, a runny, bitter-tasting concoction, remained a family joke for years. The family ate out for special occasions, choosing Chifa El Dorado (Chinese) or a pizza place, as the family explored international cuisine experiences for the first time. In this posting, Anne's primary roles were mother, manager of the food, and then wife and secretary for her husband's work as a translation consultant; she was a skilled secretary who could type in six languages. She managed the house with assistance from live-in staff—a Latin American tradition for those who could afford it—cared for the children—and typed her husband's correspondences, theses, and reports.

Figure 3. Lusaka, Zambia Market, 1972, D. J. Pauls, Photo.

In the 1970s, Anne, her husband, and youngest child, a son, transferred to Africa, living first in Zambia and later without children in Togo. In Africa, Anne shopped at open-air markets, bargaining in English in Zambia and French in Togo. Peanuts were sold in the market for protein, so Anne adapted and made African peanut soup, baked peanuts, and peanut stew. She had access to local stores with fixed prices for staples and purchased supplies, such as long-life milk and oil from a vendor who delivered. Because of availability, Anne cooked using only fresh fruits and vegetables—bananas, papayas, mangoes, and an African variety of squash. Male helpers assisted with kitchen and household work in both countries because French and British colonials had trained local men as servants. Although she appeared equally comfortable with male or female help, in Africa she felt safer with a male helper on the premises during her husband's frequent work trips. She continued to maintain responsibility for all food decisions, doing the bulk of the shopping.

Anne returned to Abbotsford, BC. Canada in retirement in the early 1980s. In this urban community, with pockets of Mennonites, South Asians, and East Asians, Anne blended her foreign food experiences, traditional Mennonite recipes, and familiar North American standards. She culled recipes from magazines and newspapers, carefully glued or typed them onto 3 x 5 cards for her recipe box that had always travelled with her. She baked buns and cinnamon rolls for her grandchildren following her Mennonite tradition. At her children's request, she wrote out her chicken borscht recipe, an adaptation, as beef was too fatty, measuring her cooking-by-taste process for the next generation. She regularly treated her family to feasts of cottage cheese and blueberry varenike with cream sauce and shared her recipes.

Figure 4. Anne Loewen Giving a Varenike Tutorial to Children and Grandchildren, Abbotsford, BC, circa 2004, D.J. Pauls, Photo.

Her experience with market shopping had conditioned Anne to the benefits of fresh produce for cost, nutrition, and taste, so she enjoyed BC farm fruits, eating blueberries, apples, peaches, strawberries, raspberries, and blackberries and freezing them for winter use in lieu of canning. She continued to make dishes she learned overseas. Two Vietnamese immigrant women, whom Jacob and Anne sponsored, walked into the house one day as she was cooking Jasmine rice for dinner. Son Bill recalls the women inhaling deeply, exclaiming "Oh my, you even know the best rice to cook." Eating out for Anne generally meant visiting ethnic restaurants, such as Thai, Indian, Italian, Mexican, and Greek.

Some of Anne's siblings had grown beyond traditional Mennonite cooking, which allowed food to be a comfortable and common denominator in social exchanges. However, travel and life overseas had shifted Anne's cultural and spiritual outlook from insular to global, and she chafed at those who could not appreciate or accept her growth as a woman of faith. The struggle to find her place back in the Mennonite community with relatives, former friends, and places of worship was filled with tension: "I feel almost estranged from the people with whom I grew up" (A. Loewen, Journal Book III, August 10). Time did not dilute the tension, leaving a chasm between Anne and some of her siblings—an unforeseen painful outcome of her adherence to God's call.

Analysis

The *World Community Cookbook* series offers a chronology of twentieth-century Mennonite food shifts, which was strongly influenced by Mennonite mission workers returning to North America with stories of how other cultures live and eat. These cookbooks demonstrate that international food experiences influenced Mennonite food choices; international recipes were added to traditional Mennonite food while adhering to the core Mennonite values of living frugally, eating simply, and sharing generously with others.

There appear to be four different stages in the twentieth-century Mennonite food experience. The first stage is closely linked to the Mennonite values of simplicity and frugality; women cooked without recipes from their gardens, preserving food for winter. During this time, Mennonites tended to live in closed communities insulated from modernization as a way to protect their religious and cultural heritage. Food was recognizable from home to home, as traditional recipes were culturally approved, and most families stayed within the boundaries of what was acceptable and known.

The second stage was shaped by changes following WWII; women entered the workforce, and the transportation of food became easier through the increased use of railroads, trucks, and airplanes (Montanari 158). Mechanization revolutionized the food industry, increasing food choices year round and creating a high demand for animal protein (Montanari 157). Women spent less time in the kitchen, as they enjoyed the convenience of processed food; can openers replaced canning jars. These changes weakened "the economic and cultural links between food and territory" (Montanari 158). Mennonites were not immune to these changes, as they joined mainstream North Americans in embracing the innovations in food convenience. *More-with-Less* was a clarion call to resist the push for processed food, encouraging women to continue cooking from scratch with natural, simple ingredients. The cookbook included traditional Mennonite dishes, so younger women could cook as their mothers and grandmothers did, but it also delved into new territory by touting some economical international recipes such as "Vietnamese Fried Rice, African Groundnut Stew, Japanese Rice, and Pakistani Kima" (Mock 267), which could be made in North America. Women liked the fresh ingredients, the nutritional value, and novel flavours but felt the pull of convenience as modern working women.

The third stage strongly endorsed the addition of international foods into family meals, as mainstream stores began carrying foreign spices, fruits, and vegetables. *Extending the Table* promoted international food recipes as nutritious, tasty, and healthy and added vignettes about the cultural traditions of each recipe, using food stories as a common denominator to interconnect people around the globe. This cookbook allowed women to experience international flavours at home without working or travelling overseas, which was facilitated by easy access to international products on store shelves.

The fourth stage was a shift back to organic, locally grown whole foods, adjusting international recipes to available ingredients and creating a healthy fusion cuisine. *Simply in Season* honoured the Mennonite values of simplicity and frugality, viewing seasonal, local, and organic as a way to maintain healthy bodies, healthy lifestyles, and a clean environment. The themes of this cookbook are parallel to a later non-Mennonite publication, *The 100 Mile Diet: A Year of Local Eating* (Smith and Mackinnon), which promoted eating foods produced and prepared within one hundred miles of home as a way to support local vendors and protect the environment.

Anne's journey paralleled these four stages for the most part. She was raised on a farm, and like Mennonite women of her day, she cooked without recipes and preserved food for off-season consumption in her mother's house. She lived in a religious community, sheltered from the outside world. As a married woman with a child, Anne moved to South America to begin mission work with little understanding of what she would encounter and how that might impact her life. The Colombian jungle forced her to make adaptive food changes; she incorporated tropical fruits, rice, lentils, cilantro, yucca, and plantains into her family meals and lived frugally with limited food supply, much like the *More-With-Less* approach. She was still eating close to the ground, similar to her farm heritage.

When she relocated to North America, it did not take Anne long to join the masses of women exchanging homemade for store-bought processed food for the convenience. Blending Mennonite, Colombian, and convenience food was her norm, following the pattern in *Extending the Table*. In retirement, Thai, Greek, and Mexican food became Anne's favourite foods, alongside the old standards of borsht, varenike and platz. She froze local summer fruit for use in winter, never returning to canning as a way of preserving food.

Anne had been a strict adherent of food portion control but now paid attention to the food she ate and its impact on her health, preferring fresh and local fruits and vegetables. The knowledge she gained over the course of nine decades led her to healthy eating as espoused by *Simply in Season*. Even though her mothering spanned more decades than her mission work, it was the experience of living overseas and seeing her own culture and religion through the eyes of others that profoundly changed her outlook. Age, wisdom, and life experience— the progression of her Mennonite values from the insular to the international— challenged her to rethink her culture, religion, and food borders, not by choice but by necessity.

Immigrants and missionaries find themselves on the forefront of cultural adaptations and changes in order to manage life in a foreign place. In this non-normative framework, they often pioneer food shifts that become the norm or, at a minimum, new food options for succeeding generations. As Anne wrote in her journal about her first missionary posting in Colombia: "Our religion packaged in a culture would never, never work here. So my religion and culture had to be separated—my first insight" (A. Loewen, Journal Book III March 12). She embraced the cultural shifts, which had an impact on her food choices and belief system, incorporating them into an internal identity; she saw herself as a global citizen and separated food from her spiritual identity. The definition of being Mennonite for her no longer was synonymous with eating borsht, varenike, and platz. Those foods remained part of cultural traditions, separate from the spiritual, while for her extended family, the traditional Russian foods remained an unchanged part of their Mennonite identity. Detaching food from religion was a steppingstone to questioning other church rules, such as dress and baptism, and to detaching cultural practices from theological beliefs and identity.

For Anne, food without borders began as a circumstantial shift as she began mission work, living in four countries on two continents. The experience of seeing her own culture and religion through the eyes of others created a profound internal shift in Anne's understanding and thinking; it challenged her to rethink her cultural borders of food, customs and spirituality. Despite these changes, Anne reflected her Mennonite upbringing in language, frugality and enjoyment of Mennonite foods while holding faith at the center of her life.

Conclusion

Outwardly, Anne's food choices mirror the food shifts of the *World Community Cookbook* series from a closed Mennonite world to an international Mennonite experience, demonstrating how women's relationship with food and food preparation can break down food borders. Anne had all the characteristics of a Mennonite mother. She was born in Russia, spoke Low German as mother tongue, and cooked and made borscht, varenike, and zwiebach from memory with faith a focal point in her life. However, she differed from many North American women who explored international food shifts by choice from the comfort of their homes. Anne recognized the divergence of her food path and understood it came from living abroad and her exposure to differing lifestyles and beliefs. The food shift may have been the first domino to fall simply because food is central to survival, yet it set in motion an unpredictable succession of internal shifts that reverberated through all parts of her life.

Her missionary experience, a calling at the heart of the MB Church, did not bring her closer to the centre of her cultural heritage. Instead through exposure, Anne evolved into a global citizen with Mennonite roots, living outside the boundaries of her heritage in many aspects of her life. Indeed, Mennonite "women often became outsiders in their own communities.... Women often renegotiated their place both inside the community and in opposition to it" (Schmidt, Umble, and Reschly 3). Anne, through life circumstances, changed not only food borders but also her views on religion and culture. Although Anne typified her Mennonite upbringing in numerous ways, her acceptance of multiple truths across cultural and religious borders placed her at the boundary of the Mennonite community. Thus, in response to answering God's call as a young woman, Anne found herself at the margins of her own cultural and religious community, renegotiating her place as she was no longer assured of a comfortable fit.

Endnotes

1. Platz is a coffee cake covered with fruit and streusel topping.
2. Perishki is a meat or fruit pie, often shaped into squares of pastry for individual servings.
3. Moos is a cold soup, with fresh or dried fruit often used as a dessert.
4. Borscht or borsch is a cabbage based soup made from chicken or beef stock and vegetables.
5. Zwieback is a two-tiered white bun to be pulled apart.
6. Varenike or vareniky is a dumpling filled with cheese or fruit, known as perogies in Ukraine.
7. Mennonite Central Committee (MCC) is an inter-Mennonite, North American organization focused on humanitarian aid and development projects worldwide. MCC distributed aid to Mennonites in Russia and Russian Mennonite refugees resettling in the Americas.
8. Scrapple is scraps of meat left over from butchering, which is then added to cornmeal and flour and congealed to make a loaf shape, then sliced and pan fried.

9. Shoofly pie is a pie made with molasses.

10. Plantain or platano is a type of cooking banana as it is not eaten raw.

11. Guama is a large green pod the length of a forearm, with big dark seeds inside covered with a soft fleshy, edible white membrane.

12. Panela chips are unrefined cane sugar shaped into a hard block for cooking.

13. San Cocho is a traditional Colombian soup flavoured with cilantro and yucca.

14. Porcupines are ground beef balls studded with rice and cooked in a tomato sauce.

15. A bodega is corner store.

Works Cited

Anderson, E. N. *Everyone Eats: Understanding Food and Culture.* New York University Press, 2005.

Ashforth, Blake, and Fred Maelm. "Social Identity Theory and the Organization." *Academy of Management Review,* vol. 14, no. 1, 1989, pp. 20-39.

Bender, Harold, Sam Steiner, and Richard D. Thiessen. "World Mennonite Membership Distribution." *Global Anabaptist Mennonite Encyclopedia Online,* 30 June 2014, gameo.org/index.php?title= World_Mennonite_Membership_Distribution. Accessed 3 June 2021.

Braude, Ann. "Faith, Feminism, and History." *The Religious History of America: Reimagining the Past,* edited by Catherine Brekus. University of North Carolina Press, 2007, pp. 232-52.

Enns, Annie. *This is My Personal Diary.* 1942-1946. Bill Loewen Personal Collection. South Dakota.

Epp, Margaret. *But God Hath Chosen: The Story of John and Mary Dyck.* Mennonite Press, 1953.

Epp, Marlene. *Mennonite Women in Canada: A History.* University of Manitoba Press, 2008.

Epp, Marlene. "Pioneers, Refugees, Exiles, and Transnationals: Gendering Diaspora in an Ethno-Religious Context". *Journal of the Canadian Historical Association / Revue de la Société historique du Canada,* vol. 12, no. 1, 2001, pp. 137-53.

Epp, Marlene. "The Semiotics of Zwieback: Feast and Famine in the Narratives of Mennonite Refugee Women." *Sisters or Strangers? Immigrant, Ethnic, and Racialized Women in Canadian History*, edited by M. Epp et al., University of Toronto Press, 2004, pp. 314-40.

Fischler, Claude. "Food, Self, Identity." *Social Science Information*, vol. 27., no. 2, 1988, pp. 275-92.

Gumerman, George IV. "Food and Complex Societies." *Journal of Archaeological Method and Theory*, vol. 4, no. 2, 1997, pp. 105-39.

Howard, J. "Social Psychology of Identities." *Annual Review of Sociology*, vol. 26, 2000, pp. 267-393.

Kauffman, Thelma Reimer. "Hop Season." *Village of Unsettled Yearnings*, edited by L. Neufeldt, TouchWood, 2002, pp. 175-83.

Kauffman, Thelma Reimer. "Our Raspberry World." *Village of Unsettled Yearnings*, edited by L. Neufeldt, TouchWood, 2002, pp. 164-74.

Lind, Mary Beth, and Cathleen Hockman-Wert. *Simply in Season*. Herald, 2005.

Loewen, Anne. Journal Book III. March 7, 2007–January 31, 2008. Bill Loewen Personal Collection. South Dakota.

Loewen, Anne. Personal interview. 17 Sept. 2011.

Loewen, Jacob. *The Christian Encounter with Culture*. World Vision International, 1967.

Loewen, Jacob A., and Anne Loewen. "The Missionary Role." *Culture and Human Values. Christian Intervention in Anthropological Perspectives*. William Carey Library, 1985.

Loewen, Jacob A., and Wesley Prieb. *Only the Sword of the Spirit*. Kindred Productions, 1997.

Loewen, William, et al. "Who's Cooking the Borscht? A Perspective on Social Identity." *Mothering Mennonite*, edited by R. Epp Buller and K. Fast, Demeter Press, 2013, pp. 120-41.

Longacre, Doris Janzen. *More-with-Less*. Herald, 1978.

Mead, George H. *Mind, Self, and Society*. University of Chicago Press, 1934.

Mock, Melanie Springer. "Mothering, More with Less." *Mothering Mennonite*, edited by R. Epp Buller and K. Fast, 2013, Demeter Press, pp. 256-72.

Montanari, Massimo. *The Culture of Food*. Translated by C. Ipsen. Blackwell, 1988.

Neufeldt, Leonard. "Village between River and Mountain." *Before We Were the Lands*, edited by L. Neufeldt, TouchWood, 2002, pp. 22-42.

Neufeldt, Leonard, Arthur Block, and Jack Derksen. "The Dynamics of Business in Yarrow." *Village of Unsettled Yearnings*, edited by L. Neufeldt, TouchWood, 2002, pp. 148-64.

Penner, Peter. "The Foreign Missionary as a Hero." *Village of Unsettled Yearnings*, edited by L. Neufeldt, TouchWood, 2002, pp. 50-61.

Rawlyk, G. A. *The Canada Fire. Radical Evangelicalism in British North America 1775-1812*. McGill-Queens University Press, 1994.

Schalbach, Joetta Handrich. *Extending the Table... A World Community Cookbook*. Herald, 1991.

Schmidt, Kimberly D., Diane Zimmerman Umble, and Steven D. Reschly. "Introduction: Insiders and Outsiders." *Strangers at Home: Amish and Mennonite Women in History*, edited by Kimberly D. Schmidt, Diane Zimmerman Umble, and Steven D. Reschly, John Hopkins University Press, 2002, pp. 1-21.

Smith, Alisa, and J. B. MacKinnon. *100 Mile Diet: A Year of Eating Local*. Vintage Canada, 2007.

Staebler, Edna. *Food that Really Schmecks: Mennonite Country Cooking*. McGraw-Hill, 1968.

Turner, J. C. "Towards a Cognitive Redefinition of the Social Group." *Social Identity and Intergroup Relations*, edited by H. Tajfel, Cambridge University Press, 1982, pp. 15-40.

Umble, Diane Zimmerman. "Who Are You? The Identity of the Outsider Within." *Strangers at Home: Amish and Mennonite Women in History*, edited by Kimberly D. Schmidt, Diane Zimmerman Umble, and Steven D. Reschly, John Hopkins University Press, 2002, pp. 39-52.

Chapter 5

Traversing the Mythology of the Female Home Cook: Jewish-Israeli Mothers "Cooking" Homes in New Zealand

Hadas Ore

I am a very aware mother, but I am a polania, and I am a sensitive Polish mother to the extent that if my child tells me she is still hungry after eating two pitot [sing. Pita], I have difficulties saying "no!" [to her requests for more pitot].—Yasmin

In 2007, at the outset of my fieldwork in the homes of Jewish-Israeli migrant mothers who live in Auckland, I noticed that they all increased their cooking to recreate a feeling of being at home in New Zealand. In my analysis, I looked into the changes they engender in their everyday domestic food practices, focusing on cooking—their everyday practice of providing meals and snacks for the family and themselves at home. Additionally, my fieldwork included participant observation of their experiences of grocery shopping, baking, providing casual and festive hospitality, and dieting for weight management. Similarly to the mothers of various cultural groups in this volume, the women in my study deal with a form of food system migration, which alludes to their way of coping with the contextual changes that relate to

115

food. Yet it was only towards the end of my analysis in 2012 that I understood how their nostalgia—the pain of longing to return home as conveyed through their cooking—is related to mythical figures that revolve around the female home cook.

It was the pervasive nature of the mothers' rhetoric—as demonstrated in the opening quote by Yasmin[1]—which grabbed my analytical attention. Due to her longing for home following migration, Yasmin, like the other mothers in the study, began to cook more at home; in her case, she bakes pitot to enact intimacy and care towards kin. Yet in feeding her family nostalgic foods, Yasmin is also concerned with her daughter's weight gain. Referencing the myth of the polania (Polish woman), Yasmin mocks herself, because although she is concerned with her daughter's weight gain and over eating, she is more concerned with not feeding her enough. In many cultural contexts, when mothers are confronted with uncertainties regarding feeding their children, they are first concerned with the quantity of food to ensure their survival. The quality and the variety of food are secondary concerns to mothers.

Indeed, the twenty-five Jewish-Israeli migrant mothers, aged thirty-five to fifty-five at the time of the study are all well aware that the mythical figure of the *polania* is associated with negative attributes such as overbearing care in feeding and guilt. Hence regardless of their ethnic affiliations they all employed such associations to convey intimacy and care in feeding their children as well as self-mockery. But how and why do these mothers grapple with such myths through their home cooking following their migration, and how is their nostalgia related to these myths? In this chapter, I show that Jewish-Israeli migrant mothers grapple with feminine mythical figures that revolve around home cooking by employing their nostalgic emotions and memories to lay claim to being "good enough" mothers in New Zealand. I examine their actions regarding cooking, as well as their memories and rhetoric, and build on the social anthropology literature on migrant mothers' home cooking. Inspired by the recent theoretical development in the literature on nostalgia, I also focus on the mothers' ambivalence in order to understand how they convey tension and make their claim to being good enough.

Earlier studies in the literature on migrant mothers' home cooking examine their everyday experiences to show how home-cooked dishes are mythologized over time as identity markers of ethnicity (Fischler 287; Williams 114-15; Shine-Rakavy, 64-68). Such studies suggest that unexplained or mysterious ingredients are part of this mythology (Fischler 287) as well as gestures and cooking methods that disappear in time due to technological innovations. Mothers' home-cooked dishes are usually understood as cooked from scratch in terms of the methods of the previous generation (Williams114-15; Gvion). Indeed, as seen in this volume in the study on Mennonite family recipes, cooking from scratch is a way to transfer women's cooking skills and knowledge to the next generation and to preserve tradition. The mythology of iconic ethnic dishes is a phenomenon seen, for example, in the Ashkenazi cuisine of Eastern and Central European Jewish women living in Israel over the past three generations regarding foods such as blintzes, chicken soup with matzo balls, and gefilte fish (Shine-Rakav 64-68).

The later studies in the literature on migrant mothers' home cooking, however, emphasize that despite the feminist revolution in many Western countries, middle-class women remain the main home cooks in the household—a division of labour that does not change following their migration (for example Halkier; Hage; Harbottle; Ray; Law). More importantly, by relating to women in first-generation migrant groups of various cultures, these studies illustrate how mothers enact kinship relationships through home cooking in order to constitute the familial home. The importance of keeping the family intact through home cooking is an idea supported by Rodriguez's study (in this volume) on Puerto Rican mothers, whereby mothers are near migrants in their own country due to drastic changes in their food system caused by Americanization. In comparison with this study I illustrate that following migration, mothers turn their home cooking into a nostalgic practice that aims to relieve the pain of longing to return home, stirring up memories of past familial homes. As the complexity of their kinship relationships unfolds, I show that the Jewish-Israeli mothers turn dishes and recipes, cooking gestures, and objects into metonyms of female kin from the past two generations, thus feeding themselves and their children nostalgic memories. In this way, the women materialize a feeling of being at home and lay claim to being good enough Jewish-Israeli mothers in New Zealand, as they often claim.

In focusing my analysis on these mothers' ambivalent feelings that convey kinship tension, I draw my inspiration from the recent theoretical development in the literature on nostalgia. This development relates to ambivalence as part of the connection with the national home by examining the reformulation of citizen-nation relations following the disintegration of the Soviet Union in 1989 and the subsequent political changes in Eastern and Central Europe (Bach; Berdahl; Boyer; Bohlman; Boym; Haukanes and Pine; Haukanes and Trnka; Parla). Daphne Berdahl's work in social anthropology has been mainly associated with ambivalent feelings as the social critique or the counter memory that people express through their nostalgia. Based on analysis of the everyday ritualized consumption that middle-class East Germans engaged in after the shift to postsocialism, Berdahl identifies three consecutive emotive steps in the nostalgic consumption of East Germans: first, they long for and idealize their socialist past; second, they articulate social critiques by contesting Westernization and capitalism; and third, they express self-irony or self-parody as they embrace the consumption of things that represent their socialist past home, altogether reconstituting a feeling of being at home and recuperating their shared past (xviii-xix). Rather than focus on how social relationships are negotiated regarding past national homes through a nostalgic practice, by asking to whom and how the mothers in the study direct social critique as part of their nostalgic cooking, I highlight their connection with past familial homes. This connection, I claim, is also important for the home of their children, as it is realized through the food they eat in New Zealand on an everyday basis.

In the following, I present the cultural-historic background of the Jewish-Israeli mothers who participated in my study and describe their social profile. I then move to an ethnographic extract that illustrates the experience of Inness, one of the study's participants, while cooking blintzes. The analysis that follows focuses on the memories and emotions evoked in Inness in comparison to the other mothers' experiences. The section that follows the analysis demonstrates that it is the migrant mothers' nostalgia that infuses home cooking with longing while remembering and imagining female close kin through their cooking skills, gestures, the cooking utensils they gifted and, of course, the recipes of their dishes. I illustrate how all these aspects of home cooking are used as metonyms for female kin from the past two generations by elaborating on the ways in which mothers enact both intimacy and tension in their relationships with kin. In the next two sections, I further illustrate how mothers grapple with the mythical figures of the polania and the bashlanit (cooking woman). I show that as mothers materialize their longing and pleasure in home cooking to convey intimacy with kin, they also idealize them. In contrast, the mothers convey tension by denigrating their female kin's intentions, efforts, and emotional investments in home cooking. Moreover, although the idealization of the bashlanit varies subtly according to class and ethnicity, it is the gender and the nature of the kinship relationships that matter most to the acts of home cooking and the mothers' choice of dishes.

The Historic and Cultural Background of the Study Group

Waves of Jewish migration to Palestine—first arriving mainly from Eastern and Central Europe (Ashkenazim) prior to the establishment of the state of Israel in 1948 and then from North African countries and the Middle East (Mizrahim)—were propelled by Zionist ideology to establish a migrant-settler society. By embracing Zionist ideology during this process of resettling Jewish migrants, the Ashkenazi elite colonized and marginalized the Mizrahim to various extents first in Palestine and then in Israel (Khazzoom; Clifford; Shenhav; Shohat). At the time of conceding the Jewish state Zionist ideology integrated socialist and liberal ideals and was premised on a unique nostalgia that recasts prominent Jewish values and messianic beliefs as secular, modern, and civilized means of ensuring the survival of the Jewish people through political upheavals and transformations.

Ensuring survival, for example, was prioritized by lower- to middle-class Ashkenazi and Mizrahi mothers alike during the early food rationing period (1949–1952) by putting their children first when feeding and cooking (Rosin 179-81). Yet Zionist policymakers and state authorities modelled Jewish-Israeli motherhood on a premise of problematic care: the excessive care of overanxious yet good Ashkenazi mothers and the poor level of care of Mizrahi mothers (Tene; Rosin; Bendrihem). State demands for food abstinence during the rationing period, and the associated sacrifice of pleasure on the part of lower- to middle-class mothers, contrasted with the fundamental value in Judaism that celebrates life by eating (Anderson 107).[2] In addition, these demands conveyed a sense of threat, since policymakers and Zionist ideologues portrayed Jewish mothers as providing unsatisfactory levels of care. Without a doubt, such demands intensified the hierarchy of gender, class, and ethnicity among the Jewish population that had already begun to form before the establishment of the state.

The sense of threat to the survival of the Jewish people in Israel strengthened, as evidenced by the mythical Jewish feminine figure of the polania that was formulated during that time by Zionist ideologues and policymakers, which depicted mothers as housewives and sacrificial sufferers who attempt to control others through guilt and blame. Historically, however, it is hard to pinpoint the exact period when this mythical figure arose, with some studies implying that the polania may have been a response to the gendered denigration of Jews in Europe as effeminate (Gluzman; Khazzoom). The figure of the polania depicts European upper-class aspiration through emphasis on education and economic mobility and the desire for respect. The desire for respect is manifested by the importance placed on making a good impression, table manners, and appearance. Studies that examine the sociohistoric conditions in the lives of Jews in Britain and the United States prior to the First World War relate to the formation of an equivalent myth—the "Yiddish Mama" in English speaking cultures (Ravits; Prell; Samuel and Thompson 17-18; Antler). Despite its prevalent role in popular culture, particularly in humour, literature and the media to this day, the mythical figure of the polania remains distinctly overlooked in social research on the everyday life of mothers in Jewish-Israeli society. Minor exceptions are found in two MA theses, which show that the polania is a persistent figure against which Jewish-Israeli women measure themselves, regardless of their ethnicity and class (Bendrihem; Gil-Tin).

From the 1960s to the 1980s, a period of relative prosperity and economic mobility for middle-class Jewish-Israeli women, Ruth Sirkis and Nira Rousso, who are two Ashkenazi women, became renowned role models in regard to cooking in the domestic sphere (Calò 50-3). In their publications, Sirkis and Rousso recast another mythical figure, the bashlanit. The myth of the bashlanit is the result of the unique coalescing of Jewish values with Zionist ideology in response to second-wave feminism. In its modernized guise, the bashlanit echoes at least two earlier Jewish feminine myths: Eve in the Garden of Eden and eshet chayil ("a woman of great valour"). This figure epitomizes feminine prowess and modernity: Not only is she technically able, well equipped, and pragmatic (she uses convenient ingredients, such as tinned food and makes one-pot meals), but she is also capable of successfully synchronizing her womanly obligations, all the while emanating love. This ideal is premised on the wish for an omnipotent femininity depicted through the pleasures of cooking and feeding. Sirkis and Rousso conjured this figure by publishing cookbooks and other forms of culinary texts that were, and still are, highly popular among Israeli domestic cooks, including the mothers who participated in my study. Sirkis and Rousso deliberately base their model of the bashlanit on the American success of Julia Child (Calò 66), targeting middle-class women working in paid employment and cooking on a daily basis. Whereas the model of Julia Child revolutionized American middle-class domestic cooking by emphasizing the personal and visceral pleasure in cooking for the sake of cooking (Hollows 33-36), the model of Sirkis and Rousso created an idealized image of a family woman.

The twenty-five mothers in my study group grew up in cities and rural settlements in Israel during the second-wave feminist era (the 1960s). They became part of a social network of around 1,600 Jewish-Israelis in New Zealand, who immigrated there in the early 2000s, with the majority settling in Auckland. They also became part of a minority group of Israeli migrants, a small portion of the total estimated one million Jewish-Israeli emigrants worldwide (Lustick 6). These mothers self-identify as secular women, apart from one woman who self-identifies as traditional.[3] The majority of these women are tertiary educated, and two thirds of them are either affiliated with mixed Jewish ethnicities or ethnically intermarried. The ethnic diversity in the study group means that most mothers beginning to recreate the home-cooked dishes of their female close kin learned to cook dishes and improvise on recipes, spices, and cooking methods that epitomize Jewish ethnicities other than their own. As mentioned earlier, they commonly increase their home cooking in order to relieve the pain of longing for home; they also do so for health and taste reasons as well as for the pleasure they derive from fostering good and healthy food habits in their children. Next, I describe and analyze how following their migration to New Zealand, these mothers learned to cook the familiar dishes they longed for.

The Home-Cooking Experience of Jewish-Israeli Migrant Mothers

By imitating their close female kin, mothers in this study learned to cook both Mizrahi and Ashkenazi dishes in New Zealand. Inness, for example, acknowledged that she had learned to cook the dishes of her Ashkenazi mother-in-law and Mizrahi grandmothers, since she and her children greatly desired them following migration. These dishes were visceral reminders of these close female kin and their past familial homes. In order to analyze and compare her cooking experience with that of other mothers in the study, I focus on her cooking blintzes, Ashkenazi thin pancakes by which Inness expresses both her intimacy and critique towards female kin. Blintzes are the last dish Inness prepared over the course of an intensive six hours.

> Inness had learned how to make blintzes from her Ashkenazi mother-in-law on her last visit to New Zealand. While Inness was cooking, she remembered and compared the behaviours of her mother-in-law and her mother during their separate visits to New Zealand. She depicted her mother-in-law as a loving, caring, supportive, know-ledgeable, and accomplished home cook, contrasting her behaviour with that of her mother, who always cooks in haste to get it over with—"to be exempted from an obligation." During the last visit of her own mother, she hid quietly behind her husband (Inness's father) for two "stifling" months while offering little financial help and hardly any help in the kitchen. In contrast, her mother-in-law bought Inness a special blintz-sized frying pan, watched over her shoulder while Inness learned to make them, and warned Inness not to despair over the first two, which usually spoil (stick and tear) and "do not count." This truism appears as the "Rousso Rule" in her cookbook Secrets from the Kitchen of Nira Rousso (Rousso 30) and acts to protect the iconic status of the bashlanit. An initial and relative failure in cooking is required to secure future success in mastering the skill. In cooking her blintzes, Inness followed the advice of her Polish mother-in-law: she used the first two blintzes to check on the consistency of the batter and then corrected it by adding some water. She then let her children eat the torn practice blintzes. Since her family loves blintzes, Inness made about fifty in an hour and a half for her hospitality event and to feed her family in the week that followed.

She swiftly dipped the ladle in the batter and then spread its contents around the frying pan in circular motion while tilting the pan to spread the mixture evenly. She then waited for the edges to detach from the pan before moving the blintz to a plate nearby.

In a manner akin to other mothers in my study, by learning new practical cooking gestures, Inness enacted kinship relationships. Inness conveyed intimacy towards kin—an emotive element that figured in the actions of mothers, regardless of their ethnicity, cooking skills, or the level of pleasure they derived from cooking and eating. They materialized this intimacy in their dishes thanks not only to the practical cooking gestures they had learned but also to the recipes for the dishes and the equipment that they had turned into metonyms for close female kin, which provoked their nostalgic remembering. Their longing to return home is illustrated by the idealization of their female kin from past generations, which Inness shows towards her mother-in-law. As is the case with other women, nostalgic feelings drive Inness to imitate her mother-in-law's cooking gestures while her mother-in-law is portrayed as conveying care by looking over Inness's shoulder, gifting cooking utensil (frying pan), and being involved in kitchen work. In addition, the new belief Inness adopted in the two first blintzes as tokens for success sustains her self-perception as a chef in home cooking. This belief supports Inness's general increase in home cooking, which causes her to feel more of a mother in New Zealand, similarly to other women in the study. In such a way, these women lay their claim to being a good enough Jewish-Israeli mother in New Zealand.

During this cooking session, it is also clear that although Inness idealizes her mother-in-law as a home cook, she denigrates her own mother who cooks more hastily. Her use of the Israeli-Hebrew idiom "to be exempted from an obligation," which means cooking to get it over with, articulates an accusation of false or nongenuine care and expresses her bitterness and anger. This denigration attested to a fraught relationship, which were common to women in the study with their female kin. As a result, some of these women skipped a generation: They imitated the dishes of their grandmothers instead of their mothers. In fact, when talking about her grandmother's home cooking, Inness shed a few tears out of the intensity of her nostalgic memories. Moreover, many mothers like Inness refrained from acknowledging their own mothers' teachings while magnifying the intensity of relationships with their grandmothers through their nostalgia and sometimes by preferring dishes typically associated with their mothers-in-law. As shall be further developed in the next two sections, skipping a generation and preferring the mother-in-law's typical dishes are only two ways in which mothers in the study grappled with the myth of the polania and the bashlanit.

Mothers Grappling with the Myth of the Polania

The case of Inness illustrates that mothers usually employed complaint, avoidance, and humour, often in self-irony, as discursive and situational strategies in relation to home cooking. These strategies are historically and culturally associated with the myth of the polania, who is renowned for self-sacrifice, overcaring, and emotional manipulation (Gil-Tin; Rosin). However, mothers often contested this character-ization by cooking food for their own pleasure, as Inness exemplifies in cooking blintzes, and to enjoy remembering their past homes.

Interestingly, the identification with and contestation of the myth of the polania figured in women's cooking practice, behaviour and rhetoric, as women commonly referred to the polania directly. For example, Yvette blamed her husband for having become a polania by saying: "I am not a polania! If anyone is a polania, it is my husband; he worries about our son's eating, and still spoon-feeds him at the age of five." In such a way, Yvette warded off the worry over feeding her son and redirected it towards her husband, similarly to a few other women in this study. Another rhetoric example through which some women remembered the polania was makne mame (literally "to make a mother" in Yiddish). This term was used by Inness, for example, to enhance her centrality as a homebuilder and to show care for herself by prioritizing her own eating and health.[4] Historically, this term was debated in political discussions in the Israeli parliament during the 1960s and 1970s as the parliament sought to legalize abortion for the sake of securing "healthy mothers" (Bloomfield 254-55). The logic was that securing the health of women as mothers would contribute to the security and survival of the family and the nation.

The denigration of mothers by women in my study was also articulated via the practice of cooking as they explicitly conveyed resentment and anger through "haunting memories" of their mothers' polania-like behaviour (Duruz 58). For example, Yvette claimed of having been forced to learn to cook by her mother, since she was the firstborn and had to care for her younger sibling when her mother went to work. Similarly, to several other women, Yvette described having fraught relations with her mother, but Yvette was explicit in saying that she hates cooking simply because she hates her mother. She expressed great resentment towards her mother also by associating her with the myth of the polania; Yvette argued that since her Mizrahi mother prioritized her career, education, and economic interest she had "turned Ashkenazi." Following migration, rather than acknowledging what her mother had taught her, Yvette began imitating the dishes of her Mizrahi grandmother, as she longed for home. Indeed, associations with the myth of the polania led some women to denigrate their mothers by disregarding their input in their education and avoiding acknowledging their teaching and influence, even in cases where they had clearly taught their daughters to cook. Grappling with this mythical figure was also evident when women referred to themselves as being a bashlanit, as the previous experience of Inness and the following experience of Geffen illustrate.

Mothers Grappling with the Myth of the Bashlanit

The myth of the bashlanit appeared in the narratives of most of the women in the study—memories of cooking from their childhood through to adolescence as well as memories of female kin from the past two generations. Geffen, for example, proclaimed she has been a bashlanit since an early age, and like Yvette, she did not acknowledge any positive influence from her mother regarding cooking. Geffen felt that her own "home cooking is a love tainted by other emotions" and "an obsession" because she can only cook from scratch. At the same time, Geffen commented about her best friend in New Zealand, whom she treats as family: "They have this appalling thing [chuckling]; they can have a can of spaghetti on toast for dinner! And she [her friend] is looking at me and thinking I'm cholat nefesh [crazy or mad, literally meaning "sick in the soul/spirit"]." Because Geffen felt that she always has to cook a full meal "from scratch," she critiqued mothers in New Zealand while ridiculing herself for her obsessive approach to home cooking. Geffen reinforced her own self-image as a bashlanit and rejected an action typical of women in New Zealand who are responsible for feeding their family: She characterized her own approach to cooking as obsessive. Simultaneously, since Geffen conveyed love and care for her family by feeding them dishes that she cooked "from scratch"; her home cooking worked to her advantage. Home cooking became a personal point of difference, turning it into a means of claiming who she is as a mother in comparison to other New Zealand mothers. She asserted her idea of a good enough Jewish-Israeli mother, similarly to other women in the study.

However, not all the women referred to themselves as bashlanit; some contested this myth in their memories of their female kin by claiming that these set up unrealistic expectations in terms of their own priorities when settling in New Zealand. Although these mothers joked that they promote buying ready-made foods or ingredients for the making of nostalgic foods with their own two hands, they also conveyed a sense of self-irony towards their minimized cooking labour. In cases in which they took shortcuts rather than cooking meals from scratch, these women still regarded home cooking as part of their good enough mothering, especially since in doing so, they imitated the close female kin they admired. This was clear in the case of Rotem, for example, who followed her mother by using frozen vegetables rather than fresh ones, as she said that "if this is good enough for my mother, whom I regard as a good mother, it is good enough for me."

Moreover, the idealization of the *bashlanit* in relation to female kin from the past two generations subtly varied according to the class and ethnicity of the women-kin. Often when mothers described an Ashkenazi kin as a *bashlanit*, they emphasized her vast knowledge, drive for perfection, use of written European recipes, and accurate measurements. Some Ashkenazi bashlaniot (sing. bashlanit) were remembered as artistic and even as culinary pioneers. These memories resulted in expression of ambivalence when mothers in my study felt threatened by the high cooking literacy of their female kin. Moreover, Ashkenazi dishes were mostly constrained to festive meals, whereas as self-made skilled cooks, the women emphasized their own creativity, choice, and skill in creating a hybrid fusion of dishes. In comparison, Mizrahi female home cooks were remembered and idealized with distinctive abilities to feel foods, spices, textures and measurements and to cook by intuition, instinct, and senses without using recipes and cookbooks. One may even identify their dishes according to their unique smells, colours, and tastes, which serve as personal signatures. These depictions emphasize cooking gestures and knowledge that are embedded in the senses and the body of the cook. Expressions such as "add as much flour as the dough can take" or "put a handful of" are common examples of unfamiliar gestures and measurements that made it difficult to imitate their dishes and required improvisations, a situation that contributed to their process of idealizing these home cooks. Their abilities to improvise resourcefully and overcome poverty were remembered and admired by women in my study.

Conclusion

In this chapter, I showed that Jewish-Israeli migrant mothers recreate home-cooked dishes they associate with female close kin from the past two generations, feeding their children and themselves nostalgic foods due to longing for home following migration to New Zealand. In doing so, they aim to recreate a feeling of being at home, but they also turn recipes, dishes, cooking gestures, and utensils into metonyms of their female kin according to the nature of their kinship relationships. They also idealize their memory to convey longing and intimacy in subtle differences, according to ethnicity and class of the women-kin who are remembered; however, it is their kinship relationships that matter most. Through their memories and imagination, as provoked and materialized by their home cooking, the mothers grapple with the Jewish mythical figures that revolve around the female home cook of their culture: the polania and the bashlanit. The mothers' ambivalence regarding their female kin's efforts, knowledge, and skills in home cooking becomes a means to convey kinship tension and critique. Thus, traversing the mythology of the female home cook also reveals how migrant mothers realize and negotiate connections between four generations (including their children) through home cooked dishes. Although longing and tension reside side by side in their memories of familial homes, it is the migrant mothers' nostalgic cooking that not only provokes memories of home and imagination but also materializes their claim to being good enough. Contrary to the women in this study, migrant mothers in other New Zealand settings, such as the postnatal ward, have less autonomy to use their home cooking to reconstitute a sense of being at home, as seen in a later chapter. It is my hope that future studies will identify the mythical figures that migrant mothers from various cultural groups grapple with in their daily lives and their reasons and ways for doing so.

Endnotes

1. I use pseudonyms to protect the privacy of the participants in my study.

2. E.N. Anderson compares Christianity with Islam and Judaism and asserts that Judaism in particular endorses the pleasure of eating to celebrate life (107).

3. Jewish secularism and religiosity are fluid affiliations that Jewish-Israelis set on a spectrum. The main reason for the majority of the mothers in my study to self-identify as secular is that they do not adhere to kashrut rules or practice Judaism religiously according to the Halacha. Moreover, seven out of the twenty-five mothers purposely increased eating pork and crustaceans in New Zealand. Further explanations about their choice to explicitly identify as secular can be found in the work of Joseph Loss.

4. A similar mentioning of the term "makne mame" was made by a Jewish-Israeli mother who participated in an MA study on middle-class dual-income families in Israel (Gil-Tin 22-23). In this study, the informant argued she prioritizes feeding herself each morning before feeding her children by following the principle of makne mame.

Works Cited

Anderson, E.N. *Everyone Eats: Understanding Food and Culture.* New York University Press, 2005.

Antler, J. *You Never Call! You Never Write!: A History of the Jewish Mother.* Oxford University Press, 2007

Bach, J. P. G. "'The Taste Remains': Consumption, (N)Ostalgia, and the Production of East Germany." *Public Culture*, vol. 14, no. 3, 2002, pp. 545-56.

Bendrihem, Reut. *Hybrid Motherhood: Motherhood as a Faction in the Feminine Identity of Mizrahi Women in a Peripheral Town.* 2006. Ben Gurion University, MA thesis.

Berdahl, Daphne. *On the Social Life of Postsocialism: Memory, Consumption, Germany.* Indiana University Press, 2009.

Bloomfield, Elana. "Conceiving Motherhood: The Jewish Female Body in Israeli Reproductive Practices." *Intersections*, vol. 10, no. 2, 2009, pp. 227-69.

Bohlman, Philip V. "To Hear the Voices Still Heard: On Synagogue Restoration in Eastern Europe." *Altering States: Ethnographies of Transition in Eastern Europe and the Former Soviet Union*, edited by D. Berdahl, M. Bunzl. and M. Lampland, The University of Michigan Press, 2000, pp. 40-69.

Boyer, Dominic. "*Ostalgie* and the Politics of the Future in Eastern Germany." *Public Culture*, vol. 18, no. 2, 2006, pp. 361-81.

Boym, Svetlana. *The Future of Nostalgia.* Basic Books, 2002.

Calò, Emanuela. *Change of Taste in Israeli Food: The Case of "Italian Cuisine," 1980-2000.* 2005. Tel Aviv University, MA thesis.

Clifford, James. "Diasporas." *Cultural Anthropology*, vol. 9, no. 3, 1994, pp. 302-38.

Duruz, Jean. "Haunted Kitchens: Cooking and Remembering." *Gastronomica*, vo. 4, no. 1, 2004, pp. 57-68.

Fischler, C. "Food, Self and Identity." *Social Science Information*, vol. 27, no. 2, 1988, pp. 275-92.

Gil-Tin, Shlomit. *Food and Feeding the Family: An Analysis of the Discourse in Dual Earner Families.* 2005. The Ben Gorion University, MA thesis.

Gluzman, M. "Longing for Heterosexuality: Zionism and Sexuality in Herzl's Altneuland." *Theory and Criticism*, vol. 11, 1997, pp. 145-62.

Gvion, Liora. *Culinary Bridges Versus Culinary Barriers: Social and Political Aspects of Palestinian Cookery in Israel.* Carmel, 2006.

Hage, Ghassan. *White Nation: Fantasies of White Supremacy in a Multicultural Society.* Pluto Press, 1998.

Halkier, Bente. "Suitable Cooking? Performances and Positionings in Cooking Practices among Danish Women." *Food, Culture and*

Society: An International Journal of Multidisciplinary Research, vol. 12, no. 3, 2009, pp. 357-77.

Harbottle, Lynn. *Food for Health, Food for Wealth: The Performance of Ethnic and Gender Identities by Iranian Settlers in Britain. The Anthropology of Food and Nutrition.* Vol. 3. Berghahn Books, 2000.

Haukanes, Haldis, and Frances Pine. "Ritual and Everyday Consumption Practices in the Czech and Polish Countryside: Conceiving Modernity through Changing Food Regimes." *Anthropological Journal on European Cultures*, vol. 12, 2004, pp. 103-30.

Haukanes, Haldis, and Susanna Trnka. "Memory, Imagination, and Belonging across Generations: Perspectives from Postsocialist Europe and Beyond." *Focaal—Journal of Global and Historical Anthropology*, vol. 66, 2013, pp. 3-13.

Hollows, Joanne. "The Feminist and the Cook: Julia Child, Betty Friedan and Domestic Femininity." *Gender and Consumption: Domestic Cultures and the Commercialisation of Everyday Life*, edited by E. Casey and L. Martens, Ashgate Publishing Group, 2007, pp. 33-48.

Khazzoom, Aziza. "The Great Chain of Orientalism: Jewish Identity, Stigma Management, and Ethnic Exclusion in Israel." *American Sociological Review*, vol. 68, no. 4, 2003, pp. 481-510.

Law, Lisa. "Home Cooking: Filipino Women and Geographies of the Senses in Hong Kong." *Empire of the Senses: The Sensual Culture Reader*, edited David Howes, Berg, 2005, pp. 224-44.

Loss, Joseph. "Buddha-Dhamma in Israel: Explicit Non-Religious and Implicit Non-Secular Localization of Religion." *Nova Religio: The Journal of Alternative and Emergent Religions*, vol. 13, no. 4, 2010, pp. 84-105.

Parla, Ayşe. "Remembering across the Border: Postsocialist Nostalgia among Turkish Immigrants from Bulgaria." *American Ethnologist*, vol. 36, no. 4, 2009, pp. 750-67.

Prell, Rivka-Ellen. "Why Jewish Princesses Don't Sweat: Desire and Consumption in Postwar American Jewish Culture." *People of the Body: Jews and Judaism from an Embodied Perspective*, edited Howard Eilberg-Schwartz, State University of New York Press, 1992, pp. 329-60.

Ravits, Martha A. "The Jewish Mother: Comedy and Controversy in American Popular Culture." *MELUS*, vol. 25, no. 1, 2000, pp. 3-31.

Ray, Krishnendu. *The Migrant's Table: Meals and Memories in Bengali-American Households*. Temple University Press, 2004.

Rosin, Orit. "Leben and Lebenia: About Food, Femininity, and Nation-Building at the Rationing Times." *A Full Belly: Rethinking Food and Society in Israel*, edited by Aviad Kleinberg, the University of Tel Aviv and Keter Books Ltd., 2005, pp. 155-204.

Rousso, Nira. *Table Talk or Secrets from the Kitchen of Nira Rousso*. Modan, 1984.

Samuel, R., and P. Thompson. *The Myths We Live By*. Routledge, 1990.

Shenhav, Yehouda. *The Arab-Jews: Nationalism, Religion and Ethnicity*. Am Oved Publishers, 2004.

Shine-Rakavy, Tamar. *Food, Symbolism and Group-Identity: Aspects of Perception of Polish-Jewish Food Culture among Israeli Women of Polish Descent*. 1999. The Hebrew University of Jerusalem, MA thesis.

Shohat, Ella. "The Invention of the Mizrahim." *Journal of Palestine Studies*, vol. 29, no. 1, 1999, pp. 5-20.

Shohat, Ella. "The Narrative of the Nation and the Discourse of Modernization: The Case of the Mizrahim." *Middle East Critique*, vol. 6, no. 10, 1997, pp. 3-18.

Tene, Ofra. "'This Is How We Will Cook' a House in Israel: A Reading of Cookbooks from the 1930s to the 1980s " *A Full Belly: Rethinking Food and Society in Israel*, edited by Aviad Kleinberg, University of Tel Aviv and Keter Ltd, 2005, pp. 92-130.

Williams, Brett. "Why Migrant Women Feed Their Husbands Tamales: Foodways as Basis for a Revisionist View of Tejano Family Life." *Ethnic and Regional Foodways in the United States: The Performance of Group Identity*, edited by L.K. Brown and K. Mussell, University of Tennessee Press, 1984, pp. 113-26.

Chapter 6

Symbols and Sel-Roti: The Taste of Return in Women's Nepali-Bhutanese-Hindu Refugee Identity and Ritual Performance

Dorothy Abram

Foods that are prepared for and used in ritual contexts reveal cultural systems of significance that are sustained with devotion by their participants. Whereas some scholars have characterized Swasthani, which is an annual ritual for Nepalese women, as a means of social subjugation and oppression, other scholars prefer to explore the complexity of gender relations and varying expressions of prestige and power in non-Western contexts.[1] From this perspective, ritual food preparation offers a unique insight into women's construction and experience of meaning and agency, particularly in the role of mother. Accordingly, women's religious practices provide a public performance of those sources of significance. When these rituals and associated foods are brought with refugees to their resettlement communities, mothers, as ritual specialists, are challenged to maintain and transform traditional meanings while sustaining the integrity of purpose, practice, and performance. In this chapter, I consider these issues in the making of a Nepalese bread called sel-roti in the practice and performance of the Nepali-Bhutanese-Hindu refugee mothers during Swasthani.

Drawing from ethnographic fieldwork conducted among Nepali-Bhutanese-Hindu refugees in 2009 in Providence, Rhode Island, this chapter focuses on sel-roti in the beliefs and practices of Nepali-Bhutanese-Hindu refugees who have recently resettled in Providence from refugee camps in Nepal. My introduction to this family came about through community theatre. I had recently established the AWARE Alliance Refugee Theatre as a stage for community and student awareness of refugee issues and concerns by the refugees performing their stories from sources of strength. Since the first challenge of assimilation for many recently arrived refugees is English language acquisition, this theatre project served to provide motivation for the difficult process of foreign language acquisition. The Acharya family were one of the first to get involved in this project, and a happy coincidence appeared in the process of getting to know them. I discovered their intense involvement with food and ritual—that is, with sel-roti and Swasthani. Working together provided many opportunities for interaction and engagement, resulting in friendships that continue to this day.

Sel-roti signifies what I call "the taste of return." Circularity is an existential belief and experience manifested in the shape of sel-roti and in the ritual contexts in which it is used, especially at Swasthani. The name "Swasthani" refers to the holy month as well as the text, ritual, performance, and goddess. All are called Swasthani, meaning "established in your own place." [2] I use the ritual, text, and my experience with this family's performance of Swasthani to explore the capacity and use of sel-roti to express existential beliefs and concerns.

I examine this significance through the lives and words of the Acharya family. As their name ("scholarly or learned teacher") reveals, the Acharya family belongs to the Brahmin caste of the Hindu social hierarchy. This identity, however, is complicated by their Bhutanese nationality, their Nepali ethnicity, their recent move to the United States (US), and it will be further complicated by their eventual American enculturation. I had the good fortune of becoming friends with this family after their initial arrival to the US in September 2009 and the subsequent arrival of additional members of their family from the refugee camps in Nepal, where they had lived for the past eighteen years. The core of this extended family is five adult brothers and their wives and children. Consistent with US refugee policy, Laksman (the oldest brother), as a survivor of torture, was given priority resettlement with his wife, Chandra, and their four sons (Monarath, Tara, and the twins Lok and Laksmi). Two years later, in 2011, most of the rest of the family joined them with the grandmother. One brother, his wife, and two children remain in Bhutan. This group of the Acharya family in Providence numbered twenty-one.

On several occasions over the course of my fieldwork, selected members of this family shared their knowledge and experience of sel-roti and Swasthani with me. Chandra, the mother of the immediate family and the wife of Laksman, who is the patriarch of the extended family, generously introduced me to Swasthani and patiently brought me into its practice. Jhuma, the next to the youngest brother of Laksman, whose proficiency in English positioned him in the role of culture and language translator for the entire group, helped me understand the interrelationship of food, text, and performance. Monarath and Tara, the two eldest sons of Chandra and Laksman, also improved my understanding of this Himalayan Shaivite belief system and their mother's role and responsibility within it.

Sel-Roti and the Taste of Return

Sel-roti is a distinctive bread from Nepal (Pathak; Katawal and Subba) and is featured in the Swasthani preparations, text, and ritual performance. Made predominantly from rice flour, the sel-roti batter is poured in a circle into hot mustard oil, creating its distinctive form. The metaphoric significance of sel-roti is rendered through its shape: a circle with overlapping ends. Jhuma explained it in this way: "We always serve sel-roti when we want someone to return to us. Just like the circle of sel-roti, the end meets the beginning. We will meet again." Jhuma also added that mothers make sel-roti for the children when they go out so that they will return: "Our mothers always put sel-roti in our packs whenever we children left the house for the day. From when I was a little boy going to school every day, to when I left for college far away. It was her hope for my return." And the taste of memory. More specifically, it was the anticipation of return that gives sel-roti its intense flavor, as Jhuma explained:

> It's occasional and auspicious—when you leave, when you come, at festivals, at ceremonies. It captures the most exciting times in

our lives. It signifies togetherness, that we will make the reunification again. Like at the marriage, when the daughter leaves her mother and family to move to her husband's home, sel-roti assures the family that she will return. It's the circle that keeps us intact.

The sel-roti, made for the family by mothers who would remain in the refugee camps, signalled the reunion of the entire family—the return of a united group—wherever they may end up. As Jhuma explained: "The last day we are together is very important; it's our memory of parting. On that day, we make a dinner together and say prayers. We share the same table, the same food, and the same hope. Our mothers serve the sel-rotis so we'll meet together again." Sel-roti, in this way, is cited as an emblem of identity—that is, in whichever community, nation, or context that family is sent or travels, sel-roti promises the hope of return and reunion through having this important meal at departure. The taste of sel-roti is the memory and promise of return.

Of course, reunification and return to Bhutan are now no longer possible because of the ethnic cleansing of the non-Buddhist citizens of the southern area of the country (called Lhotsampas) by the Buddhist government to reduce this Hindu population by a third (Bird). Fleeing to refugee camps on the border with Nepal and living there for more than twenty years, the Hindu Bhutanese have been refused return to their homes in Bhutan. With Nepali ethnicity, they would prefer resettlement in Nepal, but the Nepalese government will not grant this permission due to internal politics. Thus, the refugees have only two choices available to them currently: to move to another country for resettlement or to remain in the refugee camps indefinitely.

Chandra, the mother of this extended resettlement family, was the authority on the making of sel-roti. I have had several occasions since 2009 to watch her advise, instruct, and supervise the sel-roti production. She tested the texture of the flours—she mixed three different flours to achieve the correct consistency—and checked and double-checked the flow of the batter. Chandra's secret ingredient was to use milk instead of water; she claimed that it enabled the breads to absorb less oil. The mothers dominated the kitchen activity, but every so often one of the men of the family would come into the kitchen to taste a sample, to joke and amuse the cooks, or to make suggestions. Chandra's oldest son, Monarath, was quite skilled in Nepalese cuisine. Their three younger sons (who had grown up primarily or solely in refugee camps), however, had no interest in cooking and even, sometimes jokingly, sometimes not, claimed to prefer American fast food to home-cooked Nepalese cuisine.

Given the need for specific Himalayan food products to perform and complete the Swasthani ritual, the refugees face a particular challenge in the US. Without these foods, the ritual cannot be performed, which puts the participants into a dangerous ritual space—not only has the devotee not honored the goddess to achieve her blessings and boons, but she now also risks offending the goddess and perpetuating the very suffering that has brought her to invoke the goddess for her assistance. Specifically, this dilemma arose for the refugees through their need for unhusked rice grains and bael flowers. Rice in US supermarkets has been processed long before even arriving on supermarket shelves, and bael flowers are not native to North America. Given the priority of the observance of the ritual, the Hindu priest from a neighbouring city allowed for substitutions for this refugee population: Unhusked barley was found to replace the rice and coconut to replace the bael flowers. Substitutions represent one of many adjustments between ritual and memory for the refugees once they arrive in the US and attempt to perform and perpetuate their traditions. Moreover, some ingredients that they need to enact the Shiva rites may not be legal in the US, reinforcing their separation from their sources of meaning, identity, and culture. For example, at the end of the series of rituals at Swasthani and Shivatria, the final offering to Shiva, typically performed using marijuana, was replaced with camphor leaves. The reasoning behind such accommodation was that Shiva's great gift is the removal of fear, so camphor could serve the same religious and narrative purpose of this worship even if it does not contain identical sensory and pharmacological properties.

On the altar space for the Swasthani ritual, the mother places the sacred objects in units of 108, including 108 sel-rotis as the ritual requires (*SVK*; Iltis; Birkenholtz). However, the 108 sel-rotis are handled differently than any of the other 108 sacred artifacts. According to tradition, the mother, at the end of the ceremony, distributes one hundred of the 108 breads to the community. Eight sel-rotis are given to her husband. In no other ritual or use of artifacts is the sacred number of 108 divided. As the iconography of Swasthani shows—the central Mother Goddess surrounded by her eight manifestations of power—it is reasonable to claim that the sel-roti division that emphasizes the eight is related to this maternal identity of agency and authority. In the Swasthani stories that accompany this ritual, the eight sel-rotis are shared equally between wife and husband, marking their return, reconciliation, and the reunification of the family.

Swasthani, thereby, provides the model and method of unity on both physical and metaphysical levels. The refugees had worked within the traditional division of labour within an agrarian economy in which women tended household gardens and domestic duties and men accomplished the heavy plowing and large field work. Migrating from that framework into a post-technological, consumer-capitalist economy of their new homeland has been neither comfortable nor uncomplicated. Because it is easier for women to secure jobs here, marital relationships oftentimes become strained, creating unfamiliar responsibilities and unequal authority within the home. In addition, the ease of language acquisition by the youth and children in contrast with the older generation has created additional cultural disruptions of relationships with age and social status. With the easy affordability of alcohol, the rising suicide rate within the US Bhutanese community has become a crisis (Preiss; CDC). Even so, through the endurance of the current generation of mothers, the practice of Swasthani persists in the US as a source of equanimity, identity, agency, and authority (Doniger; Pulla).

The Promise of Swasthani

The focus of the practices and performances of the ritual of Swasthani is to gain the blessing of the goddess for the purpose of securing a human return, such as the return of loved ones from travels or the return of calm to the household through reconciliation and the return of good health (Iltis). She may also bestow the gift of a handsome bridegroom for a girl and other requests. The month-long practice centres on the mythical tales of the transformations of Swasthani: "Do the Swasthani ritual offering and listen to her story. Tell the story to others; if there is no one to listen, tell yourself. Listen to yourself. Tell your mattress, tell your bed, tell your spindle, tell your carding tool.... After doing this ... by the power of Sri Swasthani's vows, all your troubles will disappear; don't believe otherwise" (*SVK* 647).

Reiterating and practicing the Swasthani myth through acts of ritual purification, the petitioner believes she creates favour with the goddess, who, thereby, grants the petitioner's request: "because of single-minded concentration on Swasthani, all the things became real" (*SVK* 567).

Swasthani is a deeply revered deity (associated with the goddess of good fortune and prosperity, the Goddess Laksmi) (Rhodes). The woman who desires to make a request to Goddess Swasthani for the first time—in this case, it was Jhuma's wife Durga (Chandra's sister-in-law)—must be accompanied by a woman (a mother) who previously has been granted a wish by the goddess. Durga, the first-time petitioner here, was requesting the boon of pregnancy from Swasthani. Chandra had performed Swasthani, and she told me that the goddess had given her the release of her husband from Bhutanese imprisonment and his return home. The fact that Laksman, her husband, had already been tortured and jailed in Bhutan for five years at the time of his release was irrelevant for Chandra. She had performed the Swasthani ritual, and her husband had been released at that time. For Chandra, this correlation was enough to demonstrate the efficacy of her ritual performance and prayers to the Goddess Swasthani and the validity of the rites.

Swasthani: The Sacred Text, Holy Day, Ritual, Performance, and Goddess

The name Swasthani refers to multiple manifestations of holiness (Bapat; Birkenholtz; Doniger; Iltis; Shemkhada). It is a text titled Swasthani or *Swasthani Vrata Katha* (*SVK*, referring to the ritual protocol [vrata] and the collection of stories [katha] this scripture contains) that is used to provide instructions for how to carry out the annual ritual. Organized by the mother, the Acharya family (males and females, young and old) read, recite, and listen to Swasthani every year and their Swasthani text is reverentially stored within their home shrine to Shiva. The first chapter presents instructions for performing the month-long rite:

> Therefore from today onwards, bathe three times a day in this Salinadi River, at noon perform puja [worship] ... and tell ...

Swasthani ... stories.... Then after one complete month, on the full moon of the month of Magh, to do the ... Swasthani dharma, gather together 108 *apa madhi*—["fried breads"]—and the other 108 offerings ... according to your means. (*SVK* 564-65)

SVK presents an extensive collection of Hindu myths and is used to recite these stories during the month of the rite. Swasthani is also the name of the goddess for whom the ritual is performed in order to gain her blessings and the specific gift that is requested by the initiate. "If you keep [the ritual of] Swasthani," Jhuma instructed, "your wish will come true." Most importantly, Swasthani, the name of all these religious expressions, translates literally to mean "in your own place," a meaning that holds particular poignancy for these migrant mothers. Swasthani is the goddess of the centre space of consciousness (Daryn; Walker).

Swasthani—text, ritual, practice, holy day, and goddess (all by the same name)—is particular to Nepal and is virtually unknown outside of its borders, even within the broader Hindu world. This lack of notoriety does not diminish its importance. Swasthani translator Pallav Ranjan claims that Swasthani is even more important in Nepali homes than the great Hindu epics: "The scriptures of Swasthani has [sic] been read in Nepal for many generations. Its stories are derived from the oral tradition as well as from the *Puranas* (the roots of which go back to 1200BC). The Swasthani is as important as, and in many homes more important than, the *Ramayana* or the *Mahabharata*." For Hindu refugee families in Rhode Island, the festival of Swasthani is one of the most important celebrations of this exiled diaspora community, which is held in even higher esteem than the great Mahashivastri celebration that commemorates the birth of Shiva, the patron deity of the Hindu Himalayas.

Swasthani Background and Worship

Swasthani appears to have originated in the Indigenous Hindu Newari religion and culture and carried on as an oral Sanskrit tradition in Nepal until the printing of Swasthani texts in the sixteenth century and subsequent translations into various Nepali languages (Iltis; Birkenholtz). The *SVK* is read only once a year, between two full moons in the months of January and February. The Swasthani ritual is performed by women and involves ritual bathing three times a day, fasting, prayers, daily reading of a single chapter of the thirty-one chapters of *SVK*, and an all-night on-going repetitive reading of the entire text by the female petitioners, mothers, daughters, family, friends, and community as culmination of the rite. The sacred scripture is then closed until the next annual celebration of Swasthani. The reading of the text during the night-long ritual that I observed was performed by both men and women who read until they tired or until someone else requested a turn. Consistently present within the recitation group was Jhuma's wife, Durga, who had the specific request of motherhood of the Goddess Swasthani, and Chandra, her guide or maternal mentor through the process. At the entrance to the shrine room, each worshiper (even if she is not specifically petitioning the goddess) reiterates silently her request to the goddess. Clarity of intention is seen to activate the request's potential reality.

As Nepali-Brahmin-Hindus, the Acharyas, including the women, are literate, knowledgeable, and experts on Hindu texts, beliefs, and rituals. Their particular religious practice is defined by worship of Shiva, which has been influenced by their Buddhist coreligionists and, for the ritual that is the focus of this chapter, the historical incorporation of Tantrism into this belief system (Iltis; Rhodes). It is not just Brahmins, associated with priestly performance, who honour Swasthani. Throughout the Nepali ethnic and caste groups of Newaris, Thakalis, Gurungs, Chhetris, immigrants, refugees, and nationals, Swasthani is a deeply revered deity (associated with Laksmi, the goddess of good fortune and prosperity and called the Mother of the Universe). These influences provide the context for understanding the religious and spiritual significance of sel-roti with this particular refugee family. Sel-rotis reveal and demonstrate the capacity for food to sustain identity and culture through global crises, and, alternately, to witness the diminishment of cultural practices as refugees enter the American mainstream (Abram).

The Swasthani rites are strenuous, especially in terms of diet for the petitioner and her guide. They emulate the acts of the Goddesses Shakti, Sati, Parvati, Goma, and Swasthani (like the other women, Swasthani is a manifestation of the powerful Mother Goddess), who demonstrated single-minded concentration and a capacity to perform austere rituals of purification in order to retrieve her absent husband

and secure his return to their marriage and family. The Swasthani petitioner eats according to the guidelines of the Brahmin priestly regimen; for example, she eats rice without salt, spices, garlic, or onions. She may eat fruits and milk product, but no meat. However, she may only have one bowl of rice daily and that is consumed after the reading of the daily chapter of SVK is completed at noon ("It's the time of Shiva's wakefulness," I was told). This diet is maintained throughout the month of the Swasthani ritual.

The fasting diet is said to provide spiritual purification for the petitioner; the single most important concern for Swasthani is that the petitioner is in a state of purity and must prepare and eat her own meals separately from the family lest they contaminate her ritual condition. Jhuma's wife, Durga, told me how much easier it is to complete fasts in Nepal. In an agricultural setting where the fruits and foods are easily and readily available, fasts are easier to accomplish than having to shop for food at a supermarket. Additionally, this ritual is performed within a community of women practitioners. The fasting, renunciation, and the separation that the worshipper undertakes are told in the Swasthani text through the actions and experiences of the goddess by which the petitioner's practices and identity gain salience as part of a larger group. In the US, work commitments make this communal experience impossible to achieve on a daily basis. Professional (paid) work exacerbates the demands of motherhood for the Nepalese women. Whereas the Swasthani ritual offered periods of respite from daily mothering work within the home, the Western workplace annuls these opportunities for relaxation. In addition, since motherwork necessarily involves directing ritual practice, the workplace challenges the per-petuation of this central ritual to women's, particularly mothers', cultural identity.

The Long Night

The Swasthani text is read during the month of the ritual only and not opened at any other time during the rest of the year. The intensity of the final night of repetitive reading (from sundown to dawn) is palpable. Recited under conditions where focus, awareness, and the story itself are wavering and periodic due to the sleeplessness of the participants and the diversity of levels and skills of readings (including

traditional chanting), the textual narrative shifts in and out of awareness and develops a sort of heightened but fragmented consciousness.
Mythical tales appear, disappear, and then reappear, whole or in part,
with varying attention levels throughout the night. The metaphors and
meanings of the text also achieve a sort of hallucinatory flow that is
consistent with the aesthetics of Shiva consciousness. In this sense, the
listener or reader may notice that there is a reduplication of form in the
serpent and the sel-roti shape in the following mythical tale as it
repeats in retellings across the night. This story is told as a story within
a story within another story of Swasthani and sel-roti and reveals
crucial features of sel-roti, narrative form, maternal identity, and
Swasthani significance. It also pays witness to the ideal of an equitable
and loving marital relationship, which is foundational to the construction of motherhood according to this cultural tradition.

The four of the breads [of the eight sel-rotis] and which [the
petitioner, a mythical royal mother] *Candravati* had floated in the
river were found and caught by a [serpent] *Naga* named
Sankhasila. But, being unable to catch the other four breads, they
floated away. Meanwhile, the *Naga* thought: "Oh, what exceptional breads I've caught! Now, without my wife *Sankhavati*, how
can I eat these breads all by myself? It's been twelve years since I
left *Nagini*. I'm going to search for her whether she is alive or
dead!" Thus he went down to the Salinadi River to look. Then the
other four breads which the Naga was unable to catch, and which
floated away, were caught by *Sankhavati Nagini*. At that time, the
Nagini thought: "Oh, oh, how did these exceptional four breads
get here? Now, if I only could feed these breads to my husband!
How could I eat them alone? Where could my husband have
gone? I'm going to search. If I find him, we'll share these breads
and eat two each. If I don't find him, I will certainly abandon my
life-breath." Having said this, the *Nagini* went to search for her
own husband. Then, at the confluence of the Ganga and Jamuna
Rivers, they met each other. At that time, Nagini saw her
husband's face; and bowing to him affectionately, she asked: "O
Svami, since you left me, where did you go to live? Are you well
or not? O *Svami*, I want to tell you one thing. If you ask what, it
is that today I caught four exceptional breads. At that time, with
you gone, I was wondering how I could eat those all alone, and

thus I came to search for you. It took a long time. Finally, I came here to look in this *Salina Ganga,* thinking that if I didn't find you here, I would certainly abandon my life-breath. With my luck, I found you." Hearing his wife, *Sankhavati Nagini,* tell this, *Sankhasila Naga* smiled impishly and said: "O Wife, I also caught four exceptional breads, just like you. At that time I thought: 'How can I eat these exceptional breads all by myself?' So I went searching for you in the Gandaki Rivers, in the rivers, and in the streams, and I thought I would come to look in this river, and came. O *Nagini,* through fate, I have met you. Therefore, I have peace of mind. Now you eat two of these breads, and I'll eat two." Thus he gave two breads to the *Nagini.* Then the *Nagini* likewise gave two of the breads which she had caught to her husband; and, distributing two and two each, they shared them as they ate, gazing at each other's faces, and smiling and laughing affectionately (*SVK* 569-72).

Told in this tale, as in many others, is the gift of the goddess as Mother of the World to respond to the requests for reunion of separated husbands and wives, and, thereby, to unite families. If there is no surviving husband or the husband is absent, the role of accepting the sel-roti offered by the mother falls to her son. When Jhuma first told me this story of the married Naga serpents and sel-roti, his intention was to provide an example of the return motif with sel-roti, as both the myth and the food demonstrate that the end comes again to the beginning. Just as the participants experience in the reading of the text throughout the month and throughout the final evening, circularity characterizes narrative, mythic, and ceremonial time and space (Daryn; Walker). The serpents' successful reunion was signaled by the accumulation of eight sel-rotis that the royal serpents share together. This gives them the power to bestow blessings on the mythic petitioner who floated the sel-rotis for her own desires and is told throughout the holy day of Swasthani. Return, as a cultural value, is demonstrated in Chandra's oldest son Monarath's consolation message to me about their decision to leave Providence: "Departing is the lesson of life; the possibility of return is its hope."

In both the ritual and the myth, sel-rotis are featured as the means of achieving the goals of Swasthani. Chandra, as I mentioned, connects the release, return, and reunion with her husband and reuniting of the family during the ethnic cleansing of the Hindu-Bhutanese as Swasthani's response to her fasting, prayers, reading and fulfillment of these ritual practices—her motherwork. The serpent reunion is a myth and model for the practice and proof of Swasthani. Yearly, the refugees hear that story many times and many times over their lifetimes. During the night-long culmination of the ritual, the participant listens to the stories over and over again through varying states of wakefulness, or the visitor hears selections when he or she is present for a time and returns later. Of course, the Swasthani worshiper and her guide are present for the entire time. Hearing the story and telling the story is crucial to this holy day (SVK).

At the end of Swasthani, tradition requires that the ritual objects are deposited in a river with prayers rendered for the fulfillment of wishes. The sand lingi of Shiva from the altar and other offerings were gathered and brought to deposit. Led by Chandra, the mother of the group, together with the entire family, we dipped our fingers in vermillion powder and grasped grains of rice that became stained with the red powder. Arms over each other's arms, we stretched together towards the river and let the rice fall into the water. I was given two explanations for this practice, and both seemed relevant. The red-dyed rice was to carry our wishes on the river for their fulfillment as told in the text. Chandra offered another interpretation. The rice is for the dead, she explained or, more precisely, for the souls who have not yet been reincarnated into their next bodies. They linger, hungry, in the water. We feed the hungry souls, she told me, which we hope will also be done for us through our reincarnation into our next lives. The souls also eat the sel-rotis floating in the water (offered by those women without husband or son) in order to make their return. Motherwork not only spans generations in life but also in death.

From Food to Philosophy

Through her status as mother and previously initiated, Chandra acts as mentor to Durga, her sister-in-law, and together they prepare and cook the sel-rotis to be used as prasad (blessed food) on the final holy day. Completion—the return of the end to its beginning—is believed to be achieved through the precise enactment of every Swasthani gesture, act, and tale. Each recitation of the text, act of purification, and ritual performance brings one closer to the divine being who is Mother of the World:

> First she drew the letter Om on a ritual mirror, to be ... Swasthani ... and did the invocation; and being very pure, she performed the ... puja according to the traditional procedures. Fully absorbed in meditation and recitation, she wished for the accomplishment of her heart's desire.... Then, after joining her hands to recite ... in single-minded concentration, she then recited the following *stostra*: Om, Praise to Swastha Devi [Goddess of She who has Everything Within Her], Mother of the World, who is filled with good auspiciousness; "Fulfill my heart's desire, Mahesvari" ... who is present in the hearts of all living creatures. (*SVK* 567-8)

These retellings of the basic myth lead to a crescendo. The ultimate manifestation of the Goddess Swasthani, the reader and listener is informed, is at the end of the performance when Swasthani appears in the form of the woman who worships her: "Then, to the one called... Swasthani who is Swastha Devi ["the goddess within yourself"] in yourself, establish her in her own true form as the letter Om, written on a ritual mirror, and worship her" (*SVK* 565).

When I questioned Jhuma for a further explanation, Chandra interrupted. She told Jhuma, her brother-in-law, that he was making the simple practice of Swasthani too complicated in his explanation to me. Chandra instructed him to say it directly and simply, she offered, in place, a description that was obvious to her: "Through Swasthani, we are the bride of Shiva."

There are deeper echoes to Chandra's explanation. In fact, Chandra's belief derives from the very foundation of Swasthani ritual and Hindu philosophy (Johnson). Swasthani is believed to have the power to make each participant divine. Just hearing the text bestows blessing, even if you are not the petitioner or the worshiper:

> Whoever keeps [Swasthani] in their heart and does puja or tells the story, or even listens to the story, or has the story told by another, or whoever writes a book of these stories, or keeps this book in their home, those persons will always have well-being, their pain and misery will be eliminated, they will be protected.... Laksmi [the goddess of luck, wealth, and prosperity] will reside

in their home ... they will be able to overcome their fears ... those persons will enjoy supreme happiness and fortune, and in the next world, will never be reborn and die, but live with the gods on Kailasa.... Devotion to Swasthni through recitation, meditation, reciting sotras, puja, and stories, is the highest and greatest thing in the whole world. (*SVK* 596)

Chandra explained to me that the ritual serves to purify the human female, transforming her into the goddess; thus, the initiate transubstantiates into the divine. Through her month-long performance and recitation of the *SVK*, the petitioner achieves the power to create her own agency and identity. When Chandra clarifies an explanation of Swasthani with the simple phrase, "We are the goddess," she speaks from a cultural and religious depth of a lifetime of focus and single-minded concentration on this framework for constructing and expressing the many manifestations of her personal and maternal identity.

For Chandra and Durga, this is the message of Swasthani: She is you. You are Swasthani, the goddess in your own place, who resides at the centre of being and blessing. The end has now returned to its beginning and sacred source. We must give the final word to Chandra, who instructed me: "Don't ask why. Just do it [Swasthani]. Explanations lead you down the wrong path into falsity. When you do, you understand." However, the next generation of refugee children seems to express little interest, or profess belief, in the old rituals. One can predict that this challenging ritual performance will eclipse as this community assimilates into American society.

Chandra, as wife of the eldest brother and mother of the family, is moving towards the role of matriarch of the extended family, as the elder generation ages. Her son Tara explained that with four adult sons, Chandra should not have to work. His comment reflects the Nepali respect for age. Yet Chandra had the best work situation in the US of her family, as her job offered health insurance and retirement plans. Chandra, however, was not the matriarch of this family yet; the grandmother's desire to have her entire family around her necessitated that Chandra give up this job to move with the family to Ohio. What sense, then, could be made of her decision to uproot twenty-one people to move across the country to Ohio?

Conclusion: Coming Full Circle

The grandmother chose to move the family to Ohio, where her brother had already settled. Her reliance on her brother and her decision to displace the entire extended family was also modelled on that traditional Swasthani narrative of return. This arrangement of reunion provided coherence and comfort for the family, especially the grandmother, who claimed the protection of her brother during a difficult period of adjustment in a new land. A week after the move was completed, the grandmother died, and the entire extended Acharya family was together to perform and to complete her funeral rites.

These influences provide the context for understanding the religious and spiritual significance of sel-roti with this particular refugee family and community. The mothers' productions of sel-rotis reveal and demonstrate many capacities for food to sustain identity and culture through global crises: to reconfigure their places in everyday family life, and, alternately, to witness the diminishment of cultural practices as refugees enter the American mainstream. Clearly, with the change to the American cultural context, this perpetuation of cultural practices holds both comfort and difficulty. The family must adjust to a new social and economic setting while also respecting the grandmother's central place and authority in the family. The role of the mother is pivotal to this adjustment and transformation.

Since the family moved to Ohio, a number of events have moved them along in their self-definition and cultural identity. Durga became pregnant—the gift, she insists, of her practice of Swasthani. The two older sons married. Prohibited from performing the Swasthani ritual that year because of a death in the family, their wives became pregnant anyway. Chandra ascended into her role as the true matriarch of the family, which their cultural framework allowed once the grandmother had passed. Chandra now stays home to care for the family without the burden of outside work. And sel-rotis continue to be made, shared, and eaten at the Nepali-Bhutanese marriages, births, and celebrations.

Endnotes

1. Lynn Bennett proposes that sisters are celebrated, whereas wives are subjugated. Linda Iltis, though, convincingly argues for a different understanding of women's experience in Nepal. And

Wendy Doniger asserts that any imposition of duality indicates an oppressive social identity and proposes that cultures that hold multiple models and mythological variants of female identity indicate a flexible and resilient identity for women and a positive demonstration of women's status in culture—and this is what the Swasthani text offers. As Doniger explains:

> To tell these stories for positive purposes.... [Women] tell them to validate the many, not just two, parts of themselves and to construct other selves into which they move in their lived lives.... They tell and listen to these stories both to revise their histories and to express their imaginative view of possible futures. They tell them to celebrate the infinite the Swasthani text offers varieties of ways in which men and women have used storytelling to storm the oppressive barricades of gender and culture. (308)

I have also reexamined similar interpretive models (Abram).

2. At the time of this writing, only two dissertations have been written specifically on Swasthani—one by Iltis in 1985 and one by Jessica Valentine Birkenholtz in 2010. Since her dissertation, Birkenholtz has published an extensive study of Swasthani and Nepalese Hinduism. The only English translation of the Swasthani text available to date may be found in Iltis's dissertation along with her excellent analysis of the entire institution of Swasthani. I refer to that translation as *SVK* for citations in this chapter.

Works Cited

Abram, Dorothy. *Girls' Dolls and Women's Gravestones. The Artifacts and Experiences of Women's Transitions in Ancient Greece.* 1991. Harvard University, MLA thesis.

Abram, Dorothy. *The Suffering of a Single Child: Uses of an Image from the Holocaust.* 2003. Harvard University, EdD dissertation.

Abram, Dorothy. "The Cooking Lesson: Identity and Spirituality in the Lives of Hindu Refugees in America." *What's Cooking, Mom? Narratives of Food and Family*, edited by Tanya M. Cassidy and Florence Pasche Guignard, Demeter Press, 2015, pp.185-93.

Bapat, Jayant Bhalchandra and Ian Mabbett (eds.). *The Iconic Female.*

Goddesses of India, Nepal and Tibet. 2008. Victoria, Australia: Monash University Press.

Bennett, Lynn. *Dangerous Wives and Sacred Sisters. Social and Symbolic Role of Women in Nepal.* Columbia University Press, 1983.

Bird, Kai. "The Enigma of Bhutan." *The Nation,* 7 Mar. 2012. www.thenation.com/article/archive/enigma-bhutan/. Accessed 6 June 2021.

Birkenholtz, Jessica Valentine. *Reciting the Goddess Narratives of Time in the Making of Hinduism in Nepal.* Oxford University Press, 2018.

Birkenholtz, Jessica Valentine. *The Swasthani Vrata Katha Tradition. Translating Self, Place, and Identity in Hindu Nepal.* 2010. University of Chicago, PhD dissertation.

Cassidy, Tanya M., and Florence Pasche Guignard, eds. *What's Cooking, Mom? Narratives of Food and Family.* Demeter Press, 2015.

Centers for Disease Control. "Suicide and Suicide Ideation among Bhutanese Refugees—United States, 2009-2012." *CDC,* 5 July 2013, www.cdc.gov/mmwr/preview/mmwrhtml/mm6226a2.htm. Accessed 5 June 2021.

Daryn, Gil. *Encompassing a Fractal World. The Energetic Female Core in Myth and Everyday Life—A Few Lessons Drawn from the Nepalese Himalaya.* Lexington Books, 2006.

Doniger, Wendy. *Splitting the Difference. Gender and Myth in Ancient Greece and India.* Chicago: The University of Chicago Press, 1999.

Gray, John. *Domestic Mandala. Architecture of Life Worlds in Nepal.* Ashgate, 2006.

Iltis, Linda L. 1985. *Women and Ritual in Nepal. The Swasthani Vrata.* 1985. University of Wisconsin, Madison, PhD dissertation.

Johnson, W. J. *Oxford Dictionary of Hinduism.* Oxford University Press, 2010.

Katawal, Surendra Bahadur, and Dilip Subba. "A Survey Study on Technology of *Sel-roti*: A Traditional Food of Nepal." *Journal of Food Science and Technology Nepal,* vol. 4, 2008, pp. 23-30.

Pallav, Ranjan. *Swasthani.* Spiny Babbler, 1999.

Pathak, Jyoti. *Taste of Nepal.* Hippocrene Books, 2007.

Preiss, Danielle. "Bhutanese Refugees are Killing Themselves at an Astonishing Rate: How Unemployment, Depression, and Lack of

Family Ties Lead to Extreme Desperation." *The Atlantic*, 13 Apr. 2013, www.theatlantic.com/international/archive/2013/04/bhutanese-refugees-are-killing-themselves-at-an-astonishing-rate/274959/. Accessed 5 June 2021.

Pulla, Venkat. *The Lhotsampa People of Bhutan: Resilience and Survival.* Palgrave Macmillan, 2015.

Rhodes, Constantina. *The Goddess Lakshmi in Song and Ceremony.* State University of New York Press, 2011.

Shimkhada, Deepak. "Goma: An Embodiment of the Goddess." *The Constant and Changing Faces Of the Goddess*, edited by Deepak Shimkhada and Phyllis K. Herman, Cambridge Scholars Publishing, 2007.

Shimkhada, Deepak, and Phyllis K. Herman. *The Constant and Changing Faces Of the Goddess* edited by Deepak Shim-khada and Phyllis K. Herman, Cambridge Scholars Publishing, 2007.

Subba, Dilip, and Sudrendra Bahadur Katawal. "Effect of Particle Size of Rice Flour on Physical and Sensory Properties of Sel-roti." *Journal of Food Science and Technology*, vol. 50, no. 1, 2011, pp. 181-85.

Swasthani Vrata Katha (SVK). (undated) In Nepali.

PART III
Meanings and Experiences of Migrant Maternal Meals

Chapter 7

Intersections of Discursive, Social, and Material Contexts of Good Mothering: Asian Immigrant Mothers' Experiences with Infant Feeding in Metro Vancouver

Gwen E. Chapman and Sanzida Habib

The effects of migration on the experience of motherhood have been largely neglected by researchers, and immigrant women's experiences of infant feeding have specifically received little attention (Liamputtong 26; Liamputtong and Naksook 46). Our exploratory qualitative study fills this gap by examining women's experiences of nourishing infants in the context of migration from Asia to Canada.

In this chapter, we explore how Asian immigrant mothers' experiences of infant feeding in general and breastfeeding in particular were shaped by the interplay between scientific discourses about infant feeding and traditional feeding approaches, moral constructions of good mothering, and the socioeconomic constraints of being immigrants in a new country. We argue that women's infant feeding and childrearing practices in Canada reflect processes of governmentality, or the social and moral regulation of mothering (Coveney 15-24; Foucault, "Governmentality" 87-104). Decisions women make about feeding themselves and their families are shaped by authorized knowledges of food, nutrition, and medical sciences, especially those around breast-feeding. Through the moral constructions of good mothering that come to be defined through these discourses, mothers are required (and require themselves) to meet certain obligations in relation to feeding their infant. The techniques of governmentality also include programs of the state, which work to create and circulate these discourses, especially through its healthcare system, and ensure that new immigrant mothers adopt the expected practices of responsible parenting.

Framing the Research: Theoretical Background

Our analysis is informed by critical poststructuralist theory, particularly as it has been applied to the understanding of nutrition practices and breastfeeding. Foucault's interpretations of the inextricable linking of power/knowledge and how scientific and technical knowledge come to form the basis for moral judgments we make about ourselves and others are highly relevant to understanding dominant food choice practices in North America and other Western countries (Coveney 1999, 15-24; Foucault, *Power/Knowledge* 109-133; Foucault, "Governmentality" 87-104). Foucault introduced the notion of governmentality to explain how the conduct of populations is controlled through self-regulation and the term "biopower" to describe how power operates through social control of bodies (Foucault, "Right of Death" 258-272). As further explicated by Paul Rabinow and Nikolas Rose, biopower operates through three elements: specific truth discourses about the character of human life, legitimated by accepted authorities, such as scientists and medical professionals; intervention strategies aimed at improving the health and lives of the population; and technologies of the self, or moral practices of self-regulation, through which individuals govern and produce themselves as ethical subjects (197-98; Foucault, "Technologies of the Self " 16-49). The combination of science and moral conduct thus forms a self-regulatory process whereby individuals are required to meet certain obligations set out by authorities and require themselves to meet these obligations. At the same time, the authority of expert knowledge devalues and delegitimizes other ways of knowing, or what Foucault referred to as "subjugated knowledges," which become buried or invisible (*Power/Knowledge* 109-133).

All of these processes have been well described in analyses of dietary practices (Chapman, "Making Weight" 211-20; Chapman, "From 'Dieting'" 80-83; Coveney, 122-56; Ristovski-Slijepcevik, Chapman, and Beagan 472-78). The emergence of nutritional science and dietary guidance over the past 150 years has provided knowledge and standards for what and how a healthy population should eat. As noted by DeSouza in this volume, nutritional messages reflect a reductionist science approach, in which foods are understood in terms of the nutrients they contain and the scientific expertise of health professionals is privileged over cultural traditions and lay knowledge. In many contexts, this technical and rational knowledge has taken on moral overtones, becoming a social standard whereby people judge themselves and others based on what they eat and regulate their own diets as a moral health imperative.

Women's experiences of mothering and feeding their infants are particularly subject to processes of governmentality. Mothers in contemporary society are increasingly constructed as having a moral responsibility to be conscious about risks (for example, the health risks to their baby if they do not breastfeed) and to be able to manage those risks with the help of professional guidance and expert opinion (Knaak 345-47). Infant-feeding knowledge becomes a set of factual information that women are expected to know and believe, and various medical, psychological, and other professionals, rather than mothers, are seen as the primary experts of childrearing (Hays 54; Knaak, "Contextualising Risk": 345-47; Wall 593-94; Wallace and Chason 406, 409). Within such a framework, mothers' consciousness of risk in relation to infant feeding becomes an ideologically infused moral discourse of good mothering as defined by the dominant scientific-medical discourse. Through her critical analysis of health education material, Glenda Wall has pointed to the involvement of the state in this construction of the good mother through its educational materials and other efforts to promote breastfeeding and proper infant-feeding practices (604-05).

In addition to viewing infant feeding through the lens of governmentality and technologies of control, we also understand mothering and breastfeeding as complex social experiences that are shaped by structural conditions and material realities. There is no homogeneous "Asian immigrant mother experience"; instead, experiences vary with women's diverse social locations as they intersect along the lines of race, class, religion, sexuality, ability, and culture (Varcoe and Doane 297-99; Esterik 258; Wallace and Chason 409-12).

Method and Sample

Data were collected through in-depth individual interviews conducted between December 2010 and August 2011 with a convenience sample of Asian immigrant mothers (n=16) with an infant between three and twelve months old. We used the term "immigrant" broadly, including any woman who was born in Asia and had lived in Canada for one to ten years. Our study was open to women with different official statuses in Canada, including refugees, women who came through student visas or work permits, as well as permanent residents and new citizens. The women ranged in age from twenty-four to thirty-nine, lived in Metro Vancouver, and were originally from China (n=6), Iran (n=3), the Philippines (n=2), India (n=2), Bangladesh (n=2), and Pakistan (n=1). All were well educated with at least a bachelor's degree, but the sample varied in terms of household income, religion, length of time in Canada (between one and nine years) and number of children (between one and three). All infants were healthy term infants who were predominantly breastfed (<1 feeding of formula per day) for at least three months. The study was approved by the University of British Columbia Clinical Research Ethics Board, and written informed consent was obtained from all mothers.

Interviews were conducted in Farsi, Mandarin, Cantonese, and English by one of three bilingual interviewers, all of whom are immigrant women and two of whom are mothers. Interviewers were also able to speak Bangla and Hindi; however, most women were comfortable speaking English, and almost half of the interviews were conducted in English. Topics included women's experiences of giving birth, breastfeeding and mothering, their knowledge, beliefs and practices regarding diet and infant feeding, and nutrient supplementation. All but one interview was audio-recorded; extensive notes were taken during and immediately following the interview with one participant who did not want to be recorded. Interviews were transcribed by the interviewer, with the Farsi, Mandarin, and Cantonese interviews being translated at the time of transcription. Using an inductive process, the transcribed texts were categorized according to codes and subcodes and examined for emerging themes. Several broad themes and patterns as well as contradictions and variations within those themes were identified through iterative and reflexive readings of not only what the texts actually contained but also the implications (Mason 147-72).

As feminist qualitative researchers, we were attentive to our own positionality in relation to the research topic and participants. Both authors are mothers and academics with a PhD. One of us (GC) is a white tenured professor who has always lived in Canada, while the other (SH) is a naturalized Canadian citizen of South Asian ethnic background. Generation and analysis of research data were shaped by both our academic-theoretical orientations and personal-social locations.

Findings and Discussion

The findings illuminated the ways in which the mothers drew on and negotiated with the authorized (medical/scientific) and subjugated discourses of infant nutrition available to them. Women's perspectives and decisions about infant feeding were imbued with moral expectations of good mothering, and their experiences were further complicated by the socioeconomic consequences of migration to Canada.

Negotiating with Different Discourses of Parenting and Health Practices

The participants' discussions of why they fed their babies as they did revealed two interconnected discourses they negotiated: authorized knowledge grounded in biomedical concepts and subjugated knowledge based in personal experience and wisdom associated with their culture. As shown in Table 1 (next page), the authorized knowledge content was consistent across participants regardless of their country of origin and echoed current Canadian infant-nutrition guidelines that advocate exclusive breastfeeding for six months and continuation of breastfeeding for up to two years (Health Canada). Participants described gaining this knowledge through contact with Canada's public healthcare system, including visits with doctors, midwives, public health nurses, and lactation consultants as well as other community-based resources. They also described accessing the authorized knowledge through books, pamphlets, the internet, and family and friends. This information was not specific to Canada, however, as they noted much consistency between formal information provided from their home and from Canadian sources. For example, a Farsi-speaking woman who regularly visited the Canadian BabyCentre website (www.babycentre.ca) and the Iranian NiniSite (www.ninisite.com) confidently said: "All of the information is the same, and there isn't any difference among them. For example, 'Try to breastfeed your baby for six months' is on every site." Other participants echoed this, especially the international emphasis that breastmilk is the best food for babies.

Table 1: Discourses of Infant Nutrition

Authorized Knowledge	Subjugated Knowledge
Consistent across participants, regardless of country of origin:	Some variations between participants:
• Exclusive breastfeeding for six months	• Breastfeeding supported but less specific timelines and in some cases for shorter duration
• Continued breastfeeding for up to two or more years	• Earlier introduction of (different) complementary foods
• Vitamin D supplementation	
• Introduction of iron-rich complementary foods starting at six months	

Subjugated knowledge was mostly learned informally through communication with extended family, including mothers and mothers-in-law, friends, and other mothers of young babies. This was not a unified discourse, as the specific advice varied depending on participants' backgrounds and circumstances. As with the authorized knowledge, breastfeeding was generally viewed as the best way to feed the baby but sometimes for a shorter length of time, with earlier introduction of solid foods. This was illustrated by a mother from China:

> When the baby was three or four months old, my mother-in-law asked me to start solid food. She said in China, some babies, when they are three, four months old, they start eating some of the solid food ... [She] even advised me to stop breastfeeding when the baby is nearly nine months old ... because she believes that when the baby is nine months old or older, the mother's milk is no longer nutritious.

Given the contradictions in the advice women received about how to feed their babies, participants had to develop strategies for deciding what to do. Most tended to follow the instructions prescribed by the authorized discourses. For example, the woman quoted above said: "I just listened to the nurses here instead of taking my mother-in-law's advice." Nurses and doctors were seen as providing "information that has been studied and proven to show [that] it is better for the baby" (mother from Iran) and government sources, such as the *Baby's Best Chance* book published by Health Canada, were considered reliable: "This is a publication by the government ... so I thought this was a more responsible authority than other authors who I don't know, right?" (mother from Bangladesh). Other participants, especially those with the highest levels of education, relied on their own medico-scientific knowledge and research skills: "I'm a PhD in biomedical sciences, so yeah, basically I do know the advantages of breastfeeding. ... Baby gets really good amount of immunity if the baby is breastfed as compared to the formula, and it gives protection in all forms and it's good nutrition, everything."

However, some participants were less sure that the authorized knowledge was always right or that cultural practices that contradicted those medical recommendations were always wrong. A mother from Iran decided to follow her mother's advice to feed her baby almond purée, which "makes the baby strong." She justified her decision by saying: "This information belongs to our culture, and we don't have it here, and I cannot get it from anywhere else.... I haven't heard anything against feeding these foods to the baby or [that] feeding almond may cause allergies." The implication was that the culturally specific practice could be followed unless or until science finds it to be harmful.

A mother from Bangladesh dealt with conflicting advice by trying to be consistent in following one set of guidelines: "I consciously didn't mix up these two knowledges because otherwise if I follow partly this knowledge and partly that knowledge and if anything goes wrong I cannot seek advice from anybody, right? So that was my conscious choice, but at the same time, I don't know whether the other knowledge is right or wrong or whatnot."

Overall, the study data illustrate that participants were living in hybrid spaces in an era of globalization of information and technology, and they readily accessed information about infant nutrition from various sources. These young, well-educated women tended to rely on the dominant, expert-guided discourses reflecting the scientific and medical foundation of parenting and childrearing in contemporary parenting culture, wherein various medical, psychological, and other professionals, rather than mothers, are deemed the primary experts of childrearing (Foss 298-99; Knaak, "Contextualising Risk" 346-47; Wall 593-94). Similarly, Vallianatos (in this volume) noted that immigrant mothers' experiences with food were shaped by tension between traditional teachings of elders and the authoritative knowledge of medical professionals, with some women discounting traditional knowledge as nonscientific and therefore untrue.

Infant Feeding, Morality, and Being a Good Mother

Despite contradictions in some aspects of the information they received about infant feeding, participants were unequivocal in their understanding that breastfeeding is "best for babies," "the number one choice," and "healthier" than formula feeding. This conviction mirrors findings of the "increasingly hegemonic and homogeneous character of pro-breastfeeding discourse" (Knaak, "Contextualising Risk" 346). Although both breastfeeding and formula feeding are officially acknowledged as acceptable choices, there is an ever-increasing discursive gap between these two options, as breastfeeding has become more and more idealized and formula feeding ever more devalued (Knaak, "The Problem" 412-413). Much research has found breastmilk to be healthier than formula, but the magnitude of the differences observed is in fact relatively small, particularly when compared to the risk of feeding something other than either formula or breastmilk (Knaak, "The Problem" 413). Probreastfeeding discourses, however, tend to frame breastfeeding as the only appropriate, acceptable, or moral choice, restricting women's ability to freely choose alternative feeding approaches.

The belief that breastfeeding is indeed the only option seemed to be shared by all study participants, as articulated by this mother from India: "I was very determined that I will be breastfeeding her.... I mean I never gave it a second thought." Most women thought that breastfeeding was well supported in Canada by public health services, community-based resources, such as parenting classes and support groups, and policies, such as longer maternity leaves. Nevertheless, establishing and maintaining breastfeeding was not easy. Many women talked about experiencing certain challenges, such as lack of sleep, physical exhaustion, and demands on their time. Almost all had taken special ethnic or traditional food to increase milk production, and a few had consulted a lactation specialist. Some also discussed how they had not been very health conscious before becoming a mother, but that the experience of pregnancy and breastfeeding made them become conscious of their own health and diet for the sake of the best possible development of their children.

The efforts and transformations that participants went through to ensure that their babies were well nourished speaks to their sense of being responsible for producing healthy, intelligent, and perfect babies as well as to ways in which the authorized discourses and actions of Canada's public health system recruited their participation in practices of good mothering. One participant alluded to this when she said: "In China, you can expect the babies to grow up by themselves without much worry. But here, people will teach you specific topics on babies' safety, diet, their sleeping habit, and even on how to manage your family relationship ... I feel that taking care of a baby here is done very carefully."

This comment supports the findings of other studies that mothers in contemporary society are increasingly viewed and constructed as "builders of better babies" (Wall 604). Women internalize this as a moral imperative; they feel compelled to transform their own lives and diets and to work hard to ensure that they can successfully give birth and breastfeed for an extended period of time, thus establishing their identities as good mothers. One participant pointed to the moral responsibility women (now but perhaps not a generation ago) feel to take proper care of their own and their children's bodies when she said her mother was inundating her with nutrition information from Bangladesh during her pregnancy because she (her mother) was trying to compensate for her own guilty conscience for not taking good care of herself during pregnancy: "When she was pregnant with me and my brother, she thinks that she didn't take the best care of herself, and she thinks there was a lack of knowledge and lack of awareness from her side and also the people around her. So she was really conscious that it wouldn't happen in my case."

A woman from the Philippines specifically named her pride in being able to identify herself as a good mom after persevering with breast-feeding and thus producing what other people could see as a healthy, happy baby: "I didn't expect it [to be] as hard ... like, the hardest part is like I don't have sleep in the nighttime.... But I think it's rewarding, that every time I see him, that he's smiling with me, and he's healthy and other people say that he's in good condition ... I think, you know, I'm a good mom, yea!" Similar to these indications of the personal responsibility the mothers felt for ensuring the wellbeing of their babies, Pranee Liamputtong also found that becoming a mother was experienced by Southeast Asian immigrant women in Australia as a "moral transformation of self," where they felt pressed to perform a "moral career ... influenced by an ethic of care and responsibility for others, particularly their children" (25).

Intersections of Discursive, Social, and Material Contexts of Immigrant Mothers' Lives

As the immigrant mothers in our study negotiated with the discourses and expectations of mothering, their experiences were also shaped by the social and material contexts of their individual lives. Similar to what is described by Vallianatos elsewhere in this volume, the lack of extended family support combined with strong gendered divisions of labour regarding childcare and tight family finances—which, to a large extent, are linked to their position as immigrant women—were particularly relevant.

Like the women interviewed by Vallianatos, some participants in our study talked about having parents or in-laws come and stay with them for extended periods after the baby was born, whereas others said that not having extended family nearby increased the challenges of infant feeding and childcare. Most women acknowledged support received from the Canadian public health system, especially through community health nurses and other community resources, but some also said there were few people to turn to for immediate advice or to share the load of childcare. This situation seemed to be especially draining for women who had older children as well as the newborn.

The isolation and hardship of being a mother were often increased by strong norms regarding the gendered division of labour. The majority of participants were doing almost all of the childcare by themselves. In a couple of instances, the father was working and living in another country (China and the United States), while the mother was raising the infant with the help of her parents and in-laws. Even when the fathers were living at home, many were away working long days and did not see parenting as their role. As one woman explained: "I cannot rely totally on him because men cannot always do a lot of work like women do, like taking care of the kids maybe. I don't think he is very interested in doing this and very capable of doing this. I can get some support from him but not very much."

Although some of the fathers' lack of involvement can be attributed to gender ideologies, it is also related to the material conditions of their lives, as immigrants are often unable to obtain professional employment and have to work long hours for low pay (Zaman 39-89). When the mothers in the study were at home with young infants, the fathers needed to be earning as much income as they could to support the family. A few women were able to receive paid maternity leave, but most were unpaid stay-at-home parents either because they were not able to secure a job in Canada due to a lack of accreditation of their academic qualifications and employment experiences from home countries, or they did not have the financial and extended family support to manage a paid job along with the parenting responsibilities.

The resulting tight finances influenced living arrangements and the accessibility of extended family as mentioned above. For example, a woman from India said, "We were living in a small one bedroom apartment so having a newborn baby and at the same time having my parents over, it would be quite overwhelming for us." Moreover, financial solvency is a major determinant of the ability to sponsor extended family members to Canada—something most participants (like most new immigrants) could not sufficiently demonstrate, despite their needs for personal support (Habib 140-165; Koehn, Spencer, and Hwang 80). Postmigration financial hardship was also raised in participants' comments about the expense of healthy foods and vitamin supplements. However, all the women regardless of financial status said that they did not compromise on these items, especially for their children. As one explained: "Well, we're living on credit cards! Our financial situation is quite tight now, but we're not making any compromise with our food and health and the health of our baby!"

Other researchers have also documented how women's experiences of mothering are shaped by the diverse and intersecting social locations of race, class, religion, immigration status, culture, and other dynamics (Varcoe and Doane 304-08). Experiences of migration, uprooting, and lack of extended family support intersecting with financial and other stress and language barriers create special challenges for many immigrant mothers in accessing health and other information, resources, services, and care in their new country (Guruge and Khanlou 33; Liamputtong 44; McLaren and Dyck 41-44; Vissandjée et al. 233-37). Immigrant women are subjected to ideologies of good motherhood, but the implementation of those ideologies can be experienced as difficult because of the intersecting economic, social, and cultural conditions of their lives as immigrant women (Liamputtong 49).

Conclusion and Implications

The findings presented in this chapter highlight ways Asian immigrant women living in Metro Vancouver are recruited into practices of good mothering through widespread nutritional science and parenting discourses and related material practices of the state that promote specific modes of infant and self-care. For immigrant mothers, however, the expected practices may be in tension with subjugated knowledges based on cultural and personal wisdom as well as with the conditions of their lives as immigrants, which may be marked by isolation from extended family, a rigid gendered division of labour, and significant financial constraints. The moralizing discourses of good mothering, though, may be so powerful that they create physical, mental, and financial hardships for immigrant mothers who are implored to prioritize the mothering and welfare of their children over other issues.

The study data can be read as indicating that current public health processes operate effectively to support immigrant mothers in Greater Vancouver and ensure that their infants are provided with optimal nutrition. However, from our critical feminist perspective, the data also demonstrate pervasive and somewhat pernicious processes of governmentality that not only coerce immigrant women into gendered roles of motherhood but also shape their subjectivity and identity (Knaak, "Contextualising Risk" 347, 352; Varcoe and Doane, 301-304; Wall 604). DeSouza (elsewhere in this volume) similarly describes how healthcare practices—in her case, interactions between nurses, midwives, and a Korean immigrant who had just given birth in a New Zealand hospital—act as disciplinary mechanisms to produce self-regulating compliant immigrant mothers who replace traditional food practices with behaviours expected by healthcare experts. Showering immigrant mothers with health information and services thus serves neoliberal ideologies of health reform and self-responsibilization for raising future productive citizens. Neoliberal ideals of motherhood expect women to invest in their children's health and "generate human capital in their children to meet the neoliberal idea of citizen self-sufficiency" (McLaren and Dyck 47). Immigrant women's participation in the dominant discourses of mothering in Canada allows them to demonstrate themselves as responsible parents and citizens or as ideal as opposed to deficient immigrants who are in charge of their own and their children's health and can contribute in producing an efficient future work force and healthy Canadian citizens.

In interpreting these findings, it is important to acknowledge some limitations of our study. Our sample was small, well educated, and did not include voices of women who did not predominantly breastfeed their newborns. Despite our efforts to use a variety of recruiting venues, most participants were recruited through the public health system (community maternity services and programs), and thus immigrant women who are unable to access such services were not included. All mothers were from a dual-parent heterosexual family, and no single or lesbian mothers were included.

Despite these limitations, the study points to the need for nutrition and public health professionals and others working with immigrant mothers to critically reflect on their own assumptions about health, nutrition, and mothering, including consideration of the Eurocentric, biomedical framing of the knowledge being promoted. Individually focused interventions emphasizing provision of health information and professional advice may ignore barriers that make it difficult for immigrant mothers to implement what is being advocated. At the same time, those working with immigrant mothers should challenge stereotypical assumptions about the mothers' knowledge and practices. One cannot assume they are unaware of current biomedically framed recommendations or that they are steeped in traditional practices of their culture. The mothers in this study did not come to Canada with static and traditional cultural knowledge but with an understanding of scientific, evidence-based nutrition education and recommendations. This reality demonstrates the global nature of current knowledge, challenging binary assumptions of the West as the locus of modern scientific knowledge and the East as the locus of traditional cultural knowledge.

Works Cited

Chapman, Gwen E. "Making Weight: Light-Weight Rowing, Technologies of Power, and Technologies of the Self." *Sociology of Sport Journal*, vol. 14, no. 3, 1997, pp. 205-23.

Chapman, Gwen E. "From 'Dieting' to 'Healthy Eating': An Exploration of Shifting Constructions of Eating for Weight Control." *Interpreting Weight: The Social Management of Fatness and Thinness*, edited by Jeffery Sobal and Donna Maurer. Aldine de Gruyter, 1999, pp. 73-87.

Coveney, John. *Food, Morals and Meaning: The Pleasure and Anxiety of Eating*. Routledge, 1999.

Esterik, Penny van. "Contemporary Trends in Infant Feeding Research." *Annual Review of Anthropology*, vol. 31, 2002, pp. 257-78.

Foss, Katherine A. "Perpetuating 'Scientific Motherhood': Infant Feeding Discourse in Parents Magazine, 1930–2007." *Women & Health*, vol. 50, no. 3, 2010, pp. 297-311.

Foucault, Michel. "Governmentality." *The Foucault Effect: Studies in Governmentality with Two Lectures by and an Interview with Michel Foucault*, edited by Graham Burchell, Colin Gordon, and Peter Miller, University of Chicago Press, 1991, pp. 87-104.

Foucault, Michel. *Power/Knowledge: Selected Interviews and Other Writings, 1972-1977*. Pantheon, 1980.

Foucault, Michel. "Right of Death and Power Over Life." *Foucault Reader*, edited by Paul Rabinow, Pantheon Books, 1984, pp. 258-72.

Foucault, Michel. "Technologies of the Self." *Technologies of the Self: A Seminar with Michel Foucault*, edited by Luther. H. Martin, Huck Gutman, and Patrick. H. Hutton, University of Massachusetts Press, 1988, pp. 16-49.

Guruge, Sepali and Nazilla Khanlou. "Intersectionalities of Influence: Researching the Health of Immigrant and Refugee Women."

Canadian Journal of Nursing Research, vol. 36, no 3, 2004, pp. 32-47.

Habib, Sanzida. *South Asian Immigrant Women's Access to and Experiences with Breast and Cervical Cancer Screening Services in Canada.* 2012. University of British Columbia, PhD dissertation, hdl.handle.net/2429/42855. Accessed 5 June 2021.

Hays, Sharon. 1996. *The Cultural Contradictions of Motherhood.* Yale University Press, 1996.

Health Canada. "Infant Feeding." *Health Canada*, 2014, www.hc-sc.gc.ca/fn-an/nutrition/infant-nourisson/index-eng.php. Accessed 5 June 2021.

Knaak, Stephanie. "The Problem with Breastfeeding Discourse." *Canadian Journal of Public Health*, vol. 97, no. 5, 2006, pp. 412-14.

Knaak, Stephanie. "Contextualising Risk, Constructing Choice: Breastfeeding and Good Mothering in Risk Society." *Health, Risk & Society*, vol. 12, 2010, pp. 345-55.

Koehn, Sharon, Charmaine Spencer, and Eunju Hwang. "Promises, Promises: Cultural and Legal Dimensions of Sponsorship for Immigrant Seniors." *Diversity and Aging among Immigrant Seniors in Canada: Changing Faces and Greying Temples*, edited by Douglas Durst and Michael MacLean, Detselig Enterprises Ltd., 2010, pp. 79-102.

Liamputtong, Pranee, and Charin Naksook. "Infant Feeding Practices: The Case of Thai Immigrant Women in Australia." *Australian Journal of Primary Health-Interchange*, vol. 7, no. 1, 2001, pp. 46-55.

Liamputtong, Pranee. "Motherhood and 'Moral Career': Discourses of Good Motherhood among Southeast Asian Immigrant Women in Australia." *Qualitative Sociology*, vol. 29, no. 1, 2006, pp. 25-53.

McLaren, Arlene T., and Isabel Dyck. "Mothering, Human Capital, and the 'Ideal Immigrant'." *Women's Studies International Forum*, vol. 27, 2004, pp. 41-53.

Mason, Jennifer. *Qualitative Researching.* 2nd ed. Sage, 2002.

Rabinow, Paul, and Nikolas Rose. "Biopower Today." *BioSocieties*, vol. 1, 2006, pp. 195-217.

Ristovski-Slijepcevic, Svetlana, Gwen E. Chapman, and Brenda L. Beagan. "Being a 'Good Mother': Dietary Governmentality in the Family Food Practices of Three Ethnocultural Groups in Canada." *Health*, vol. 14, no. 5, 2010, pp. 467-83.

Varcoe, Colleen and Gweneth Hartrick Doane. "Mothering and Wo-
men's Health." *Women's Health in Canada: Critical Perspectives on
Theory and Policy*, edited by Marina Morrow, Olena Hankivsky, and
Colleen Varcoe, University of Toronto Press, 2007, pp. 297-323.

Vissandjée, Bilkis, et al.. "Women's Health at the Intersection of
Gender and the Experience of International Migration." *Women's
Health in Canada: Critical Perspectives on Theory and Policy*, edited by
Marina Morrow, Olena Hankivsky, and Colleen Varcoe, University
of Toronto Press, 2007, pp. 221-43.

Wall, Glenda. "Moral Constructions of Motherhood in Breastfeeding
Discourse." *Gender & Society*, vol. 15, no. 4, 2001, pp. 592-610.

Wallace, Lora Ebert, and Holly Chason. "Infant Feeding in the Modern World: Medicalization and the Maternal Body." *Sociological
Spectrum*, vol. 27, no. 4, 2007, pp. 405-38.

Zaman, Habiba. *Breaking the Iron Wall: Decommodification and Immigrant
Women's Labour in Canada*. Rowman & Littlefield Publishers, 2006.

Chapter 8

Going Without: Migrant Mothers, Food, and the Postnatal Ward

Ruth De Souza

ospital admission signifies the induction into a distinct patient subculture in Western medical healthcare systems (Yarbrough and Klotz). Clothes, belongings, and identity are relinquished, and autonomy over everyday activities and routines is ceded to health professionals and institutional processes. The dominant mode of biomedicine emphasizes the individual and the physical body, shifting a person from a socially integrated member of a community into an object who receives care. Food structures both our daily lives and life transitions, such as maternity, and is an arena where powerful values and beliefs about being a human are evident. More than sustenance and nutrition, food has social, cultural, and symbolic meanings. Practices relating to food demarcate cultural boundaries of belonging and not belonging on the basis of religion, nation, class, race, ethnicity, and gender (Wright and Annes; Bell and Valentine). Being unable to access one's own food can result in cultural disadvantages, in which a person is separated from their own cultural context and cannot provide for themselves within an institutional environment (Woods).

Examining the significance of food in the institutional context of health highlights how people are racialized by the foods that they eat and how institutions and staff working within them regulate migrant bodies. This chapter analyses literature related to food and provides an excerpt from a study of migrant maternity in New Zealand. It shows how food habits are shaped by everyday institutional practices, which maintain order and simultaneously impose disciplinary processes on migrant bodies. The preparation of food represents the continuity and affirmation of tradition and culture, a mechanism for promoting wellness within the physical, emotional, and social transitions of birth. Food as an analytic shows how ethnic identity is performative and processual—that is, it reacts and is reacted to by the host culture. I propose that health services can provide care that is more culturally safe by developing a better understanding of the importance of culture and food in constructing, maintaining, and transforming identities and by providing facilities and resources to facilitate food preparation during the perinatal period.

An Excerpt about Food and the Postnatal Ward

Young-Ja's account shows how food is a mechanism for the disciplining and normalizing of maternal subjectivity in the hospital site. She attaches meaning to the food that is available for her postbirth, but in the case of the universally available hospital food in New Zealand, this food is limited. Her cultural food preferences mark her as an other-mother (who is not a "Kiwi"). Korean food represents more than nutrition for Young-Ja; it connects her to cultural beliefs about what is health giving and life affirming as she brings new life into the world:

> I'm not picky with food, and I still enjoyed food even after giving birth. The Kiwis said that the food had all the nutrition, but the portion was too small for me. Kiwis probably eat the same thing, but how would I produce milk with a portion like that? They gave me the same amount of food (it was sort of watery...) as if I was an ordinary person, and it wasn't quite enough. I couldn't bring my own food under the circumstances and didn't want to bother the other mums with the smell of my own food—when I had my first child, the nurse had told me off for the smell. In both children's birth, I had to share a room with another mother, as there were too many patients, and the midwives showed an obvious sign of dislike. They even said to me if I had "brought fish." This experience after my first child put me off from bringing food again. This is why I was hungry.

Young-Ja's experience in a New Zealand maternity hospital shows how food structures both daily events and the life event of becoming a mother. How much food, what kind of food, and the quality of that food all affect her perceived capacity to provide adequate milk to feed her baby. The new mother has undertaken a tumultuous transition, and for Young-Ja, this means that she needs food that will return her to health and give her the nutrients she requires to feed her new baby. She is not an ordinary person. The institutional context of the postnatal ward limits her agency for resistance or getting her own needs met, and previous negative verbal and nonverbal feedback about the odour of her traditional food prevents her bringing in more nutritious food to the ward. Young-Ja exercises vigilance over herself and surveils herself to fit the norm, as regulation becomes self-regulation.

Identity and Consumption

People are racialized by the foods they eat (Mannur). The saying "We are what we eat" refers to not only the nutrients we consume but also to beliefs about our morality (Bell and Valentine). Similarly, we are also what we do not eat; hence, our food practices mark us out as belonging or not belonging to a group. Elspeth Probyn argues that "As that which both viscerally segregates us and radically brings us together, without doubt, eating takes us into a hugely powerful system of values, regulations and beliefs" (65). Therefore, food has an exclusionary and inclusionary role with affective consequences, which range from curiosity and delight to disgust.

For the migrant, identity cannot be taken for granted, it must be worked at to be nurtured and maintained. It becomes an active, performative, and processual project enacted through consumption (Kalcik). Food provides an anchor during a tumultuous event, where history, memory, feelings, and social status can be activated in a mouthful. An imagined diasporic group identity is produced, maintained, and reinforced with every taste. The rituals of food preparation represent continuity through the techniques and equipment that are used to affirm family life (Bell and Valentine), and in sharing this food hospitality, love, generosity, and appreciation can be expressed. However, the food that is a comfort for the dislocated, lonely, and isolated migrant also sets her apart, making her stand out as visibly, gustatorily, or olfactorily different. The resource for her wellbeing also marks her as different and a risk. If her food is seen as smelly, distasteful, foreign, or abnormal, these characteristics can be transposed to her body and to those bodies that resemble her. As Martin Manalansan observes:

> Struggling with the upheavals in rotating to a new culture and environment, sensory memory can be a balm against loneliness. Aromas celebrate the sensorial knowledge of one's heritage and preserve cultural continuity but also make one's residence and body as distinctly other and vulnerable to being targeted. Finding ways to accomplish the former without invoking the consequences of the latter becomes a challenge requiring ingenuity and constant self-monitoring. (15)

Therefore, smells are political. In the postnatal ward, detergent and antiseptic smells are acceptable, but organic smells pose a problem and must be contained. The body that produces the food aromas and odours must be the one to negotiate both the smell that is out of place and the identity that does not belong. Typically, migrant bodies have been viewed as a vector of disease, crime, and immorality by virtue of their olfactory differences. Food smells are a means of categorizing groups of people who are different, and those viewed as negative are seen as a marker of non-Western primitiveness. The emotion of disgust is emblematic of the too-near proximity of others and the fear that we might be invaded through our mouths. Probyn writes: "Disgust reveals the object in all of its repellent detail, it causes us to step back, and, in that very action, we are also brought within the range of shame" (139). However, nutritional assimilation or sanitization to become odourless, and modern, does not guarantee belonging; like citizenship, it remains thin when compared to the affective power of ethnic identity.

Cultural Safety and Food

Cultural safety offers healthcare practitioners a framework for considering the significance of food practices for people outside of the dominant culture, where a combination of nutritional assimilation, ethnocentric thoughtlessness, and lack of awareness of the distinctive cultural significance of food results in a failure to meet dietary expectations (Gerrish, Husband, and Mackenie; Harbottle).

Meals are critical to the wellbeing and recovery of patients, furnishing physical and emotional support. In an unfamiliar environment, meals provide a link with normal life and provide routine. However, issues of cost, satisfaction, acceptability, nutrition levels, wastage, and undernutrition in hospitals are endemic. Little autonomy can be exercised by patients, as the choices of meal and mealtimes are inflexible (Bell and Valentine). Larger infrastructural issues drive mass production, and they must be cognizant of regulatory structures, efficient production, medical individualization, hygienic food service, and safety-oriented caregiving. Diets driven by discourses of medical and financial risk strip food of its social and cultural meaning and limit individual variation (Wu and Barker).

The food culture of hospitals is dominated by "the ideology of nutritionism," or nutritional reductionism (Ferrie). This view developed from science and sees food in terms of nutritional composition rather than in terms of whole foods or meals or foodways. Required nutrients and their effects on one another and on the body are identified. Nutritionism colonizes and undermines other knowledge about eating, which creates a dependence on nutrition experts rather than the sensual, aesthetic, cultural, and environmental factors that determine food choice. Eating for pleasure is pathologized, and it is expected that people will compromise on flavour or satisfaction in order to be healthy. Hospitals embody the ideology of nutritionism, with hospital meals planned according to nutrient goals set by the government. Mass-produced meals are provided for patients either from a central processing unit or from a hospital kitchen (Ferrie). In such settings, cultural preferences, such as for hot or cold foods, are viewed as personal preferences or habits. Hospital food is devoid of reciprocity, interaction, choice, and surprise as well as the sights and sounds of ceramic cups and chopsticks and evocative odours (Wu and Barker).

Food service systems in hospitals tend to only make minor concessions to cultural diversity because they predate the expanded cultural and religious diversity of the population being served (Ferrie). Often family or friends are discouraged from caring for loved ones by providing food, as there is a lack of facilities, such as kitchens, microwaves, or implements, so family are discouraged from eating with their loved ones in a culturally meaningful way (Wu and Barker).

Surveillance and Labelling: Creating Docile Bodies

The significance of food is accentuated for migrants or people identified as ethnic who experience institutional processes differently (Ferrie). Hierarchical power within hospitals is exercised through processes that lead people to be isolated, assessed, labelled, surveilled, and transformed. These processes also strip the patients of their social and cultural identities so that they can be fed into the machinery of the institution. Thus, migrants who might not conform to the Anglo-centric norms of individualism and autonomy can experience hospitalization as a process that tears them from their family and community, exacerbated by controlled contact, limited visiting times and number of visitors, and limited telephone access. Decision making, clothing, and possessions are removed and replaced by those of the hospital. In addition, limited food choices become available and the patient has to assimilate for the period that they are in the hospital.

Young-Ja's excerpt also shows how bodies become docile through performing self-disciplining, compliant, and docile behaviour. Panopticism, or the ever-present threat of potential or continual surveillance, is a mechanism for translating technologies of disciplinary control into an individual's everyday practices (Rolfe and Gardner). Foucault uses the metaphor of the panopticon, which was a type of prison designed by the philosopher Jeremy Bentham. In this prison, the central observation tower could potentially view every cell and every prisoner. However, the prisoners could not view the observers or guards, so the prisoners could not tell if or when they were being observed. Consequently, they came to believe that someone may always be watching them, so they begin to discipline themselves (Rolfe and Gardner). This threat of surveillance has been transferred to other institutional settings and to power relations in society. Not only do kinds of disciplinary techniques produce distinctive institutions of modern nation states, but they also produce modern individuals who are constructed as "isolated, disciplined, receptive and industrious political subject[s]" (Mitchell xi). For the docile body to be successfully created, the subject has to internalize and embody these types of discipline, which consist of social standards, routines, practices, beliefs, and behaviours that ensure conformity with society's disciplinary regimes. We can see how Young-Ja produces herself as a docile subject who has nutritionally assimilated into the culture of Western healthcare.

Young-Ja's words highlight another discursive gap between her view of maternity and that of the health professionals that care for her. Midwifery discourses position birth as natural and the maternal subject as physically capable of caring for her baby from the moment it is born, requiring minimal intervention and protection. The maternal body is represented as strong and capable of taking on the tasks of motherhood. In contrast, Young-Ja, along with many of the Korean women in my study, discursively positioned birth as a process that made the body vulnerable, which required careful surveillance, monitoring, as well as a period of rest and nurturing with special foods before the new mother could take on new or additional responsibilities. The vulnerable maternal body requires special care. Consequently, as a racialized maternal subject, Young-Ja's body was subject to modes of governing that were normalizing (and seen to be empowering). However, she experienced these modes as disempowering because she was not defined in her uniqueness and particularity but in relationship with the technical knowledges deployed by nurses and midwives: She was made to regulate herself accordingly. Ultimately, becoming a white mother is a subject position that will forever be unavailable to her despite her rebuttal of her traditional food. These processes result in the experience of a differential quality of care, which contributes to dissatisfaction with her maternal experience, and detrimental practices associated with colonial and assimilatory discourses are reproduced.

Discussion and Conclusion

The globalization of borders has seen the movement of people and products, and consuming ethnic food has become a feature that represents a form of palatable multiculturalism (Gunew) or "ethnicity at its most sharable" (Van den Berghe). However, this "cosmo-multiculturalism" or "multiculturalism without migrants" (Hage) requires few adjustments from the dominant culture. Yet food and food smells are political and illustrate a complexity of power relations; they construct human difference as well as boundaries between "us" and "them." Hospitals are not odourless or neutral, so analyzing how food is provided and consumed in the postnatal ward of the hospital highlights the limitations of sharable ethnicity and palatable multiculturalism. These limits point to the ways in which understandings of the politics of food and smells can enhance service provision for multicultural populations within an assimilatory health system so that dietary expectations can be better met.

Works Cited

Bell, David, and Gill Valentine. *Consuming Geographies: We Are Where We Eat*. Routledge, 1997.

Ferrie, Suzie. "Invasion of the Body Snatchers: Food, Feeding, and Power in Hospitals." *Cultural Studies Critical Methodologies*, vol. 106, 2010, pp. 437-44.

Gerrish, Kate, Charles Husband, and Jennifer Mackenie. *Nursing for a Multi-Ethnic Society*. Taylor & Francis, 1996.

Gunew, Sneja. "Introduction: Multicultural Translations of Food, Bodies, Language." *Journal of Intercultural Studies*, vol. 21, no. 3, 2000, pp. 227-37.

Hage, Ghassan. "At Home in the Entrails of the West: Multiculturalism, 'Ethnic Food' and Migrant Home-Building." *Home/World: Space, Community and Marginality in Western Sydney*, edited by Helen Grace, et al., Pluto Press, 1997, pp. 99–153.

Harbottle, Lynn. *Food for Health, Food for Wealth: The Performance of Ethnic and Gender Identities in Iranian Settlers in Britain*. New York. Berghahn Books, 2004.

Kalcik, Susan. "Ethnic Foodways in America: Symbol and the Performance of Identity." *Ethnic and Regional Foodways in the United States: The Performance of Group Identity*, edited by Linda Keller Brown and Kay Mussell, University of Tennessee Press, 1984, pp. 37-65.

Manalansan, Martin F. "Immigrant Lives and the Politics of Olfaction in the Global City." *The Smell Culture Reader*, edited by Jim Drobnick, Berg, 2006, pp. 41-52.

Mannur, A. "Culinary Fictions: Immigrant Foodways and Race in Indian American Literature." *Asian American Studies After Critical Mass*, edited by Kent A. Ono, Blackwell, 2008, pp. 56-70.

Mitchell, T. *Colonizing Egypt*. University of California Press, 2004.

Probyn, Elspeth. 2000. *Carnal Appetites: Food Sex Identities*. Routledge, 2000.

Rolfe, Gary, and L.Y.N. Gardner. "'Do Not Ask Who I Am': Confession, Emancipation and (Self)-Management through Reflection." *Journal of Nursing Management*, vol. 14, no. 8, 2006, pp. 593-600.

Van den Berghe, Pierre L. "Ethnic Cuisine: Culture in Nature." *Ethnic and Racial Studies*, vol. 7, no. 3, pp. 1984, pp. 387-97.

Woods, Martin. "Cultural Safety and the Socioethical Nurse." *Nursing Ethics*, vol. 17, no. 6, 2010, pp. 715-25.

Wright, Wynne, and Alexis Annes. "Halal on the Menu?: Contested Food Politics and French Identity in Fast-Food." *Journal of Rural Studies*, vol. 32, 2013, pp, 388-99.

Wu, Shirley, and Judith C. Barker. "Hot Tea and Juk: The Institutional Meaning of Food for Chinese Elders in An American Nursing Home." *Journal of Gerontological Nursing*, vol. 34, no. 11, 2008, pp. 46-54.

Yarbrough, Susan, and Linda Klotz. "Incorporating Cultural Issues in Education for Ethical Practice." *Nursing Ethics*, vol. 14, no. 4, 2007, pp. 492-502.

Chapter 9

Infant-Feeding Practices among Chinese Mothers in Ireland

Qianling Zhou and Haoyue Chen

According to the World Health Organization, exclusive breast-feeding is the optimal feeding practice for infants within the first six months of life, and complementary foods with continued breastfeeding should be given to infants up to two years of age or beyond (*The Optimal Duration*). Migration to another country may induce changes in infant-feeding practices of the mothers as the social environment and maternal sociodemographic status differ. For Chinese mothers, the first one month after childbirth is considered as a critical and vulnerable period for the newborn and the mother. They will follow a traditional practice (called "doing the month") during this period. A number of restrictions on behaviour (e.g., avoid drinking cold water) should be followed (Liu, Petrini, and Maloni). The consumption of a special postpartum diet has been traditionally regarded as beneficial to the quantity and quality of breastmilk. Such a cultural belief is still prevalent among Chinese mothers living in China and abroad (Tarrant, Dodgson, and Choi, "Becoming a Role Model"; Zhou et al.), as doing the month can have a positive influence on breastfeeding practices (Tarrant, Dodgson, and Choi, "Becoming a Role Model"; Zhou, Younger, and Kearney).

Data related to infant feeding among immigrant Chinese mothers in Europe is scarce. Thus, this chapter aims to provide more information about the infant-feeding practices of Chinese immigrants in Ireland, regarding their breastfeeding rates, weaning practices, and influences that affect their infant feeding practices. In addition, the successful experiences of Chinese immigrants who had exclusively breastfed for four to six months are also detailed. A sequential explanatory mixed method study was conducted among Chinese immigrant mothers in Ireland. Phase 1 was a cross-sectional self-administered retrospective mailed survey, which was conducted between September 2008 and March 2009 in the Dublin area and explored infant-feeding practices and the determinants of breastfeeding among a convenience sample of Chinese mothers living in Ireland (n=322). Phase 2 consisted of seven semistructured focus groups (n=33), which were conducted between October and December 2009 in Dublin and explored the influence of living in Ireland on breastfeeding among Chinese mothers who had given birth there. Phase 3 comprised qualitative in-depth interviews (n=14), which were conducted between December 2009 and February 2010 and investigated the experiences of Chinese mothers living in Ireland who managed to breastfeed exclusively for four to six months. Ethical approval of each phase was obtained from the Research Ethics Committee of the Dublin Institute of Technology. Confidentiality was assured, and the participants' written consent was sought before any assessment. Each phase is described in detail in the following paragraphs.

In this chapter, breastfeeding is understood as "any breastfeeding"—that is, feeding a child with any breastmilk (WHO, *Indicators*). Breastfeeding initiation is defined as putting the child to breast at least once after birth or feeding the child with breastmilk at least once (WHO, *Indicators*). Exclusive breastfeeding means the infant receives only breastmilk (including breastmilk expressed or from a wet nurse); the infant may also receive oral rehydration solutions, drops, and syrups (vitamins, minerals, or medicines) if needed but nothing else (WHO, *Indicators*). Zuo yuezi ("doing the month") is the traditional Chinese postnatal practice in which women confine themselves at home for one month after childbirth for the purpose of restoring their health with rest; they avoid contact with cold matter (such as drinks and water) and consume more hot foods while receiving extended family assistance (Pillsbury).

Phase 1. Infant-Feeding Practices among a Convenience Sample of Chinese Mothers Living in Ireland

A cross-sectional questionnaire was devised to seek retrospective information on mothers' infant-feeding practices of their youngest child. Women who were born in China (including Hong Kong and Macau), who had given birth to at least one child, and who had been in Ireland for at least six months were included in the study. Potential participants were approached in Chinese supermarkets, Chinese language schools, church organizations, and a few Chinese restaurants in Dublin urban and suburban areas. The purpose and demands of the study were explained, and the questionnaire was distributed to each participant, together with instructions for completion and a stamped addressed envelope. A snowball technique was used to increase the sample size—that is, participants were required to help announce and distribute the survey to those who were known to them and met the inclusion criteria. In total, 322 Chinese mothers participated in the study, including forty-seven Chinese mothers who had given birth to their youngest child in China (CMC) and 275 Chinese mothers who had given birth to their youngest child in Ireland (CMI). The majority of mothers were married, had a university level of education, and had been born in the northern part of mainland China. Three-fifths of CMC gave birth between the age of twenty and twenty-five, whereas almost 70 per cent of CMI were over twenty-five years old. The majority of CMC had been in Ireland for no more than five years; however, nearly 60 per cent of CMI had been in Ireland between five and ten years.

Differences in infant-feeding patterns of CMC and CMI were investigated. Initially, forty-one out of forty-seven CMC (87.2%) and 208 out of 275 CMI (75.6%) breastfed their child. Rates of CMI dropped to 49.1 per cent at three months and 28.4 per cent at six months, whereas the rate among CMC at six months remained above 60 per cent. At twelve months, the breastfeeding rates of CMC and CMI fell to 17 per cent and 7.6 per cent, respectively. Significant differences in breastfeeding rates between CMC and CMI were noted from one to three months, and even more distinct differences were found from four to twelve months. Moreover, most children born in China (44.7 per cent) and Ireland (52.0 per cent) were fed with breastmilk first after birth. Breast milk was introduced sooner among CMI than CMC. For mothers who did not breastfeed at first, CMI mainly used infant formula (45.5 per cent), whereas CMC mainly used nonmilk liquids. More than 90 per cent of infants born in either China or Ireland were given water before four months. The use of other nonmilk liquids (e.g., juice and tea) before four months was more prevalent among CMC (>62 per cent) than CMI (<20 per cent). The majority of CMI introduced infant formula before four months, compared with 46.8 per cent of CMC. The early introduction of cow's milk before twelve months was found among 31.8 per cent of CMC and 8.5 per cent of CMI. Over 60 per cent of the children were fed according to a scheduled routine, with no difference between CMC and CMI. Over two-fifths of CMC gave their babies complementary foods before four months, compared with less than one-fifth of CMI. For the first solid foods introduced, egg yolk (34.8 per cent) and commercial baby foods (45.8 per cent) were commonly used by CMC and CMI, respectively. The proportions of mothers using traditional Chinese infant staples (e.g., rice porridge and soft rice) were similar between CMC and CMI. For the timing of solid introduction, fruit and egg yolk were introduced earlier (between four and five months), followed by rice porridge and vegetables (between five and six months), and meat/fish (seven months). A normal family meal was generally introduced after one year of age. No significant differences in the time of first introduction between CMC and CMI were found among most of the foods, except that egg yolk was found to be introduced earlier among CMC (4.90 ± 2.69 months) than CMI (5.78 ± 2.45 months). Multivariate analyses revealed that CMI were less likely to breastfeed for four months and above (odds ratio [OR]=0.181, 95% CI: 0.055-0.595, P=0.005) and to introduce water to their child within one week after childbirth (OR= 0.267, 95% CI: 0.073–0.979, P=0.046). However, they were more likely to introduce infant formula within four months after childbirth (OR=7.489, 95% CI: 2.242-25.019, P=0.001) in comparison to CMC, after controlling for potential confounders.

Factors influencing infant-feeding practices were compared between CMC and CMI. Over 83 per cent of CMI delivered vaginally compared with only 68.1 per cent of CMC. Most of the mothers roomed-in with their newborn during the first few days after childbirth, and CMC (44.7 per cent) were more likely to bedshare with the newborn, whereas CMI (70.4 per cent) were more likely to sleep in a different bed. CMC and CMI reported similar sources of infant-feeding information, including their own mother, doctors and other health professionals, friends, pamphlets or booklet, and the internet. A significantly higher proportion of CMC (48.9 per cent) obtained the information from antenatal/parent-craft classes, compared with only 27.0 per cent of CMI. The husband was the most important source of family support in Ireland, whereas the newborn's grandmothers played a more important role in China. For breastfeeding mothers, CMC (47.5 per cent) were more likely than CMI (22.1 per cent) to receive breastfeeding support from their mother-in-law. The majority of mothers went back to work or study during the first six months after childbirth, but 41.4 per cent of CMI stayed at home for at least one year. The benefits of breastfeeding to the babies were the main reasons given for breastfeeding, for both CMC and CMI. However, a significantly higher proportion of CMC breastfeeding mothers considered that breastfeeding promotes mother-infant bonding (72.5 per cent vs. 51.5 per cent) and that it was more convenient and easier (55 per cent vs. 30.2 per cent). About 13 per cent of CMI breastfed because they had previous breastfeeding experience, whereas none of CMC indicated this reason. The convenience of formula feeding and a fear of the baby becoming too attached were cited as the main reasons for mothers who did not breastfeed. One-fifth of CMI planned to breastfeed for fewer than four months, compared with only 2.6 per cent CMC. The majority of CMC planned to breastfeed for six to twelve months (59 per cent), and another 10.3 per cent planned to breastfeed for more than one year, whereas the corresponding figures for CMI were only 37.0 per cent and 5.8 per cent, respectively. Going back to work or study as well as the right time to stop were cited as the main reasons for breastfeeding discontinuation among both CMC and CMI. About 2 per cent of CMI breastfeeding mothers indicated sending the child back to China a few months after birth as one of the reasons for breastfeeding cessation. Over 53 per cent of CMI breastfeeding mothers indicated insufficient breastmilk as a reason, compared with 32.5 per cent of CMC breast-feeding mothers. To increase breastmilk supply, 87.5% of CMC breastfed mothers consumed a special Chinese diet compared with 68.3 per cent of CMI. A higher percentage of CMI did not use any methods to boost breastmilk compared with CMC.

Phase 2. Focus Groups of Chinese Mothers Who Gave Birth in Ireland

Phase 2 was a focus group discussion to explore the influences of living in Ireland on Chinese mothers' breastfeeding practices, in particular the reasons for the short breastfeeding duration among Chinese mothers who gave birth in Ireland. Seven focus groups were conducted. The inclusion criteria required that mothers were born in China (including Hong Kong and Macau), had been living in Ireland for at least six months, and who had given birth in Ireland. Two Chinese-language schools for children on weekend days were visited, and mothers who sent their children to the schools were approached. At the same time, a contact list generated from the survey of Phase 1 was used to contact the eligible participants. Finally, the participants consisted of mothers recruited from Chinese language schools (n=14) and mothers who were participants of Phase 1 (n=19). Groups were formed according to maternal delivery place(s) and the maternal dialect/region of their hometown; each group had four to six mothers. The focus groups, which lasted from forty to seventy minutes, were conducted in Chinese and at a convenient location in Dublin for the participants; all discussions were tape-recorded. A semistructured interview guide was developed to elicit the barriers to the initiation and continuation of breastfeeding in Ireland. The guide started with an open question on mothers' personal experience in childbirth and infant feeding in Ireland. Mothers were prompted to share how they initiated and sustained breastfeeding and why they terminated breastfeeding. Mothers who had previously given birth in China to an older child were additionally asked to compare their breastfeeding experience in China versus in Ireland. Qualitative data were analyzed by thematic content analyses, following the guidelines recommended by Janice Morse and Anne Field.

There were thirty-three participants in Phase 2; nineteen had given birth in Ireland only, and fourteen had given birth in both China and Ireland. Participants were between twenty-three and forty-nine years old (mean age: 35.1 years old) and had been living in Ireland between two to 27.2 years (mean duration: 8.5 years). Apart from the nine mothers from Hong Kong, there were twenty-four participants from mainland China, dominated by those from Liaoning province (n=8) and Fujian province (n=10). These two provinces were also the main birthplaces of participants from Phase 1. Mothers had generally relatively low socioeconomic status in Ireland because at the time of the focus groups conducted, only six participants had achieved university level of education and none had a professional occupation. Only eight out of thirty-three mothers had never breastfed, whereas twenty-five mothers had breastfed at least one child.

Theme 1. Concern about Breastmilk Quantity and Quality

All mothers believed that breastfeeding is the optimal method of infant feeding. They stressed that breastmilk promotes immunity in the baby. The association between breastmilk quality and the child's health was a major concern. Fifteen mothers had been worried about their breast-milk quality and believed that breastfeeding should stop if breastmilk becomes watery and not nutritious. Mothers also had some doubts about the quality of expressed breastmilk, with some believing it is not fresh enough.

Mothers considered that the quantity and quality of breastmilk are influenced by maternal nutrition, health, medication, age, and mood. They believed that an older mother who takes medicine and is in a bad mood will have breastmilk of a lower quality. They also believed that the mother's diet is important for producing adequate breastmilk as well as ensuring her health and good nutrition (Figure 1). One mother attributed her cessation of breastfeeding at one month to her diet: "I did not have good diet. My breastmilk was not good. So my daughter had diarrhea at that time. Then I stopped [breastfeeding]."

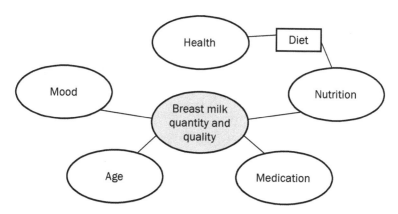

Figure 1. Perceived influences on Breastmilk Quantity and Quality

Mothers largely related their health and breastmilk supply to their postnatal diet and behaviour restrictions. According to Figure 2, due to a lack of family support and the high price of Chinese foods in Ireland, mothers were not able to follow a culturally appropriate diet. Moreover, health professionals in Ireland often knew little about Chinese culture, and mothers had to follow Irish guidelines that went against their cultural beliefs. Consequently, living in Ireland did not allow mothers to follow Chinese postnatal rituals correctly and, thereby, was considered a negative influence on maternal breastmilk supply. The following three subcategories, as described in Figure 2, explain how living in Ireland triggered concern among the Chinese mothers about their breastmilk supply.

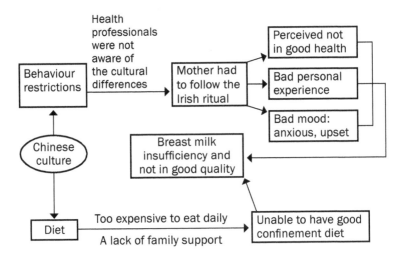

Figure 2. Negative Influences on Breastmilk Production

(a) A Lack of Family Support

Mothers generally believed that zuo yuezi is the most important period for maternal healing and for regaining their strength and health. Mothers should stay at home, have plenty of rest, and avoid doing housework. They should consume hot foods and avoid cold foods, including tap and icy water. They should drink various kinds of soup, such as pig feet and peanut soup, papaya and fish soup, and shellfish soup, which are considered to be effective in boosting breastmilk supply. Not observing rest during zuo yuezi was generally believed to result in illness, either immediately or in later life. During zuo yuezi, support from family members in helping with all the housework, preparing the maternal diet, and minding the child was considered to be essential.

Most mothers were living in a nuclear family in Ireland. It was too expensive to employ housekeepers or childminders. Husbands were often the only source of family support. Moreover, husbands, being the main source of financial support, had to work. Due to a lack of family support, appropriate zuo yuezi was difficult to follow, thereby triggering considerable concern about breastmilk quantity and quality. For example, a mother who had breastfed her first child for one month in Ireland but did not breastfeed her second said: "Mothers in China may receive more care and support from family, so they recover better and have sufficient milk. They can breastfeed for a longer duration. For most of us in Ireland, our parents were far away, and our husband had to work. Nobody was available to look after us during zuo yuezi." In comparison, a mother receiving sufficient family support managed to breastfeed for thirteen months in Ireland: "I stayed at home and did not go back to work. During zuo yuezi, my husband did not work either. I was accompanied by and taken care of for three months. So I did well in zuo yuezi and rested enough." Other mothers in the group were envious of the support this mother receives. Moreover, for multiparous mothers, minding their elder children and nursing the newborn without family support deprived them of rest. A mother said: "I did not have as much milk as last time ... perhaps [because] I had to take care of two children. I did not have enough sleep, and I did not eat well.... I was not in good health."

(b) A Lack of Culturally Sensitive Support and Advice from Health Professionals

In the Chinese tradition, within thirty days after birth, postnatal mothers should refrain from contact with cold water, bathing, and hair washing because these practices are seen to cause wind in the body, leading to aches and pain in later life (Pillsbury; Holroyd et al.). Women should only use warm boiled water or herb water (Cheung). However, these cultural beliefs are not understood by health professionals in Ireland. During the hospital stay, in order not to be seen as difficult, mothers followed the instruction of the nurses. They took a shower soon after birth and consumed the hospital-provided food, most of which was deemed as cold. Cultural conflicts in hospital practices made mothers worried, upset, anxious, or even depressed, as the following three quotes show:

> They prepared you a large cup of cold water after birth, one day one cup. I asked for hot water, [but] she [nurse] said "no."

> Breakfast in the hospital was cold.... They [health professionals] were not aware of the constitutional difference. Their suggestion was based on their norm but [was] not suitable to our body. If you just eat bread daily, how can you produce milk?... They [nurses] felt unbelievable. Why you were so eager for hot water?... In the hospital, I did not take a shower. Then the doctor came to examine me. She asked why I did not take a shower. She looked very angry. So I went to take a shower.

> It was my first time to have a baby. When I saw the food [in the hospital], I was quite upset. I heard that a lot of mothers got postnatal depression.... We were really in the middle. When I phoned China, my mother reminded me to avoid cold and wind. But here, the doctor ... you had to follow their ritual; otherwise, they saw you as a monster! You can see the expression from their eyes.

Negative outcomes following the hospital practices were shared by one mother: "I fainted once on the floor in the hospital. My husband wanted to lay me on the bed. But the doctor said 'no,' and let me lie on the floor [floor is considered cold matter]. Now my shoulder pains every year." After being discharged from hospital, the breastfeeding support provided by health professionals was not culturally sensitive. A mother who had sought help for insufficient breastmilk supply stated: "She [a public health nurse] said you would have enough milk if you drank more water. But we are Chinese people; we have to have soup, like fish soup. They don't understand our Chinese culture."

(c) Quality and Price of Certain Chinese Foods in Ireland Are Not Satisfactory

There are a variety of Chinese foods sold in Asian food stores in Ireland. However, they are too expensive for some mothers to afford daily. Some mothers even doubted the quality of these Chinese foods: "[Chinese food in Ireland] is not as nutritious as food in China."

Theme 2. Migrants' Socioeconomic Problems

(a) Language Barrier

As non-native English speakers, mothers had difficulties in communicating with health professionals in Ireland. Language barriers and social isolation interfered with mothers' access to appropriate infant-feeding information and education, as illustrated by the following three quotes:

> There are training classes. They will invite you to attend and teach you how to feed the baby. But my English is not good.... I did not attend.

> They [health professionals in Ireland] briefly told you that breastfeeding is good. But they didn't tell you as detailed as the doctors in China do.... I think this is because of the language problem for most of us here.

> If they think your English is not good, they have no patience to explain to you.

To promote breastfeeding in Ireland, mothers suggested setting up a Chinese infant-feeding telephone hotline and column in Chinese newspapers in Ireland; to organize Chinese breastfeeding helping groups; and to train more Chinese-speaking healthcare providers.

(b) Sending Children Back to China a Few Months after Birth

Mothers coming to Ireland for economic reasons or who have financial burdens went back to work soon after giving birth. Having no time to take good care of the child, they sent the child back to China to be looked after by other family members. Mothers who sent their child back to China indicated a prenatal intention to abandon breastfeeding or breastfeed for a short period. A mother from Fujian province of mainland China said: "Except for those who are staying here [in Ireland] permanently, most of us stay here for a short term. We come to Ireland for economic reasons. It is not good to have our baby beside us. We have to work. If we want to take good care of the baby, we have to stop working. But it is impossible." This mother still chose breastfeeding prenatally. Her family members in China suggested the following: "Breastfeeding is the best. But if you wanted to send the child back home, you had to be aware of the difficulties of weaning the baby once you start. But it is up to you."

(c) House sharing

Mothers indicated house sharing as one of the reasons for not breast-feeding. They assumed that the baby would cry more if they were breastfed. They did not want to disturb their housemates: "Some people don't like baby.... If your child cries a lot, they will not be happy.... You have not been a mother; you won't understand that feeling! Very difficult!"

Theme 3. A Preference for Infant Formula on the Irish Market

(a) Infant Formula in Ireland Is Widely Considered to Be Good, Safe, and Reliable in Quality and Reasonable in Price

Mothers had great concern about the quality and safety of infant formula on the Chinese market, while they highly valued the infant formula on the Irish market. When the Irish born child visited or stayed in China during the milk-fed period, mothers brought the Irish infant formula back to China. No mothers had fed their Irish-born child with Chinese infant formula. One mother stated the following: "Infant formula produced in China is not good.... Didn't you hear about the problem [melamine-contaminated infant formula in China] months ago?... My friend in China used imported infant formula. Her child was very fat. I doubt if it was really imported... It may be fake.... Quality control is not strict in China."

A mother who had given birth in both countries compared the quality of Irish and Chinese infant formula:

It [infant formula in Ireland] is better than that in China.... You can tell the difference from the colour. Infant formula in China appears as yellow, and infant formula here [in Ireland] is white.... Its [infant formula in Ireland] taste is quite close to breastmilk. But infant formula in China is too sweet.... I sent my second child back to China at nine months; my luggage was full of infant formula.... In China, I formula fed my first son [born in China and used Chinese infant formula]. The hospital in China suggested me to supplement him with calcium. They [health professionals] said his calcium level was not sufficient. I took my second son [fed with infant formula in Ireland] back to China. I took him for a checkup, and the doctor said he did not need to supplement with calcium.

A mother who had breastfed two Chinese-born children for twelve months and two Irish-born children for only six months said: "The weather in Guangdong [a province of China] is very hot, and the quality of infant formula is not good; a lot of children get sick if formula fed.... In Ireland, air is fresh and clean.... Infant formula (in Ireland) is good. It contains sufficient nutrients. So I do not need to breastfeed that long."

Some mothers considered infant formula good for the baby according to their personal experience: "I breastfed my child for eight months in [China], but he was very weak... perhaps my breastmilk was not good.... For the children born here [in Ireland], they were fed with infant formula and very healthy."

And some were influenced by their friends or family members, as the following two mothers explained:

We know that breastfeeding is very good. But we have not seen any disadvantages of formula feeding. If I did, I would definitely not use infant formula.... I see that children fed with formula here are healthy. They grow well and fast.

I did not breastfeed my second child.... My family members said my first son was too thin. They did not encourage me to breastfeed the second one; they said my breastmilk was not good.... My sister-in-law's child was fed with infant formula here in Ireland, and he was very strong.

Infant formula on the Irish market is not expensive, compared with the imported infant formula on the Chinese market. It is affordable for Chinese mothers even though they are not of high economic status in

Ireland: "Sometimes there is discount. Counting the postal fee, it is still cheaper [to buy the infant formula in Ireland] than buying infant formula in China."

(b) Convenience of Formula Feeding

Convenience, the widely perceived advantage of formula feeding, was acknowledged by Chinese mothers in Ireland. Due to a lack of family support, the mothers preferred the most convenient way to feed their baby. The mothers indicated that at nighttime, formula feeding allowed their husbands to help with infant feeding; moreover, babies who received infant formula cried less. Therefore, they could sleep well. Some mothers indicated the inconvenience of breastfeeding when they go outside and return to work. Inconvenience sometimes suggested embarrassment. Mixed-feeding mothers always used infant formula when they went outside: "I used infant formula when I went out. It [breastfeeding] was not convenient."

Theme 4. Less Pressure to Breastfeed in Ireland

(a) More Flexibility in Choosing Feeding Methods

When comparing the breastfeeding environment between China and Ireland, mothers indicated that there is a lot of breastfeeding promotion in both countries. Ireland has supportive breastfeeding facilities in public places, but these are rare in China. Mothers also felt that they had more freedom to choose breastfeeding or formula feeding in Ireland than in China: "They [health professionals in Ireland] told you that breastfeeding is good. But they didn't force you to breastfeed. In China, you would see the posters and slogans everywhere in the hospital. You had to attend the prenatal class, and in the class they [health professionals in China] suggested you breastfeed again and again."

In Ireland, mothers who decided to breastfeed were encouraged to try breastfeeding even if they did not have breastmilk at birth. However, some mothers reported that the hospital staff suggested using infant formula in hospital:

> The nurse saw my child crying. She said he was hungry. Then she gave me a bottle of infant formula. My child slept after having the infant formula.

My breastmilk came on the third day after birth. At first, the nurse fed him with infant formula. He got used to infant formula and disliked breastfeeding.

Two mothers who formula fed at birth indicated that their baby refusing the breast was the main difficulty in sustaining breastfeeding. One mother gave up breastfeeding. The other one used her expressed breastmilk for one month. In comparison, no free infant formula is provided in Chinese hospitals, and mothers have to try hard to initiate breastfeeding.

(b) Family Members' Attitudes Have Less Impact

Mothers indicated that their family members, especially their own mother or mother-in-law, expected them to breastfeed and for a long duration. To maintain family harmony, mothers would obey the suggestions of the elder generation. Being far away from these family members allowed mothers to feed their child per their own intention: "They [elder generation in the family] believed that it is necessary to breastfeed. It is good for the baby. In China, you could not give up breastfeeding unless you really don't have any milk…. My mom reminded me to breastfeed for one year. I would become crazy if I did so! … I did not tell her that I had actually weaned at four months."

Theme 5. Differences in Breastfeeding Attitudes and Practices between Mothers from Mainland China and Hong Kong

Differences in practices of and attitudes towards breastfeeding between mothers from Hong Kong and mainland China were found. Eight out of thirty-three mothers had never breastfed any of their children. Two mothers from mainland China intended to breastfeed; however, health professionals suggested that they not do so because of their postnatal medical condition. The remaining two from mainland China and the four who were from Hong Kong had no intention of breastfeeding. Nine out of the mothers from China who had delivered in mainland China breastfed in China. The only one who formula fed did so because she did not have any breastmilk. She was a nurse in China, and she did her best to breastfeed. In comparison, three out of four Hong Kong mothers who had delivered children in both countries had never breastfed.

All mothers, wherever they were from, perceived the superior health benefits of breastfeeding and acknowledged the better breast-feeding environment in Ireland than in China (either mainland China or Hong Kong). Mothers from mainland China were more determined to breastfeed and did so. Barriers to sustaining breastfeeding in Ireland made them stop early, in particular those who did not have a strong desire to breastfeed for long. However, Hong Kong mothers had less intention to breastfeed. The reasons for not choosing breastfeeding were more likely to be perceived rather than actual problems, such as no breastmilk, poor breastmilk quality, and painful breastfeeding experiences. One Hong Kong mother who repeatedly mentioned the protective effect of breastfeeding for maternal breast cancer said: "Breastfeeding is very good ... I am lazy. And I did not eat well. I ate too much chocolate and chips." It is obvious that she did not have a strong desire to breastfeed. Others from Hong Kong said:

Intentionally we did not choose breastfeeding.... If we did not work, we could not survive in Hong Kong. That is why most of women go back to work soon after giving birth ... The cost of living is very high in Hong Kong, and people daily life is going rapidly. ... The living speed is very fast in Hong Kong.

Maternity leave is twenty-one days in Hong Kong including prenatal and postnatal period.... I had no intention to breast-feed.... Doctors in Hong Kong said breastfeeding is the best, but infant formula is very close to breastmilk now. It is also very good.

Although the lifestyle in Ireland was considered to be more relaxed than that in Hong Kong, a housewife in Ireland said: "I did not breastfeed my first child in Hong Kong, so I was not intending to breastfeed the other child in Ireland." In addition, feelings of embarr-assment were indicated by all Hong Kong breastfeeding and formula-feeding mothers but only by two mothers from mainland China as a barrier to breastfeeding. Most mothers from mainland China did not suffer from feelings of embarrassment. They stayed at home most of the time, went to breastfeeding rooms in shopping centres, and used coverings.

Based on the above comparison, mothers from Hong Kong appeared to have less intention to breastfeed and were more likely to attribute their abandonment of breastfeeding to employment and embarrassment about breastfeeding than mothers in mainland China. These findings are supported by other scholars (Diana; Tarrant, Dodgson, and Choi, "Becoming a Role Model"; Zhou et al.) in that breastfeeding is largely tied to social class in Hong Kong, as working women are given much more status and mothering is seen as secondary; Marie Tarrant, Joan Dodgson, and Shirley Tsang Fei argue that breastfeeding is an activity that many feel must be hidden away from families and friends ("Initiating"). In addition, these authors compared the hospital practices and maternal leave between mainland China and Hong Kong and highlight how mainland China offers a more supportive environment for breastfeeding women due to its enacted legislative support ("Initiating"). The present study's findings suggest that breastfeeding promotion among Chinese mothers in Ireland should be considered separately for those from mainland China and those from Hong Kong. Apart from using different dialects, it may be effective to encourage Hong Kong mothers to initiate breastfeeding by stressing that breastfeeding is natural and not embarrassing, whereas for mothers from mainland China, it may be more important to help them build the skills required to overcome common breastfeeding problems and enhance their self-efficacy and confidence to persevere with breastfeeding if they do encounter difficulties.

Phase 3. In-Depth Interviews of Chinese Mothers Who Breastfed Exclusively for Four to Six Months in Ireland

Through using individual in-depth interviews, Phase 3 revealed the experiences of Chinese mothers who managed to breastfeed exclusively for four to six months in Ireland. How mothers overcame barriers to breastfeeding, as well as their constructive opinions on promoting exclusive breastfeeding, was also documented. The inclusion criteria were Chinese mothers born in China, who had given birth in Ireland, who had resided in Ireland for more than six months, and who had breastfed their children six months or beyond with exclusive breastfeeding for at least four months. Participants in Phase 1 who met the above inclusion criteria were contacted by telephone. Fourteen semi-structured individual interviews were conducted. All interviews were conducted in Chinese, audio-taped, and lasted between forty-five and 125 minutes. Transcribing was conducted verbatim, and the data were analyzed through content analysis. Fourteen mothers were included in this study. They were between twenty-four and fifty-four years old (mean age: thirty-four years) and had lived in Ireland from three to eighteen years (mean duration: nine years). The majority of them had university level of education. Over half were stay-at-home mothers or had part-time nonprofessional jobs, whereas others were self-employed or had professional jobs.

Favourable Factors to the Success of Exclusive Breastfeeding

Mothers indicated that many favorable factors contribute to their success in exclusive breastfeeding. Maternal confidence and determination towards breastfeeding were the main factors. Their self-confidence was enhanced by their good physical conditions, such as sufficient milk supply and suitable nipple size. The influences of Chinese breastfeeding culture as well as the numerous benefits of breastfeeding greatly increased maternal determination to breastfeed. Many mothers interviewed had no job or had part-time non-professional jobs, leaving them sufficient time for breastfeeding. Moreover, breastfeeding support from family, peers, employers, and healthcare personnel played an important role in the success of exclusive breastfeeding.

How to Overcome Barriers to Exclusive Breastfeeding

Mothers encountered many difficulties during breastfeeding, and they had solutions to overcome these barriers. First, some mothers complained that they did not produce enough breastmilk. This problem was solved by sucking immediately after birth and breastfeeding less at one time and more throughout the day. Some mothers felt worried that their baby always choked because too much breastmilk was produced. Thus, as one mother said, "Every time before feeding, some breastmilk would be squeezed out." Another mother worried that as her babies grew up, her "breastmilk might fail to meet their nutritional needs." Another said: "If I had a cold or fever, I would be afraid of infecting my babies through breastfeeding." To dispel these worries, observing the colour of the breastmilk and learning the correct knowledge may be helpful for mothers. The majority of mothers experienced breast engorgement and inflammation. Massage and applying hot treatment could relieve pains. Baby teething and cracked nipples were often mentioned by the participants. Using ointment that can be used during breastfeeding can relieve the pain resulting from nipple cracking. Some mothers were concerned about changes in their body shape after breastfeeding, but some suggested that using breastfeeding bras, since they prevent sagging.

Second, going back to work has been identified as the main reason for stopping breastfeeding (Li et al.; Li et al.). Our participants also complained about the difficulty in breastfeeding after returning to work. However, they managed to breastfeed exclusively. One mother sent her baby to a crèche: "When he was three months old, I sent him to the crèche, and I went to the crèche to feed him once every three hours.... Three months later, the staff there could feed him with spoon, so I fed him during lunch time." Another mother sought her husband's help: "I adjusted the working hours with my husband. My husband brought our baby to my workplace twice a day so that I could continue breastfeeding."

Third, mothers complained about dietary and behavioural restrictions during lactation. However, they were determined and showed a strong will for their babies' health, as one mother said: "During lactation, I couldn't eat too salty or too spicy [food], but I like spicy food very much.... Every time I saw a dish of tasteless soup [the traditional postpartum diet], I felt sick.... But I still ate it for my baby's sake."

Fourth, taking medication while breastfeeding was another major issue for mothers. Some mothers suspended breastfeeding while taking medication; some chose medication that could be taken while breast-feeding, and some did not take any medication. Some mothers reported maternal depression and irritation. Since the mothers realized that maternal depression could result in their baby's refusal to suck, they tried to calm themselves through self-regulation and self-control.

Fifth, mothers discussed their infants having breastmilk jaundice, and severe diarrhea and failing to latch. Among those whose infants had breastmilk jaundice, mothers continued breastfeeding and increased the frequency of breastfeeding to promote infant urination.

Increasing their infants' exposure to the sun was also cited as a useful method. To relieve severe diarrhea, mothers consumed a diet low in fat and sugar and resolved latching problems through rubbing their nipples around the baby's lips.

Sixth, the mothers cited the language barrier and the inaccessibility of a Chinese postpartum diet as the major barriers to accessing maternal healthcare in Ireland. Mothers indicated their difficulties in understanding terminology and strongly recommended employing Chinese healthcare professionals in Irish hospitals, as one mother stated: "In fact, there was still a language barrier. When I communicated with a healthcare professional, there were many professional terminologies that troubled me. So, I think maybe more Chinese nurses and midwives would be better."

Seventh, some mothers complained about their difficulties consuming a Chinese postpartum diet in Ireland, which would promote breastmilk production: "My mother went to a shop for fish heads twice but came back with nothing. No shops sell fish heads." No effective solutions were mentioned regarding this issue.

Finally, mothers received odd looks or negative comments from the public when they breastfed in public. They said ignoring negative attitudes was the best way to deal with the problem. Using a cloth to cover the breast during breastfeeding was also helpful. Mothers complained that in Ireland only limited breastfeeding facilities were available in public places. To solve this problem, they reduced the frequency of breastfeeding or avoided going out. They chose places near home or those that had breastfeeding facilities. They pumped milk before going out or breastfed in hidden places (e.g., the toilet and car).

Mothers' Recommendations on Exclusive Breastfeeding

Based on their successful experience of exclusive breastfeeding, mothers in our study proposed the following recommendations to Chinese immigrant mothers themselves, their family, their employers and colleagues, healthcare professionals, and the Irish government. For Chinese mothers, improving intention and self-confidence of exclusive breastfeeding for an optimal duration was of great importance, as one participant said: "You can complain, but do not give up." To ensure sound financial condition before pregnancy and to share the accommodation with those who have had babies could create suitable conditions for exclusive breastfeeding. For obtaining breastfeeding information, one participant said, "Don't exclude home visits because you cannot speak English well." In contrast, the participants suggested that Chinese immigrant mothers should obtain breastfeeding information proactively and rationally.

Sufficient family support was considered to be important to ensure the optimal duration of exclusive breastfeeding. Husband support was strongly recommended as other family members seldom visit Ireland; thus, sufficient maternity leave for husbands could be an option to support mothers. For working mothers, enough maternity leave and suitable conditions (e.g., providing hygienic venues for breastmilk storage and setting up breastfeeding rooms and nurseries in workplaces) could be beneficial to exclusive breastfeeding. Efforts from employers and colleagues to create suitable conditions for breastfeeding are required.

Irish hospitals were suggested to advocate exclusive breastfeeding. Mothers thought that recruiting and training multilingual healthcare professionals to support different ethnic groups was necessary. Combining breastfeeding knowledge and practice in the prenatal education was also recommended.

The Irish governmental agencies were recommended to set up breastfeeding rooms in order to avoid embarrassment for mothers when they breastfed in public. Since the successful experiences of peers could have positive impact, providing special places for breastfeeding groups was also recommended to promote peer communication. Mothers in our study suggested to increase breastfeeding publicity but in multiple languages and through various means (e.g., newspaper, television, and brochures). Additionally, an independent welfare policy for immigrants was also suggested.

Conclusions

This is the first and only migration study on infant feeding among Chinese mothers in Ireland. It finds that giving birth in Ireland was associated with a shorter duration of breastfeeding. The reasons for discontinuing breastfeeding were cultural conflicts, a lack of family support, linguistic isolation, and the mother's low socioeconomic status in Ireland. These findings suggest the need for culturally and linguistically sensitive breastfeeding support in Ireland. Specific solutions to barriers to exclusive breastfeeding among Chinese mothers in Ireland were also presented in this study as was the important role that self-determination plays in successful exclusive breastfeeding, suggesting a need to develop programs to enhance the self-efficacy of exclusive breastfeeding. The importance of family support revealed in the study suggests the need to involve family members, especially husbands, in breastfeeding interventions. This study also demonstrated the urgent need for multilingual healthcare professionals, breastfeeding facilities in public, sufficient maternity leave, intensive breastfeeding publicity in multiple languages and independent welfare policies for immigrants in Ireland. Our findings may have some implications for other English-speaking countries with low rates of exclusive breast-feeding.

Works Cited

Cheung, Ngai Fen. "Chinese Zuo Yuezi (Sitting in for the First Month of the Postnatal Period) in Scotland." *Midwifery*, vol. 13, no. 2, 1997, pp. 55-65.

Holroyd, Eleanor, Twinn Sheila, and Yim Ip Wan. "Exploring Chinese Women's Cultural Beliefs and Behaviours Regarding the Practice of 'Doing the Month.'" *Women's Health*, vol. 40, no. 3, 2004, pp. 109-23.

Li, Lin, et al. "Chinese Mothers' Knowledge and Attitudes about Breastfeeding in Perth, Western Australia." *Breastfeeding Review*, vol. 11 no.3, 2003, pp. 13-19.

Li, Lin, et al. "Factors Associated with the Initiation and Duration of Breastfeeding by Chinese Mothers in Perth, Western Australia." *Journal of Human Lactation*, vol. 20, no. 2, 2004, pp. 188-95.

Liu, Yan Qun, Marcia Petrini, and Judith A. Maloni. "'Doing the Month': Postpartum Practices in Chinese Women." *Nursing & Health Sciences*, vol. 17, no. 1, 2015, pp. 5-14.

Martin, Diana. *Motherhood in Hong Kong: The Working Mother and Child-Care in the Parent Centred Hong Kong Family*. Curzon Press, 1997.

Morse, Janice, and Peggy-Anne Field. *Qualitative Research Methods for Health Professionals*. 2nd ed. Sage Publications, 1995.

Pillsbury, Barbara L. "'Doing the Month': Confinement and Convalescence of Chinese Women After Childbirth." *Social Science & Medicine*, vol. 12, 1978, pp. 11-22.

Tarrant, Marie, Joan Dodgson, and Shirley Tsang Fei. "Initiating and Sustaining Breastfeeding in Hong Kong: Contextual Influences on New Mothers' Experiences." *Nursing & Health Sciences*, vol. 4, no. 4, 2002, pp. 181-91.

Tarrant Marie, Joan E. Dodgson, and Vinkline Wing Kay Choi. "Becoming a Role Model: The Breastfeeding Trajectory of Hong Kong Women Breastfeeding Longer Than 6 Months." *International Journal of Nursing Studies*, vol. 41, no. 5, 2004, pp. 535-46.

World Health Organization. *Indicators for Assessing Infant and Young Child Feeding Practices*. Geneva, 2008.

World Health Organization. *The Optimal Duration of Exclusive Breastfeeding*. Geneva, 2001.

Zhou, Qianling. *Breastfeeding Attitudes and Practices Among Chinese Mothers in Ireland: A Mixed Methods Study*. 2010. Dublin Institute of Technology, PhD dissertation.

Zhou, Qianling, et al. "'I Was Determined to Breastfeed, and I Always Found a Solution': Successful Experiences of Exclusive Breastfeeding Among Chinese Mothers in Ireland." *International Breastfeeding Journal*, vol. 15, no. 47, 2020, p. 47.

Zhou, Qianling, Katherine M. Younger, and John M. Kearney. "An Exploration of the Knowledge and Attitudes towards Breastfeeding Among a Sample of Chinese Mothers in Ireland." *BMC Public Health*, 10, no. 722, 2010, pp. 1-11.

Chapter 10

Migration, Mothers, Meals: Immigrant Mothers' Experiences and Perspectives on Feeding Children

Helen Vallianatos

Images of Indian womanhood are frequently suggestive of subjugated, oppressed individuals, whose downcast eyes and quiet or silent voices symbolize their powerless social location. These bodily practices of an inferior social location are mirrored in their food practices, such as women eating less and/or last. These stereotypical images coexist with a belief that śakti, the power of the universe, is embodied in the feminine and illustrated in powerful images of goddesses, such as Durga, or of women, such as Indira Gandhi. These polarized extremes are too simplistic to be useful in understanding women's lived experiences. In this chapter, I begin by deconstructing these simplistic renditions of women's social place, as I did during my fieldwork in India over a decade ago. During my research and to better understand women's food practices during pregnancy, I had considered not only larger political and economic contexts but also intrafamily dynamics. Women's agency in their food practices hinged on a confluence of social, political, and economic norms and realities. One social variable was family structure—the presence of elders typically correlated with a decreased capacity for women to make their own food choices and an increased likelihood that women living in such circumstances would follow traditional norms (Vallianatos). Women living in nuclear households typically had more control in everyday food decision making; the normative food rules loosened, as family bonds were stretched across space, from urban centres to rural villages. How might international migration sway women's authority in everyday food practices? Although some shifts in gender roles and responsibilities do occur postmigration (George), kitchen or food work continues to be an important way that gender is performed among many immigrant groups (Avakian; Vallianatos and Raine). Research has also shown the importance of food in marking ethnocultural affiliation; food's power as a signifier of identity results in culinary food heritage continuing three or more generations postmigration, long after language and other markers of ethnocultural identity have disappeared (Ray). But more work is needed to understand how migration affects embodiment and performances of gender in specific milieus (e.g. variations in family structure, community size, and place). In this chapter, I examine how gendered identities are understood and embodied by South Asian (Northern Indian and Pakistan) immigrant women and performed in the food work involved in feeding their families and themselves.

My analysis is centered on Arjun Appadurai's notion of "gastro-politics"—the idea that contestation over cultural or economic resources are evident in social transactions around food. Control of a material resource, such as food, is one way power is demarcated, and observing food practices can reveal family and community power relations and hierarchies. Thus, in a typical, ideal South Asian extended family structure, the mother-in-law controls food resources, and this power is symbolized through her food serving practices—men within the household typically are served first, according to an age hierarchy, but the mother-in-law may purposefully ignore this structure to silently indicate her support (or antagonism) for particular individuals during a family argument. Through food practices, acts of resistance may also be voiced (Adapon; Counihan; Stoller and Olkes).

Serving food may be viewed as a sign of oppression by some or of command and status by others. Before examining my data, I briefly consider how power has been conceptualized and how the concept may be applied to this analysis. A most basic definition of power is the ability to control others—that is, to make others behave as one wishes, either forcefully or by persuasion. As Max Weber has written, power is "the probability that one actor within a social relationship will be in a position to carry out his own will despite resistance" (53); similarly, Robert Dahl has argued that power is when "A has power over B to the extent that he can get B to do something that B would not otherwise do" (202-03). Other scholars understand power as the ability to act, such as Hannah Pitkin, who views it as "capacity, potential, ability, or wherewithal" (276). More recent scholarship has developed this view, such as Steven Lukes's theorizing of power as potentiality, and some feminist thinking on empowerment, exemplified by Jean Miller, who defines empowerment as the capacity to produce a change (241). Rather than viewing power as either the ability to control or the ability to act, I think both definitions are applicable, and an individual's power shifts depending on the unique social contexts of a specific space and time. This idea builds on Foucault's conceptualization of power as decentralized and a part of all social relationships and on feminist scholars' critiques and enhancements of his ideas, generating a more fruitful understanding of household gastropolitics. Instead of a stagnant image of an oppressed woman, we ought to see any individual woman as simultaneously subjected to a number of power relations that are located in time and space. These relations involve a simultaneous reproduction and resistance of normative gender roles and relations (Butler) at the intersections of gender, social class, ethnicity, and the like (Crenshaw; Hill Collins et al.).

This study was conducted in a large, western Canadian city, where almost one-fifth of the population are immigrants and where South Asian newcomers are one of the largest newcomer communities. In this study, the thirty-eight participants were from Pakistan or Northern India. My findings are based on open-ended individual interviews with eleven women, which were conducted in the women's homes. They took place in English, Hindi, or Urdu, and lasted between one and a half to three hours to complete. This stage of research aimed to learn more about unique individual stories of food, family, and migration and build upon findings that came from the first phase of the research project. In the first stage, six focus group interviews were conducted; findings provided a picture of general similarities in immigrant experiences, particularly around changing lifestyles (e.g., faster pace of life, both husband and wife entering the work force, and a downward shift in social status) and women's efforts to nurture through food as well as the ideals and values of the home (Vallianatos and Raine).

In this chapter, I begin by examining how women's perspectives on food work reveal gendered household gastropolitics postmigration and then investigate intergenerational household dynamics and how they affect immigrant women's place in the family.

Food Work and Gendered Gastropolitics

Domestic food work continues to be a responsibility of women in a range of cultural contexts. In South Asia, daily meal preparation is typically viewed as women's duty, although family structure and social class affect everyday practices. For example, women who live in an extended (or joint) household with sisters-in-law may divide meal preparation duties among themselves, whereas those of a higher social class often hire help. This gendered responsibility predominantly continued postmigration. When I asked a group of seven recent immigrant women about their family's cooking practices, they concurred that men hold power over family meal choices, and in turn, women's daily food work:

B: It depends upon the husbands. If they are easy going, then you can give them pita bread. I have to make curry and traditional roti every day for my husband.

[Everyone speaking at once.]

G: My husband knows how to cook basic meals because he was bachelor when he came to Canada, but after marriage he says, "I have taken retirement from the kitchen, so you cook." [Laughs]

D: My husband doesn't drink water by himself. The food should be served on the table.

E: Same with me.

Helen: I was thinking that because you are alone here [in Canada], your husband would help you with the cooking.

B: My cooking styles are changing a bit here.

F: They can help you in other things, such as ... vacuum[ing] and [buying] groceries, but not cooking.

B: Vacuuming [nods in agreement]

A: It is better if they don't cook anything, as they will make a mess.

This exchange highlights not only the expectation that women are responsible for kitchen work, but also that men do not belong in the kitchen, as "they will make a mess" and consequently cause even more work for women. What is interesting is that there has been a shift in some families, with men contributing to domestic work, but the kitchen space continues to be a women's space. Even those who did have a husband who enjoyed cooking recognized the rarity, as one woman noted: "He helps me in kitchen work. My dad also used to help my mom. [But] it is not very common in India." Gendered gastropolitics within these households continues to position women as responsible for family food work, even when there are shifts in family gender roles. Husbands, at least some the participants' husbands, assume domestic cleaning and other responsibilities, but there is something different about food work and the kitchen space, which makes them the domestic bastion of traditional gender roles. It is not uncommon for immigrant women to be primarily responsible for everyday cooking in Canada; generally in Canada, gendered food work continues to be women's work, whereas men may cook when they choose (e.g., weekend meals) or specialize in cooking meat in smokers or barbeques (Beagan et al.). This gendered distribution of food work could be viewed as symbolic of continued domestic power asymmetries. I found that immigrant women who had migrated separately from the husbands (either coming to Canada as newlyweds or once their husbands had some financial security) knew that their husbands had some cooking abilities, but upon their arrival, few men continued kitchen duties, even when their wives were employed outside the home. Thus, women effectively began working the classic second shift.

Some of the participating immigrant women, however, took pride in their expertise in cooking, and acquired social recognition for these skills within their family and even the larger community. Such women problematize understandings of household gender power dynamics, for they actively assert their expertise and skills within and outside the household by resisting men's encroachment into kitchen spaces and by actively reinforcing the notion of the helpless man who is incapable of creating anything other than a mess in the kitchen. In other words, for some women, their dominance in the kitchen is a source of power, not a prison. These women are asserting their agency, as illustrated by Saba

Mahmood, who critiques Western feminist conceptualizations of agency for narrowly defining agency in relation to challenging patriarchal norms. Instead, she views agency as women's engagement with traditional patriarchal practices (religious practices in her study), which may involve reproducing gender norms while also occasionally subtly shifting religious practices. Mahmood recognizes women's agency in choosing to follow Islamic practices:

> Different modalities of agency require different kinds of bodily capacities; it forces us to ask whether acts of resistance (to systems of gender hierarchy) also devolve upon the ability of the body to behave in particular ways. From this perspective, transgressing gender norms may not be a matter of transforming "consciousness" or effecting change in the significatory system of gender, but might well require the retraining of sensibilities, affect, desire, and sentiments—those registers of corporeality that often escape the logic of representation and symbolic articulation. (188)

Applying Mahmood's ideas to immigrant women's domestic food work suggests that we honour women's skills and sense of power and status that comes from their expertise, in which their empowerment may come not from their capacity to change traditional gastropolitical hierarchies but rather to embrace their proficiencies in the kitchen. I suggest that such application of Mahmood's ideas of agency is valuable to understanding immigrant women's gastropolitical context, but I note that immigrant South Asian women are not speaking with one voice, even within this sample, and that household gastropolitics contributed to everyday tensions for some women.

Thus, cooking continues to be an important means through which women perform their gender—an expected everyday responsibility through which typical gender roles are reproduced postmigration. Some women take pride in their capabilities, but for others, this quotidian task is approached more with resignation, even stress. In the next section, I continue to investigate how food work reveals complex family gastropolitics, moving beyond husband-wife relations to generational dynamics.

Intergenerational Gastropolitics: Age and Gender Issues

As previously mentioned, the ideal family structure in South Asia is a joint, or extended, family, in which women reside with their affinal kin upon marriage, which means that the new wife has her mother-in-law and sisters-in-law to assist with daily household management. These are not necessarily equitable relationships though; the mother-in-law is most powerful, followed by the eldest daughter-in-law and so on. The most recent addition to the family, the newest daughter-in-law, has the lowest status. In the ethnographic literature on India, the mother-in-law's high status is demonstrated through her control of resources, including money, food, and labour as well as the influence she holds over the men of the household, particularly her sons. One of the participants noted that "mother-in-law is always bad news ... [but] you have to face it." The youngest daughter-in-law's low status is exemplified by her arising first in the morning and preparing the chai. Her acceptance often is signified through food transactions, as illustrated by one young participant, who recalls feeling nervous after marriage: "I never left my mother; they were totally strangers to me." I asked her to describe the first meal she prepared for her in-laws (which was dal, fish, roti, and rice), and she related how they liked it: "They always appreciate my cooking." This acceptance helped smooth her way into the family.

Many participants discussed the challenges of shifting from an extended to a nuclear family structure, particularly due to the lack of familial support. In a focus group interview, one recent immigrant woman who was pregnant for the second time responded to another woman's description of daily life stresses that were exacerbated by the lack of familial social support postmigration:

> I will probably experience the same because my first child was born in Pakistan; my parents, siblings helped me a lot at the time of the birth. Now I am living with my brother-in-law; I am planning to move [before the birth]. Here, I know I have to work independently. Plan ahead, cook all the meals, freeze them, probably during my seventh month [of pregnancy]. I am prepared that as soon as I come home from the hospital, I have to do all the chores, but I am ready for that.

In other words, changes in family structure from a large household consisting of a mother and father, their sons, wives and children, and any unmarried children to a small and isolated nuclear family can result in an increased domestic work load and stress for many immigrant women. This is especially the case for women who had just given birth, since ideally they would be able to relax and recover for a period of time, traditionally forty days, while their female relatives look after the chores, including food work. A young woman, a mother of two, recalled the trials of having a baby in Canada without familial support:

> No, not here in Canada, at least because when I was pregnant, I applied for my mom's visit visa. But they refused her, so it's hard here to have children all alone. The visa officer refused her; she was a government worker, retired now, had sufficient funds, but still she was refused. It was very hard for me to manage all alone. My husband does night shifts. One night, I remember I was shivering, couldn't get up, and my son was crying, so you get frustrated. My [eldest] son stayed at one of my friend's house when I was in the hospital. We cried when my mom was refused a visa. They said that my mom didn't show proper ties to her country. I don't understand that.

This is not an infrequent experience for immigrant women, and it seems that larger political-economic forces conspire to further limit the social support available to immigrant women. In this case, the young mother did ask friends for help, but she noted the following: "One of my friends keeps us in such situations, but we can't expect help every week." In other words, friends differ from family; it is a different relationship, so one cannot impose on or rely on friends in the same manner one would with family.

Central to a woman's duty as wife and mother is sacrifice, as a newlywed woman adapts to life in her husband's household. This was explained to me by an older participant:

"In our culture, we are brought up in this way to sacrifice and try to make your marriage work.... We are committed, and we have kids before you can even think of something else." For some women, migration provides an escape from this normative, ideal family structure and expectations. When I asked a woman from Pakistan to name her most positive memory coming to Canada she replied "I have my whole house. I am in charge running my own house, as I left my whole family so that was the only thing that I felt positive about here because I have a big family."

The confinements some women experienced in a joint family structure were further elaborated upon by a Sikh woman and her elderly mother:

Daughter: Sometimes my great grandmother-in-law, she wants the sons to eat first because it happened once with me that my in-laws served me and my husband different food. When my kids were young and used to cry a lot at night, my mother-in-law asked my husband to sleep in another room so that he wouldn't get disturbed. I felt so sad.

Mom: My mother-in-law used to look after me when I went to India last time. I used to love her a lot. We never fought unnecessarily.

Helen: Was there any tension between you and your sisters-in-law?

Mom: Yeah. It happened, but mostly I used to keep quiet and my mother-in-law did justice between us so it was never prolonged. Also, the men never got involved in these matters. We were never abused physically; yeah, verbally it was there, but that's okay, we were used to it.

In this exchange, the complexity of gender and age relations within the household is demonstrated. Men's dominance is illustrated not only through food practices but also through the treatment of women. This participant's mother noted that men do not typically interfere in arguments between the women of the household, although women may be fighting for their husband's, children's, as well as their own interests. I was told that in India, "fights in the kitchen break the family"— it is these arguments between the sisters-in-law that can escalate, and eventually, the joint family breaks, as the brothers set up their own households. Arguably, this saying illustrates gender hierarchies, as women are blamed for the breakdown of the ideal family structure. Nevertheless, women are not a homogenous group, and the age hierarchies within women family members are also illustrated in the above quotation, which references the implicit tensions between the mother-in-law and her daughter-in-law. Mothers can have a great deal of influence over their sons, to the extent of assigning sleeping quarters (although it is unclear in the above conversation whether the mother or the son instigated sleeping in a different room, the mother could do this on her son's behalf). Thus, women are not uniformly subservient.

It should also be noted that women do not quietly sacrifice and do not merely acquiesce to idealistic gender and age norms; they also resist, and this resistance often emerges in the kitchen. One woman recalled the following:

> My mother-in-law wanted all the chores to be done on time and according to her way, without realizing that I have my kids, my priorities. So we had tensions sometimes, but mostly it was good. If meals were delayed, she used to get upset. Relations do change; [women] do become mothers-in-law [laughs]. Things were okay because I never talked back to my mother-in-law or told on her.

This woman learned to balance her own desires strategically. She neither complained to nor used her husband to challenge her mother-in-law; rather, she learned to pick her battles and bide her time. Her understanding that her day would come and that she would be in a position of power as mother-in-law one day is also revealing and echoes what women had shared with me during my earlier research in India (e.g., one mother in India, after complaining about her own experiences with in-laws reflected, "But you know, I will do the same").

For many immigrant women, their mothers-in-law come to visit, often for an extended stay, in their homes. Power relations are consequently altered, as explicated by one woman:

> She [the mother-in-law] has to share her son ... time, money; she has to compromise, and the daughter-in-law has to compromise; it's give and take.

> Helen: In your situation, was it different because they came to live with you?

> Yeah of course. They were visitors, so they said it's your house— buy, cook, and serve. I want to be free of responsibilities, so I said fine, as long as you're not interfering.

Not all in-laws would refrain from interfering, to use this woman's words. But her story does suggest that migration causes a shift in relations, as elders may not have the linguistic skills or cultural knowledge to manage simple everyday activities, so rely on their daughters-in-law in a different manner than back home.

It is through quotidian food work that tensions may emerge. As another woman explained, "They [in-laws] do say that she [the daughter-in-law] doesn't cook well; she doesn't cook in our style." This is a way of complaining about the daughter-in-law and can reflect other tensions or problems. An older participant explained further:

Most likely [there is tension] because it is turn taking for cooking, so it's your turn, [but] you didn't cook or didn't cook good, or you went away, so the fight starts. My mother-in-law was good in that way. The days were fixed for each and every daughter-in-law. So if she decides who does what, chances are there will be less conflict. Because I am the youngest and the oldest daughter-in-law is lazy, I can't say anything to her [the oldest daughter-in-law]. I will be mad all the time, doing work. Because making the roti takes a lot of work, time ... I don't know about here. I wish I could have a joint family here, but Gujrati families still prefer joint families, at least one son and daughter-in-law. The mother-in-law takes care of the house. First, we live together to pay off the house; [then] the first son moves out and the second one looks after [us]. We try to buy another house, a small unit, and all work together to pay that off, and then buy another one [if there are more sons]. So far, I visit and live like extended families when I'm visiting; it doesn't have to be a very big house, because the married couple gets the large bedroom live [to share] with all their children, like back home. The parents get one bedroom, and the bachelor son gets the third bedroom or the basement. The mother-in-law is in charge but [all the women of the household] work together.

Although the mother-in-law has the highest status and runs the household, the daughter-in-law has responsibilities and may overtly or covertly attempt to acquire more resources for her children. One woman, who was the eldest daughter-in-law, recalled the challenges of ensuring the joint family interactions went smoothly. And as eldest daughter-in-law, she felt she had a heavier burden:

> [I live in] a big house, [with] two brothers-in-law, their families, father and mother-in-law ... we are used to that kind of setting. Back home, we have a big family living together, brothers- and sister-in-law, their children; we lived together. But there, the situation was a little different because I was the eldest and had more responsibility.... Culturally, you have to watch everybody, and cook [and] make sure ... everybody is happy.

Helen: How did you manage that?

> I managed. My father used to say that "you are very diplomatic," so it became handy at that time.... My sister-in-law helped me and brother-in-law respected me, so it was a give and take. [But] that's tough, who is going to cook, who will clean, cut vegetables, etc. Back home, in joint families, they divide the tasks, [and] then you do breakfast, lunch, and dinner. I do dinner and clean; duties and responsibilities are divided. But in the [US], my first sister-in-law and I used to fight for [we wanted to do], [and] then we [learned to] share the work together.

The ideal joint family is simultaneously reified, missed, and unwanted. Younger immigrant women miss the support of female kin, and older immigrant women appreciate the company and the support of (maybe even the power over) daughters-in-law. Yet when memories are shared, particularly of food work and feeding their families, varying degrees of tensions are recalled, and some immigrant women appreciate the freedom migration provides to make their own choices and run their own households.

Intergenerational dynamics further complicating household gastro-politics and immigrant women's everyday food work are children's preferences. Traditionally, children would eat whatever food was prepared for the family, and a common shift postmigration was the increased food preferences of children. One participant from India recalled, "They used to eat whatever we used to give them in India. But here they don't eat; they want munchies and snacks." Another woman concurred that parent-child relationships had shifted, and this was illustrated with food practices: "Usually people don't cook separate meals for kids in Pakistan, but here we cook special food for kids, or whatever they like to eat." This push from children to prepare food privileging their tastes rather than those of older generations can create stress and extra work for immigrant mothers, particularly for those living in extended families (recall the pressures on women to conform to the food and tastes of their affinal kin). An added stress is that mothers, through food, impart sociocultural values. A group of women reflected on these challenges:

> L: Yeah of course. For us and for our kids it's hard, but I try to pack a snack, lunch from home. We feed them a heavy breakfast, like parathas, and teach them at home to abstain from meat, but it's hard for the kids.
>
> M: Our children also abstain from these things.
>
> N: But we can always make [halal] chicken, beef at home for them.
>
> M: Yeah, yeah.
>
> O: I think it's our teaching about our religion; we make them understand.
>
> P: Yeah, it's hard for young children to understand because when we go to McDonald's, they ask for chicken burgers, but when we say no, they don't understand.
>
> N: Yeah, it's hard because at least we can eat fillet fish burgers, but you [looking at l, who is a vegetarian Hindu], it must be hard for your family.
>
> L: Yeah it's tough, but we have no choice.

In this exchange, we see a number of strategies used by mothers to assist their children. First, there is formal teaching about religious beliefs and requirements. Second, women pack school lunches, as opposed to allowing children to purchase lunch in the cafeteria. Third, women may provide their children with substantial breakfasts in order to decrease the chance that their children will become hungry and snack on proscribed food. And finally, families rarely eat out because of the difficulties of finding appropriate food (e.g., halal).

The pressure children impart on their parents to consume new and unfamiliar food can lead to shifts in food practices within families. As one participant noted: "As far as we [my husband and me] are concerned, we are set in our food habits, but our kids brought a lot of change in our food patterns because when they eat pizza [or] spaghetti at school and they like it, I [will] try that. Now it's changed a lot; you can't stick to the same meal pattern." This was not an uncommon experience, as many women spoke of their families' increased consumption of Canadian food, which was illustrated in this exchange:

E: Pasta, burgers, pizza. I never tried these foods in India because there, we had our own traditional food all the time, but here kids want to eat [them], so we also eat [them].

A: Yeah, you eat these Canadian foods like a sandwich, pasta, etcetera, but you don't feel satisfied. But once you eat roti and vegetables, you feel satisfied.

C: Yeah, yeah. You can have one Canadian meal in a day, maybe a lunch or dinner. But then you feel like eating our traditional foods anyways.

This exchange highlights not only the inclusion of Canadian food but also the generational difference in how these kinds of food are viewed; for the immigrant mothers in this study, Canadian food did not have the same meaning as their own cuisines; consequently, this food left a different bodily experience—an emptiness compared with their own food. This reaction is a marked difference with their children, who initiate the inclusion of this food in the household culinary landscape.

An examination of intergenerational gastropolitics reveals an interesting pattern in age hierarchies postmigration. Power is traditionally held by elders in the joint family structure, which is complicated by intersecting gendered power dimensions. This dynamic shifts postmigration, as elders may not have the social and cultural capital to perpetuate traditional roles (although as elders, they were still respected and honoured). Furthermore, children's food preferences shift, as they are exposed to a greater array of food at school, friends' homes, and in advertisements. They become increasingly vocal about wanting similar kinds of food at home. Children's food desires have the power to shift family food dynamics, as many mothers spoke of incorporating their children's preferences while negotiating their husbands' as well as the elders' (if applicable) food preferences.

Conclusion

Performance of gender is fluid, shifting by time and place (Butler). An important site for the performance of womanhood is family spaces, particularly kitchens. Although women's status is broadly categorized as lower than men's in South Asia, experiences of gender alter as a woman marries, adjusts to married life, and eventually becomes a mother-in-law. Examining social relationships between women and between women and men in the household reveals power structures and dynamics within the family, and food practices are a particularly salient means of illustrating power dynamics—in other words, gastro-politics.

It is no surprise that practices do not neatly map onto norms and ideologies. What is evident in women's voices is a problematization of tradition (in terms of traditional food reproduction), various kinds of authoritative knowledge, and a tension between incorporating new or different ideas into reproductive practices while negotiating familial expectations.

Looking at food practices and beliefs during this important time in women's lives is a window into understanding how South Asian immigrant women do gender and how they negotiate traditions in a new context. As women, they have the responsibility for propagating their families, metaphorically and materially. Their performance of this responsibility comes under the watchful, sometimes critical, gaze of family, community, and experts (e.g., medical practitioners). Arguably, this gaze, and the responsibility women bear, is most intense when they are pregnant. This social gaze is important in providing the tools and support to reproduce traditional ideologies. For immigrant women, navigating this social gaze and familial gastropolitics in new social locations can be both a source of relief (e.g., more freedom to follow their own food work styles) and a potential source of conflict (e.g., when navigating food choices of children, husbands, and in-laws).

Works Cited

Adapon, Joy. *Culinary Art and Anthropology.* Berg, 2008.

Appadurai, Arjun. "Gastro-politics in Hindu South Asia." *American Ethnologist*, vol. 8, no. 3, 1981, pp. 494-511.

Avakian, Arlene V. "Shish kebab Armenians? Food and the Construction and Maintenance of Ethnic and Gender Identities among Armenian American feminists." *From Betty Crocker to Feminist Food Studies*, edited by Arlene V. Avakian and Barbara Haber, University of Massachusetts Press, 2005, pp. 257-280.

Butler, Judith. *Gender Trouble: Feminism and the Subversion of Identity.* Routledge, 1990.

Butler, Judith. *The Psychic Life of Power: Theories in Subjection.* Stanford University Press, 1997.

Counihan, Carole M. *The Anthropology of Food and Body: Gender, Meaning and Power.* Routledge, 1999.

Crenshaw, Kimberle. "Demarginalizing the Intersection of Race and Sex: A Black Feminist Critique of Antidiscrimination Doctrine, Feminist Theory, and Antiracist Politics." *Feminist Legal Theory: Readings in Law and Gender*, edited by Katharine T. Barlett and Rosanne Kennedy, Westview Press, 1991, pp. 57-80.

Crenshaw, Kimberle. "Mapping the Margins: Intersectionality, Identity Politics, and Violence Against Women of Color." *Stanford Law Review*, vol. 43, no. 6, 1991, pp. 1241-99.

Dahl, Robert. "The Concept of Power." *Behavioral Science*, vol. 2, no. 3, 1957, pp. 201-15.

Fischler, Claude. "Food, Self and Identity." *Social Science Information*, vol. 27, no. 2, 1988, pp. 275-292.

George, Sheba M. *When Women Come First: Gender and Class in Transnational Migration.* University of California Press, 2005.

Hill Collins, Patricia, et al. "Symposium on West and Fenstermaker's 'Doing Difference.'" *Doing Gender, Doing Difference*, edited by Sarah Fenstermaker and Candace West, Routledge, 2002.

Lukes, Steven. *Power: A Radical View.* 2nd ed. Macmillan, 2005.

Lukes, Steven. "Introduction." *Power*, edited by Steven Lukes, New York University Press, 1986, pp. 1-18.

Lukes, Steven. *Power: A Radical View.* London: Macmillan, 1974.

Mahmood, S. *Politics of Piety: The Islamic Revival and the Feminist Subject.* Princeton University Press, 2005.

Pitkin, Hanna F. *Wittgenstein and Justice: On the Significance of Ludwig*

Wittgenstein for Social and Political Thought. University of California Press, 1972.

Ray, Krishnendu. *The Migrant's Table: Meals and Memories in Bengali-American Households.* Temple University Press, 2004.

Stoller, Paul, and Cheryl Olkes. "Bad Sauce, Good Ethnography." *Cultural Anthropology,* vol. 1, no. 3, 1986, pp. 336-52.

Vallianatos, Helen. "Placing Maternal Health in India." *Locating Health: Explorations of Healing and Place,* edited by Erika Dyck and Christopher Fletcher, Pickering & Chatto Publishers Ltd, 2011, pp. 11-27.

Vallianatos, Helen. *Poor and Pregnant in New Delhi, India.* Qual Institute Press, 2006.

Vallianatos, Helen, and Kim D. Raine. "Consuming Food, Constructing Identities: A Symbolic Analysis of Diet among Arabic and South Asian Immigrant Women." *Food, Culture & Society,* vol. 11, 2008, pp. 355-73.

Weber, Max. *Economy and Society: An Outline of Interpretive Sociology.* Translated by Ephraim Fischoff et al. University of California Press, 1978.

Notes on Contributors

Dorothy Abram is a playwright and Professor in the Social Sciences department of Johnson & Wales University in Providence, Rhode Island, United States. She is coconvener of the United Nations Subcommittee on Refugees, Immigrants, and Mental Health.

Tanya M. Cassidy is International Convenor in the School of Nursing, Psychotherapy, and Community Health at Dublin City University (DCU). She is a Fulbright IRB (Irish Health Research Board) Health Impact Scholar, held in the Department of Anthropology at MIT. Prior to this, she held a senior EU Horizon 2020 Marie Sklodowska Curie Fellowship at the University of Central Lancashire (UCLan) She continues to be an affiliated researcher at Maynooth University in Ireland where she held her Cochrane Fellowship. She was born in Canada, where she continues to have lots of family.

Gwen Chapman, PhD, is provost and vice-president (academic) at the University of Guelph and was previously professor of food, nutrition, and health at the University of British Columbia.

Ruth De Souza is vice-chancellor's fellow at RMIT University, based in the School of Art and Design and Creative Practice Enabling Capability Platform. Ruth is a nurse, academic, and community engaged researcher in gender, race, and digital technologies. Prior to coming to RMIT, she was the academic coconvenor of the Data, Systems, and Society Research Network (DSSRN), a collaborative research network across the University of Melbourne. She has extensive experience in community and governance roles.

Abdullahi Osman El-Tom has retired from his post as head of anthropology in Maynooth University, after thirty years working in the department. He spent his career as a scholar, lecturer, researcher, and political activist, including teaching and publishing on the anthropology of food for over three decades.

Sanzida Habib, PhD, is an independent scholar and was a research assistant for Dr. Chapman's study "Vitamin D Status of Immigrant Mothers and Infants in Metro Vancouver."

Gladys Loewen is the oldest child of Jacob and Anne Loewen. She was born in Kansas and spent her formative years in Colombia, where her parents worked as missionaries. She has a MEd in counseling psychology from the University of British Columbia. Gladys has worked in higher education in positions with a focus on creating inclusive, equitable, usable, and sustainable environments for disabled people.

William Loewen is the youngest child and only son of Jacob and Anne Loewen. Bill was born in British Columbia and raised overseas in South America and Africa. Bill has a PhD in social work, focusing on the dynamics of multicultural work groups. Bill has worked in social service planning and administration, and currently directs and teaches in the Social Work Program at the University of Sioux Falls in South Dakota.

Hadas Ore received the Dame Joan Metge postdoctoral award (The Kate Edgar Educational Charitable Trust, 2016) to conduct the first study on Maori-Jewish homes in New Zealand. She is a social anthropologist interested in food studies, social theories of home and nostalgia, and women studies. Her 2015 PhD dissertation (social anthropology, the University of Auckland) focuses on the changes in the domestic food practices of Jewish-Israeli women following their migration to New Zealand as well as their nostalgic memories and emotions.

Haoyue Chen is a master's student in the Department of Maternal and Child Health, School of Public Health, Peking University, under the supervision of Dr. Qianling Zhou. Haoyue's research concentrates on exclusive breastfeeding issues and migrant mothers.

Florence Pasche Guignard holds a PhD in religious studies from the University of Lausanne. Since 2020, she has been an assistant professor of theology and religious studies at the Université Laval in Québec. Previously, she was a postdoctoral researcher at the Department for the

Study of Religion at the University of Toronto. Her work explores issues at the intersection of religion and culture, gender, media, embodiment, and ritual.

Ramona Lee Perez is a Chicana scholar, activist, mother, and medicine woman born and raised in California. A Ford Foundation Fellow, she is an instructor in the Department of Anthropology and assistant director of Latino Studies at Queens College, City University of New York. She holds a BA in cultural anthropology from University of California, San Diego, and holds a MA and PhD in cultural anthropology from New York University. She has conducted research on food habits and healing traditions in Mexico, Italy, New Mexico, New York, and Vermont and has published in the *Encyclopedia of Food and Culture*, *Gastropolis, Food and Foodways,* and *Journal of Latin American Anthropology.*

Maria Elena Rodriguez is a Puerto Rico–based food systems advocate, researcher, and small-scale farmer interested in Puerto Rican cultural foodways and land-based justice work. She holds an MS in community development from the University of California, Davis, and a BA in environmental studies from the University of Washington, Seattle.

Sharon Shepherd is the third child of Jacob and Anne Loewen. She was born in Andagoya, Colombia, where her parents worked as missionaries for the Mennonite Brethren Board of Missions. She was educated in the United States and South America. She has an EdS in community agency counselling from Pittsburg State University, Pittsburg, Kansas. Sharon currently works as a licensed clinical marriage and family therapist.

Helen Vallianatos joined the Department of Anthropology, University of Alberta in 2006 and is currently an associate dean of students, in the Office of the Dean of Students, as well as a professor in the Department of Anthropology. Her research and teaching focuses on the topics of food, gender, body, and health. She has examined food consumption during pregnancy in New Delhi, India, exploring how a confluence of individual, community, and political-economic factors shaped women's food practices and nutritional health status. Her research now focuses on migration and the construction of foodways and subjectivities of South Asian immigrant women and their families.

Qianling Zhou is an assistant professor in the Department of Maternal and Child Health, School of Public Health, Peking University. Her doctorate was completed in public health nutrition at the Dublin Institute of Technology. Her research interests include maternal and child nutrition, infant feeding, and behavioural changes interventions.

Cover Artist's Statement

Teacups
From the 2010 series *You Are Not Where You Were,*
a *Greetings From Motherland* project
by Mindy Stricke

In this photo installation, eighteen small colorful slide viewers float from two mobiles. The viewers contain images created in a series of *Greetings From Motherland* workshops, using miniature railroad figures and baby objects that loomed large. There are sixteen total images, plus two single words to welcome the viewer to Motherland.

Mindy Stricke is a photographer and a participatory artist. Working with the public and their true stories, she transforms the familiar into something new, connecting people to themselves and others in the process.

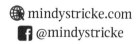

🌐 mindystricke.com
📘 @mindystricke

Deepest appreciation to
Demeter's monthly Donors

DEMETER

Daughters
Paul Chu
Rebecca Bromwich
Summer Cunningham
Tatjana Takseva
Debbie Byrd
Fiona Green
Tanya Cassidy
Vicki Noble
Bridget Boland
Naomi McPherson
Myrel Chernick

Sisters
Kirsten Goa
Amber Kinser
Nicole Willey
Christine Peets